What Terrorists Want

Understanding the Terrorist Threat

LOUISE RICHARDSON

JOHN MURRAY

© Louise Richardson 2006

First published in Great Britain in 2006 by John Murray (Publishers)
A division of Hodder Headline

The right of Louise Richardson to be identified as the Author of the Work has been asserted by
her in accordance with the Copyright, Designs and Patents Act 1988.

I

A CIP catalogue record for this title is available from the British Library.

ISBN 0 7195 6306 2

Typeset in Bembo by Servis Filmsetting Ltd, Manchester

Printed and bound by Clays Ltd, St Ives plc

Hodder Headline policy is to use papers that are natural, renewable and recyclable products and
made from wood grown in sustainable forests. The logging and manufacturing processes are
expected to conform to the environmental regulations of the country of origin.

John Murray (Publishers)
338 Euston Road
London NW1 3BH

For Ciara, Fiona, Rory

Contents

Acknowledgements

I alone am responsible for the many shortcomings of this book. Such strengths as it has are due in large part to the support I have received from a number of others. I would like to acknowledge just some of them.

I have benefited greatly from the unerring editorial eye and wise counsel of my friend Sarah Flynn, and from the charm, energy and insight of my agent Michael Carlisle.

I wrote this book at the Radcliffe Institute for Advanced Study, a vibrant hotbed of intellectual inquiry. Drew Gilpin Faust generously gave me the time I needed to write, Or-Corinne Chapman gave me invaluable research and logistical assistance, and my friends and colleagues at Radcliffe encouraged me all along the way. I am profoundly grateful to each of them.

I have had the great good fortune to teach with and learn from two extraordinary colleagues and friends, Stanley Hoffmann and Philip Heymann. My views on the subjects examined in this book, as well as on many other matters, have benefited from their influence. My views have also benefited from being questioned constantly by my students at Harvard who leave no assertion unchallenged and no argument undefended. I am in their debt.

I would also like to thank Peter James for his rigorous and incisive editorial help and my London agent Peter Robinson, as well as Roland Philipps and Rowan Yapp of John Murray for their engagement with and commitment to this book.

My biggest debt of gratitude is owed to my husband, Thomas R. Jevon, for his irrepressible enthusiasm for this project and his unfailing willingness cheerfully to pick up the pieces on the home front. This book is dedicated to our three children Ciara, Fiona and

Rory, whose mother's enduring preoccupation with terrorists remains a source of occasional annoyance and constant amusement.

December 2005

Introduction

While nothing is easier than to denounce the evildoer,
nothing is more difficult than to understand him.[1]

Dostoevsky

In September 2001 the obscure academic field in which I had quietly toiled for many years, terrorist movements, was suddenly plunged into the limelight. I have been thinking about the subject of terrorism for as long as I can remember and teaching courses on terrorist movements to Harvard undergraduates since the mid-1990s. Suddenly invitations to speak flooded in from all over the country and beyond, and I have addressed, aside from my students, countless large audiences since that time. At the end of every one of these talks one of the first questions I am asked is 'What one book should I read to get a handle on terrorism?' The disappointment of the questioner is palpable when I respond with a lengthy list of good books that address different aspects of terrorism. I always assumed that more entrepreneurial authors than I would rush to write the one good book that addresses the question of terrorism in all its complexity but with a coherent, wide-ranging and analytical approach. This book would present terrorism in a non-partisan way as an age-old political phenomenon that can be understood in rational terms. It would provide the reader with a comprehensive introduction to the field of terrorism studies as a starting point for confronting the bewildering array of books on terrorism they encounter at the bookstore. It would help readers to understand what causes people to resort to terrorism and what terrorists are trying to achieve. More than four years later I am still being asked to recommend one book, and my answer is as long-winded as ever.[2] I have written *What Terrorists Want* to try to fill this void. Drawing on years of research on the evolution of terrorist movements and counter-terrorist strategies throughout the world, it explores the nature of the terrorist threat we face today. It examines the context and the causes behind the terrorists and what drives them to fight. It explores the experiences of democracies around the world in countering terrorism and suggests lessons that can be derived from their successes and their failures to enable us, the United States in particular, to formulate a more effective counter-terrorism policy.

I have a different perspective from most experts who study terrorism. I come from the kind of background that has produced many terrorists and I have spent most of my professional life trying to understand them. When I consider a terrorist atrocity I do not think of the perpetrators as evil monsters but rather I think about the terrorists I have met, and the people I have known who have joined terrorist groups, and I rehearse in my mind their justifications for what they are doing. I grapple with how a young idealist can believe that in murdering innocent people he or she is battling injustice and fighting for a fairer world. I think, as the Protestant martyr John Bradford said 500 years ago, 'There but for the grace of God, go I.'[3] I do not find their justification for their action convincing. Far from it. In my moral code, nobody has the right to take the life of non-combatants. Nevertheless, I am struck by how futile counter-terrorist policies are likely to be when they are based on a view of terrorists as one-dimensional evildoers and psychopaths.

My perspective, like those who join terrorist movements as well as those who resolve to defeat them, is a product of my background. I grew up in a small seaside town in rural Ireland in the 1960s and 1970s. With my classmates I assembled at school every morning to pray beneath a statue of a crucified Christ and a large framed copy of the Proclamation of Independence. The text of the proclamation was surrounded by photographs of the seven men who were executed for their part in the 1916 Easter Rising which tried and failed to establish a republic of Ireland by force of arms. Their photographs were as familiar to me as the images of America's founding fathers are to my children. My classmates and I admired these seven men in much the same way that my children admire Benjamin Franklin, Thomas Jefferson, George Washington and Abraham Lincoln. The real difference, of course, is that Jefferson and Franklin and the other signatories of the American Declaration of Independence in 1776 won their war of independence, and the signatories of the Irish Proclamation of Independence lost. They did not hang together, as Franklin feared, but they were executed together.[4] The unstated message of both the crucifix and the proclamation was the same: that the good are often vilified and forced to suffer, that fighting against today's majority and being punished for it does not mean you are on the wrong side, that in time the truth triumphs. My view of the world, in other words, is very different from that of my American children who have learned to assume that the majority is right and that, as demonstrated by the War of Independence, the Civil War and the world wars, the good guys always win.

Years later, studying Irish history under the tutelage of English historians, I learned that the glorious 1916 Rising, in which we were taught that the nation rose together to overthrow the British yoke, was in fact an altogether more modest occasion. A motley crew of amateur armed insurrectionists terrorized Dublin city centre for a week by taking over the General Post Office and a few other buildings and firing at the British garrison and local police force. Two hundred and fifty-four civilians, 132 members of the security forces and sixty-four rebels were killed in the course of a week of fighting in the densely populated city. It was the reaction, or rather overreaction, of the British government that transformed the affair. The leaders were executed and thereby turned into martyrs while the footsoldiers and sympathizers were shipped off to internment camps in Britain, there to become radicalized and to return better organized, more embittered, and motivated to launch a war of independence. The resonance to today is inescapable.

The myth of 1916, however, lived on in the popular mind. My childhood was filled with stories from my mother's side of aunts secretly slipping messages into the occupied post office, of guns courageously hidden beneath food in bicycle baskets and brought to 'the lads'. On my father's side the story was that my father got his name from his uncle who died, shortly before my father's birth, at the brutal hands of the Black and Tans. These were ill-trained auxiliaries dispatched to maintain order in Ireland by Britain, whose security forces were strained by the demands of the Great War. (They were known as Black and Tans because their uniforms were made up of surplus army and police uniforms.) The story was that my uncle witnessed some thuggish Black and Tans harassing a Dublin girl and, when he went to her defence, they simply shot him in cold blood. It was only later, with the scepticism of the history student trained in research, that I discovered that most of these stories must have been apocryphal. Once while helping my grandmother clear out some drawers I came across a photo of my father's namesake, the uncle alleged to have died at the hands of the hated Black and Tans, dressed in the uniform of a British soldier. His occupation had never been mentioned in the family. I kept the secret. Less important than the facts of the history was the way this history was remembered and passed down. It is this remembered history, invariably oversimplified, with heroes and villains over-drawn, that mobilizes and motivates the next generation. The facts don't seem to matter so much.

Like many around me, I grew up with a passionate hatred of England, which was not shared by my apolitical parents, but was certainly never censored at home or at school. At school we learned Irish history as a long series of heroic efforts to throw off the evil yoke of the British. Britain was to blame for all our ills, political, cultural, linguistic, social and of course religious. I occasionally met English holidaymakers visiting our town, which shook my certi-tude, so I decided that I hated the English government rather than individual English people. As the streets of Northern Ireland exploded in the late 1960s with the civil rights movement and the overreaction of the security forces, it all seemed to be a continu-ation of the same brutal repression of Irish Catholics. I kept scrap-books of atrocities against Catholics and wrote diaries filled with invective against the latest example of Britain carrying out its his-torical role of exploiting and brutalizing Ireland. After the Bloody

Sunday massacre in 1972, my anger reached new heights. I was fourteen, and if the IRA would have had me I'd have joined in a heart-beat.[5] My bemused mother had to lock me in my room and forbid me to leave the house to prevent me carrying out my desire to travel to the North to join the civil rights march in Newry the Sunday following Bloody Sunday.

While my parents did not endorse the vehemence of my views and the political leadership did not voice them publicly in terms as extreme as mine, my views were nevertheless entirely in keeping with the surrounding culture. We all felt differently when we heard a Catholic was killed, as opposed to a Protestant, or a British soldier. A Catholic death was experienced as a loss to our side, a soldier's death a victory. The extremism I imbibed, therefore, came from school, books, popular history and songs. It came from the air around me. I was horrified to discover years later in a peaceful Boston suburb as I desperately tried to stay awake in the early hours of the morning while rocking one of my infant children to sleep that I knew only one or two lullabies, certainly not enough to get us through the night. But I knew an endless repertoire of Irish songs remembered from my childhood. I found myself sweetly singing one bloodcurdling, warmongering song after another to my restless child. These songs told simple tales of good and evil and the justice of the fight for change. These were the only songs I carried from the surroundings in which I grew up.

I arrived at Trinity College Dublin at the age of seventeen, a Catholic country girl very much out of my depth socially on the upper-crust Protestant campus. During freshman week, clubs tried to get the newcomers to join. My closest friend, another Catholic socially out of her element, and I were recruited by the student branch of the IRA. By then I had concluded that killing people was not the right way to advance the cause of reuniting Ireland. I attended meetings and discussions but said I would not join as I could not endorse the use of violence. My friend decided to join. I remained in the background arguing about methods, making sandwiches in the kitchen, until more appealing causes like anti-apartheid in South Africa attracted my attention. Those who did join were like me in almost every respect. They were young idealists wanting to do their part for their country as their forebears had (or as they thought their forebears had). They were motivated by a desire to right wrongs and to do their best for a noble cause. They knew that they were likely to suffer personally from their decisions. They justified the use of force on the ground that it was the only way to make progress towards the legitimate goals they sought.

At Trinity College I learned an entirely different version of Irish history, the British version. When I tried to present evidence to my family challenging the accepted wisdoms of Irish republicanism, it was dismissed as 'Trinity talk'. I was fascinated, and remain so, by how two entirely different versions of the same event could be believed by well-meaning people living side by side. Years later, while studying for a PhD in international relations at Harvard, I read the literature on terrorism. I was profoundly struck by how ill understood the subject was. Terrorists were portrayed as psychopaths, terrorist movements as criminal gangs motivated by desires for personal gain, the term 'terrorism' itself a loose and pejorative label attributed to one's enemies. This was not my perspective. It did not describe my fellow students who had joined the IRA, or the parents of my friends, or my teachers in the Gaeltacht (the Gaelic-speaking part of Ireland) who had joined up.

This sense of the inadequacies of the field led me into a study of terrorism to try to establish why an otherwise responsible parent, student or teacher would choose to join a terrorist movement and remain in one, and why a group of people would collectively choose to kill innocent people they do not know in order to advance some goal unlikely to be achieved in their lifetime. My research drew me to the source, to the writings of terrorists themselves. There is a great deal of primary source evidence available on terrorist motivations, aspirations and justifications for their actions. These appear in interviews with imprisoned terrorists and former terrorists, as well as in the publications and on the websites of the terrorist groups themselves. I also spoke to any terrorist I could. In the days before 9/11 this was a lot easier than it has since become.

On one occasion a few years ago, some colleagues and I convened a group of what we politely termed 'activists', representatives from a number of ethno-nationalist terrorist groups, for a secret conference in a private location. We met for several days, in which we conducted ourselves much like an academic conference. For example, I gave a paper on factors driving terrorist decisions to escalate, and a senior member of a well-known terrorist group served as commentator on my paper. He politely pointed out where he thought I was right and where he disagreed, where my generalizations applied to his movement and where they did not. We all socialized together during the conference. It was soon difficult to tell to which camp an individual belonged.

One aim of the gathering was to try to figure out what factors drive a group to escalate to a different level of violence, so we composed some scenarios to try to get at this question. We also engaged in some war games – again in an effort to establish the factors that trigger the decision to escalate. Mixed teams of academics and 'activists' participated in each role. I participated in a group that was a Chechen cell based in Moscow. The scenario called for us to be placed under increasing pressure by the authorities, as we were trying to establish what kinds of pressures would force a decision to escalate. The similarities in response between the academics and the insurgents were very striking. While the operational efficiency of those with experience was breathtaking (in a completely matter-of-fact way correcting us academics on how many individuals and what weapons would be required in carrying out a particular operation), on the more important question of when one should escalate the insurgents were not more prone to escalation than the academics. Indeed, the insurgents were quite taken aback by the belligerence of the academics in the mixed groups. The only single area in which there was a real difference was on the issue of how to respond to an incident that could be seen as an insult to our honour. I argued rationally that we were weak; we had to husband our resources and should not act. An insurgent was adamant that we had to defend our honour no matter what the cost. As to when we should target children and families, it was the academics who were prepared to take this action first. I mention this not to make light of a serious issue. Not at all – I mention it only to make the point that terrorists are human beings who think like we do. They have goals they are trying to achieve and in a different set of circumstances they, and perhaps we, would lead very different lives.

With colleagues, I helped to organize a second similar gathering, this time with representation from religious terrorist groups. We were scheduled to meet from September 11 to 14, 2001. Six weeks before the planned meeting, worried that one of the groups might make the event public and when one of the insurgent groups insisted that there could be no Jews among the academics, we decided to cancel. I have often imagined what it would have been like to have been in that company on that day.

I was drawn into teaching about terrorism by my students. As a professor of government at Harvard I taught courses on international relations and American foreign policy. In those days I did not teach or write about Ireland – I did not trust my objectivity. Coming to my office and seeing my bookshelves laden with books about terrorists, my students asked why I didn't teach on terrorism; I responded that this was my hobby, not what I taught. They talked me into it. I agreed to teach a junior honours seminar. These courses are limited in size to fifteen and usually have half that number of students. The first time I offered the course, 130 students signed up. As always happens when teaching smart students, you learn as much as they do.

Thinking of my own undergraduate days, I expected that those who wanted to take the course would be the politically disaffected, those with Che Guevara posters in their dorm-rooms. But when I went around the class the first day and asked why they were there, the responses invariably were that they wanted to be secretary of state, or director of the CIA or the FBI. They were there because they wanted to lock up the terrorists, not because they sympathized with them in any way. I required each student to choose a terrorist movement at the beginning of term and to track that movement, to consult their website, read the literature, research the leaders and the actions of the group, and then to present the group to the class at the end of term. A funny thing happened. Almost without exception the student would start his presentation (and they were predominantly males) by saying something to the effect of 'Well, all those other groups are terrorist groups but if you really look at the ETA [or IRA or Shining Path, or whichever movement he had chosen] you discover that they are not really terrorists. Do you know what happened to them?' Or 'Do you know what they do for the poor?' Or 'Do you know about their cultural programmes?' And so on. Once they learned about the terrorists, they didn't think they were terrorists any more.

The depth of student interest in the subject in the 1990s never ceased to amaze me. My small seminars clearly could not contain the demand, so I offered an undergraduate lecture course. I deliberately did everything a teacher can do to keep enrolment down. I assigned far more reading and papers than other courses, I refused to allow the course to fulfil various departmental requirements, and we met three times a week instead of two. Yet still the students poured in. Their desire to grapple with and to understand the phenomenon and to question every assertion was exhilarating and more than compensated for the scepticism of my colleagues.

Terrorism studies in the 1990s was a much marginalized field. One of my senior colleagues told me that it was academic suicide to work on terrorism, that there was no theoretical basis to the field. At the time he was right on both counts. Terrorism was studied in a range of different disciplines but was central to none. Psychologists tried to understand individual motivations; sociologists tried to understand the culture of violence; most often, individual scholars studied individual movements with little sense of how they compared to one another or to earlier movements. No major universities had positions in terrorism and very few even offered a course in the subject. There were a small number of dedicated academics around the country, however, who had devoted their lives to studying some aspect of this phenomenon. We were called the terrorism studies community. We were not so interested in counter-terrorism, not because we didn't want to counter the terrorists, but because we were more interested in other questions: Why do people do this? How do they recruit? When do they escalate? What are the underlying causes? And so on. This community had very few connections with the policy world.

Occasionally, a government official would come by to keep abreast of academic research. In early August 2001 one official came to visit me to ask why I thought no terrorist group had ever used an aircraft as a human bomb, and whether I thought they would. I'm afraid that my answer was far from helpful. I said that the tactic was very much under consideration, and I suspected that some terrorist groups would use it sooner rather than later. But I wrongly predicted that they would make some co-ordinated attack on a number of American embassies around the world.

On another occasion a member of the State Department's Office of Counter-Terrorism visited Harvard to find out what terrorism research was being conducted there. He complained bitterly that we were not being helpful, going off doing research wherever we liked, instead of focusing on the government's policy concerns. I argued just as vehemently back that it was not in our interest, and I didn't think it was even in his, to turn universities into the research arm of the government. Later, at an academic conference, in a talk entitled 'Long Live the Gap' I argued for preserving the distance between government policy and academic research. I contended that academics should be free to do their own work on the issues we consider important, rather than following the ephemeral interests of politicians.

Experience since 9/11, however, has taught me to moderate this stance. Had the American government's policy in the past few years been informed by the views of the terrorism studies community, it would have been a very different policy indeed. Human lives have been lost because of the US government's failure to understand the nature of the enemy we face and its unwillingness to learn from the experiences of others in countering terrorism. I have reluctantly emerged from my academic shell, therefore, to argue in this book that we cannot defeat terrorism by smashing every terrorist movement. An effort to do so will only generate more terrorists, as has happened repeatedly in the past. A policy informed by the work of the terrorism studies community would never have declared a global war on terrorism, because we know that such a war can never be won. A policy so informed would never have believed that Osama bin Laden and Saddam Hussein were working together against the US. A policy informed by those of us who have studied this subject for years would never have had as an objective the completely unattainable goal of obliterating terrorism and would have sought, instead, the more modest and attainable goal of containing terrorist recruitment and constraining resort to the tactic of terrorism.

After September 11 an entirely new breed of terrorism expert emerged. These were people whose priority was counter-terrorism policy and American power. They were very knowledgeable about the workings of the US government and about military and security policy. Many had formerly worked on international security issues like nuclear proliferation or the conduct of the Cold War. Others had practical experience fighting, either overtly or covertly, against terrorists, but very few had ever actually tried to understand terrorism. They found the terrorism studies community incurably soft on terrorism, ignorant of policy and blind to the threat of al-Qaeda. Members of the terrorism studies community tended to console themselves by noting how little the newly minted experts knew about their subject. It is clearly in all our interests for this gap to be eliminated.

There appears to be a popular notion that to endeavour to understand or to explain terrorism is to sympathize with it. I reject this completely. Indeed, it is a central tenet of this book that the most efficacious way of containing terrorism is to understand its appeal to those who practise it, and to use this understanding to forge effective counter-terrorist policies. The experience of a range of countries, from Britain against the nationalist IRA to the Peruvian government's campaign against the Maoist Shining Path, attests to this fact.

The Peruvian case is one example of how an effort to understand a terrorist movement can be much more effective at ending terrorism than an effort to smash it. The Shining Path was a Maoist movement with close to 10,000 members at its height in the 1980s that terrorized a large section of the Ayacucho region.[6] It was led by a ruthless academic, Abimael Guzman, who followed the Maoist prescription for revolution: mobilize the peasantry first and then move into the urban areas. The Peruvian Truth and Reconciliation Commission estimated in 2003 that 69,000 people were killed in the course of the twenty-year terrorist campaign.[7] It is anyone's guess how many of these people were killed by the Shining Path and how many were killed by the military battalions that were sent into the countryside to destroy them. I expect it was a matter of little consequence to those close to the victims which 'men with guns' killed their family members.

Successive Peruvian governments dispatched the military to destroy the terrorists, which led to an increase in casualties but no diminution of terrorism. It was only when the government established a seventy-man intelligence unit within the police force to follow the movement that they had results. Those studying the movement soon realized that the real Achilles heel of the group was its centralized dependence on the charismatic leadership of Guzman. The members of DIRCOTE, as the unit was called, decided that if they could eliminate Guzman they could destroy the movement. Again, they studied everything they could about Guzman and discovered that he had a particular skin condition. Through old-fashioned police work and good electronic intelligence they were able to track Guzman down through his medical prescription. He was captured along with several of his top lieutenants. The movement never recovered.[8] This seventy-man police unit was thereby able to achieve what wave after wave of military deployment could not.

The lesson of the Peruvian case is not that every terrorist movement will disintegrate if its leader is captured. This is not likely to be the case. There is no silver bullet for counter-terrorism. Terrorism is a complex phenomenon. Terrorism is a tactic employed by many different groups, in pursuit of many different objectives, in many parts of the world. The key is to understand the nature of the group you confront. When a group is organized around a single leader, as the Shining Path of Peru were, then it makes sense to try to decapitate the movement. Aum Shinrikyo, the Japanese group that released sarin gas on the Tokyo subway in 1995, were also heavily dependent upon their leader, Shoko Asahara. So were the PKK, the Kurdish group fighting for an independent Kurdish state. Their leader, Abdullah Ocalan, was captured with American assistance in 1999. In each case the arrest of the leader proved to be a devastating blow to the movement.

It does not follow, however, that the capture of Osama bin Laden would deal a body blow to al-Qaeda. There is no evidence to suggest that the movement is organized around him. He has clearly gone to some lengths to ensure that it can survive without him. Different terrorist movements are organized differently. Not all are dependent on a central leader; some have an organized succession plan, others have a collective leadership. The point is that it is essential to know the difference.

A central argument of this book is that in order to defeat a terrorist threat without undermining the democracy one is trying to defend in the first place, there is no substitute for learning everything possible about the terrorist movement one confronts, the nature of its organization, and the nature of its appeal, and then using that knowledge to undermine it. Radical Islamist groups have been so effective against the west in part because they have used hallmarks of our democracy against us. An al-Qaeda spokesman put it this way:

> Al-Qaeda can take over the enemy's means and use them against him, while the enemy cannot do the same. The mujahideen can do this because they have come to understand the enemy's mentality and how his society functions; yet the enemy has no way of deterring the believer or influencing his mentality.[9]

I believe that we must learn how and why they operate and learn to use this knowledge against them if we are ultimately to prevail.

I do not believe that there was a great evolutionary leap in September 2001, that the human race suddenly produced a new breed of evildoers. Rather I believe that the forces driving terrorists today are similar to the forces that have driven revolutionaries in other countries and in other times. Over the years my work has been dedicated to trying to understand the factors that drive individuals into terrorism and that drive societies to support them. Rather than start with the atrocity and move backwards, as terrorism specialists today are wont to do, I have started with the terrorists and the movements they create. By examining their words as well as their actions I have sought to discover whether there are patterns that can be discerned and generalizations that can be made.

In the first half of this book, therefore, I pay little attention to the policies of the US government and look instead to the terrorists. I spell out the meaning of the term terrorists and how terrorists themselves feel about the label. I look to the past, to the precursors of today's terrorists, to demonstrate the long lineage of the terrorist tactic and to expose the myth that terrorism, or even religious terrorism, is either new or the primary preserve of Islam. I point to the political use of the term and to terrorists who have become statesmen and to how those quite opposed to terrorism have been labelled terrorists. I argue that terrorists are neither crazy nor amoral but rather are rationally seeking to achieve a set of objectives within self-imposed limits.

I suggest that the causes of terrorism are not to be found in objective conditions of poverty or privation or in a ruthless quest for domination but in subjective perceptions, in a lethal cocktail containing a disaffected individual, an enabling community and a legitimizing ideology. I believe that terrorist behaviour can be understood in terms of both long-term political motivations, which differ across different types of groups, and more immediate short-term motives, which very different kinds of terrorists share. I also point to the fact that their record of success in attaining these secondary motives is altogether better than their record in achieving the fundamental political change they seek. When terrorists act they are seeking three immediate objectives. They want to exact revenge, they want to acquire glory and they want to force their adversary into a reaction. I call this the three Rs of revenge, renown and reaction.

With this in mind, the recent surge in suicide terrorism is seen simply as an escalation in tactics rather than any fundamental change. Those who sacrifice themselves while killing others are also seeking revenge, renown and reaction. They can continue to do so as long as they have a community that supports them and an ideology, whether secular or religious, that legitimizes their action.

Against this background, in the second part of the book I examine the situation in the US after September 11. I suggest what changed and what did not that day. The biggest change, and the one with most serious long-term implications, is the American government's reaction to terrorism. I believe that, given everything we know about the causes of terrorism and the motives of terrorists, the declaration of a global war on terrorism is a terrible mistake and a policy doomed to failure. I suggest a different approach to containing terrorism, one that relies instead on an appreciation of the factors driving terrorists and enabling them to succeed and is dedicated to depriving them of what they seek. I believe that the US can learn from the experience of other countries in countering terrorism. It should emulate their success and avoid repeating their mistakes.

Believing as I do that terrorism is a tactic that will continue to be employed as long as it is deemed to be effective, I suggest dimensions of the future we are likely to face. Technological developments will make it easier for ever-smaller groups to employ weapons of ever-greater lethality against us. We will never be able to prevent every attack against us. But we will be able to control our reactions to those attacks. If we keep these attacks in perspective and recognize that the strongest weapons in our arsenal against terrorism are precisely the hallmarks of democracy that we value, then we can reasonably expect to contain the terrorist threat.

PART I

The Terrorists

The difference between the revolutionary and the terrorist lies in the reason for which each fights. For whoever stands by a just cause and fights for the freedom and liberation of his land from the invaders, the settlers and the colonialists cannot possibly be called terrorist, otherwise the American people in their struggle for liberation from the British colonialists would have been terrorists; the European resistance against the Nazis would be terrorism, the struggle of the Asian, African and Latin American peoples would also be terrorism, and many of you who are in this Assembly Hall were considered terrorists . . . As to those who fight against the just causes, those who wage war to occupy, colonize and oppress other people, those are the terrorists. Those are the people whose actions should be condemned, who should be called war criminal: for the justice of the cause determines the right to struggle.

Yasser Arafat, November 1974[1]

I

What Is Terrorism?

Terror is nothing else than justice, prompt, secure and inflexible.

Robespierre, 1794[1]

Today our nation saw evil, the very worst of human nature.

President Bush, September 11, 2001

The best that one can say of these people is that they are morally depraved. They champion falsehood, support the butcher against the victim, the oppressor against the innocent child.

Osama bin Laden, October 7, 2001

Like pornography, we know terrorism when we see it, or do we? We know we don't like it. In fact, the only universally accepted attribute of the term 'terrorism' is that it is pejorative. Terrorism is something the bad guys do. The term itself has been bandied about so much that it has come to lose all meaning. A casual glance at newspapers reveals currency speculation being labelled 'economic terrorism', domestic violence described as 'domestic terrorism', and, in one of the sillier usages, crank telephone calls labelled 'tele-phone terrorism'. If you can successfully pin the label 'terrorist' on your opponent you have gone a long way towards winning the public relations aspect of any conflict.

Even terrorists don't like to be called terrorists. An al-Qaeda statement put it this way: 'when the victim tries to seek justice, he is described as a terrorist'.[2] Many prefer to redefine the term first. In Osama bin Laden's words: 'If killing those who kill our sons is terrorism, then let history be witness that we are terrorists.'[3] Other terrorist leaders have taken a similar perspective. Abimael Guzman, the Peruvian academic turned leader of the Maoist Shining Path, declared: 'They claim we're terrorists. I would like to give the following answer so that everyone can think about it: has it or has it not been Yankee imperialism and particularly Reagan who has branded all revolutionary movements as terrorists, yes or no? This is how they attempt to discredit and isolate us in order to crush us.'[4] Shamil Basayev, the Chechen leader responsible for the Beslan school siege of September 2004 among other exploits, declared: 'Okay. So, I'm a terrorist. But what would you call them? If they are keepers of constitutional order, if they are anti-terrorists, then I spit on all these agreements and nice words.'[5] When bin Laden was asked to respond to the fact that many in the Arabic and western media called him a terrorist he replied: 'There is an Arabic proverb that says, she accused me of having her malady and then snuck away.'[6]

Terrorism, simply put, means deliberately and violently targeting civilians for political purposes. Rather than argue about definitions, as academics are wont to do, I will simply outline what I take to be the seven crucial characteristics of the term terrorism. First, a terrorist act is politically inspired. If not, it is simply a crime. After the May 13, 2003 Riyadh bombings the US secretary of state Colin Powell declared: 'We should not try to cloak their . . . criminal activity, their murderous activity, in any trappings of political purpose. They are terrorists.'[7] In point of fact, it is precisely because they did have a political purpose that they were, indeed, terrorists.

Second, if the act does not involve violence or the threat of violence it is not terrorism. This suggests that the term 'cyber-terrorism' is not a useful one. The English lexicon is broad enough to provide a term for the sabotage of our IT facilities without reverting to the language of terrorism. Those who hack into our computers for fun or for profit are of an entirely different ilk than those who are prepared to blow up our buildings and our buses. Labelling such hackers cyber-terrorists may elevate their importance but serves only to confuse. The fear of cyber-terrorism, moreover, is overblown. Terrorists rely heavily on the internet. They use it to communicate, to proselytize, to recruit, to raise funds and to research, plan and carry out their attacks. The internet is altogether too useful a tool to become a target for terrorists.

Third, the point of terrorism is to communicate a message. It is not violence for the sake of it, or even violence in the expectation of defeating the enemy; rather it is violence to convey a political message. Writing of the September 11 attacks, an al-Qaeda spokesman declared: 'It rang the bells of restoring Arab and Islamic glory.'[8]

Fourth, the act and the victim usually have symbolic significance. The shock value of the act is enormously enhanced by the power of the symbol that the target represents. The whole point is for the psychological impact to be greater than the actual physical act. Terrorism is indeed a weapon of the weak. Terrorist movements are invariably both outmanned and outgunned by their opponents, so they employ these tactics in an effort to gain more attention than any objective assessment of their capabilities would suggest that they warrant. Bin Laden, for example, referred to the Twin Towers as 'icons' of America's 'military and economic power'.[9]

Fifth, and this is a controversial point, terrorism is the act of sub-state groups, not states. This is not to argue that states do not use terrorism as an instrument of their foreign policy. We know they do. Many states, such as Iran, Iraq, Syria and Libya, have sponsored terrorism abroad because they did not want to incur the risk of overtly attacking more powerful countries. Great powers have supported terrorist groups abroad as a way of engaging in proxy warfare or covertly bringing about internal change in difficult countries without openly displaying their strength. Nor do I wish to argue that states refrain from action that is the moral equivalent of terrorism. We know they don't. The Allied bombing campaign in the Second World War, culminating in the bombing of Hiroshima and Nagasaki, was a deliberate effort to target civilian populations in order to force the hand of their governments. The policy of collective punishment visited on communities that produce terrorists is another example of targeting civilians to achieve a political purpose. Nevertheless, it is a central tenet of this book that if we want to contain terrorism we must first understand it. Therefore if we want to have any analytical clarity in understanding the behaviour of terrorist groups we must understand them as sub-state actors rather than states. We have generations of work conducted by political scientists, historians and international lawyers to help us to understand the behaviour of states. If we want to understand terrorists we must see them operating as sub-state clandestine groups.

I use the term 'contain' rather than the more popular 'defeat' advisedly. Understood as a tactic it makes little sense to speak of defeating terrorism. Tactics are used as long as they continue to be effective. Our goal, and I believe it to be an achievable one, should be to contain the use of this tactic. To claim that we are going to defeat terrorism, whatever its motivational or rhetorical advantages, is a fairly meaningless aspiration, and an unachievable goal.

A sixth characteristic of terrorism is that the victim of the violence, and the audience the terrorists are trying to reach, are not the same. The point of the act is to use the victim as a means of altering the behaviour of the larger audience, usually a government. Victims are chosen either at random or as representative of some larger group. Particular victims are interchangeable. The identity of the people travelling on a bus in Tel Aviv or a train in Madrid, dancing in Bali or bond trading in New York was of no consequence to those who killed them. They were being used to influence others. This is different from most other forms of political violence in which security forces or state representatives are targeted in an effort to reduce the strength of the opponent.

The final and most important defining characteristic of terrorism is the deliberate targeting of civilians. This is what sets terrorism apart from other forms of political violence, even the most proximate form, guerrilla warfare. Terrorists have elevated practices that are normally seen as the excesses of warfare to routine practice, striking at non-combatants not as an unintended side effect but as deliberate strategy. They insist that those who pay taxes to a government are responsible for their actions whether they are Russians or Americans. Basayev declared all Russians fair game because 'They pay taxes. They give approval in word and in deed. They are all responsible.'[10] Bin Laden similarly said of Americans,

'He is the enemy of ours whether he fights us directly or merely pays his taxes.'[11]

Terrorists, Guerrillas and Freedom Fighters

It goes without saying that in the very messy worlds of violence and politics all actions don't always fit neatly into categories. Guerrillas occasionally target civilians and terrorists occasionally target security forces. But if the primary tactic of an organization is deliberately to target civilians, then they deserve to be called a terrorist group, irrespective of the political context in which they operate and irrespective of the legitimacy of the goals they seek to achieve. There are, of course, other differences too between guerrillas and terrorists. Guerrillas are an irregular army fighting the regular forces of the state. They conduct themselves along military lines and generally have large numbers of adherents, which permit them to launch quasi-military operations. Their goal is the military defeat of the enemy. Terrorists, by contrast, rarely have illusions about their ability to inflict military defeat on the enemy. Rather they seek either to cause the enemy to overreact and thereby permit them to recruit large numbers of followers so that they can launch a guerrilla campaign, or to have such a psychological or economic impact on the enemy that they will withdraw of their own accord. Bin Laden called this the 'bleed-until-bankruptcy plan'.[12]

It is, therefore, the means employed and not the ends pursued, nor the political context in which a group operates, that determine whether or not a group is a terrorist group.

In his famous 1974 speech to the United Nations renouncing terrorism, Yasser Arafat, Chairman of the Palestinian Liberation Organization and founder of its militant wing, Fatah, declared: 'The difference between the revolutionary and the terrorist lies in the reason for which each fights. For whoever stands by a just cause and fights for the freedom and liberation of his land . . . cannot possibly be called terrorist.'[13] A great many people, including several US presidents, have shared this view. Indeed, the main reason why international co-operation against terrorism has been so anaemic over the past thirty-odd years is precisely because the pejorative power of the term is such that nobody has wanted to pin the label on a group fighting for what are considered legitimate goals. President Reagan shared the goal of the Nicaraguan Contras to overthrow the Marxist Sandinista government, so he called them 'the moral equivalent of our Founding Fathers'.[14] America's European allies saw the Contras as a violent and unrepresentative group attempting to subvert a popular government and considered them terrorists. In fact the legitimacy or otherwise of the goals being sought should be irrelevant to whether a group is a terrorist group. Many terrorists groups and especially those that have lasted the longest, the ethno-nationalist groups, have been fighting for goals that many share, and that may even be just. But if they deliberately kill civilians to achieve that goal they deserve to be considered terrorists.

Bin Laden has only a slightly different perspective. He thinks that there is good and bad terrorism:

> Terrorism can be commendable and it can be reprehensible. Terrifying an innocent person and terrorizing them is objectionable and unjust, also unjustly terrorizing people is not right. Whereas terrorizing oppressors and criminals and thieves and robbers is necessary for the safety of people and for the protection of their property . . . The terrorism we practise is of the commendable kind for it is directed at the tyrants and the aggressors and the enemies of Allah, the tyrants, the traitors who commit acts of treason against their own countries and their own faith and their own prophet and their own nation. Terrorizing those and punishing them are necessary measures to straighten things and to make them right.[15]

Bin Laden evidently believes that terrorism is justified if it is used against those who are unjust, whereas it is unjustified if used against the innocent. His concept of innocent, however, as seen above, is an idiosyncratic one. This is a variant on the widely held position that the ends being sought determine whether or not an act is a terrorist act.

Another popular perspective is that an action is terrorist only if it takes place in a democratic state that permits peaceful forms of opposition. Liberal intellectuals made this distinction in reaction to the African National Congress (ANC) in South Africa. Conor Cruise O'Brien and others wanted to argue that the Irish Republican Army (IRA) in Northern Ireland were terrorists when they planted bombs in trash cans in Belfast in the 1970s as they had a democratic alternative to voice their opposition to the state. But the ANC, when they planted bombs in trash cans in Johannesburg in the 1980s, were not terrorists because they had no means of political opposition available to them. This perspective implies that the Basque nationalist group Euzkadi Ta Askatasuna (ETA) were not terrorists when they planted bombs and murdered tourists under the Franco regime but became terrorists when they planted bombs and murdered tourists under the democratic government of Spain. This argument is hardly compelling. I believe that the political context in which an act takes place can affect our normative evaluation of the act – the degree to which we might think it morally justified or morally reprehensible – but it does not alter the fact that it is a terrorist act.

Perhaps the most difficult case to make is that of the ANC in South Africa. If ever a group could legitimately claim to have resorted to force only as a last resort it is the ANC. Founded in 1912, for the first fifty years the movement treated non-violence as a core principle. In 1961, however, with all forms of political organization closed to them, Nelson Mandela was authorized to create a separate military organization, Umkhonto we Sizwe (MK). In his autobiography Mandela describes the strategy session as the movement examined the options available to them:

> We considered four types of violent activities: sabotage, guerrilla warfare, terrorism and open revolution. For a small and fledgling army, open revolution was inconceivable. Terrorism inevitably reflected poorly on those who used it, undermining any public support it might otherwise garner. Guerrilla warfare was a possibility, but since the ANC had been reluctant to embrace violence at all, it made sense to start with the form of violence that inflicted the least harm against individuals: sabotage.[16]

These fine distinctions were lost on the court in Rivonia that convicted Mandela and most of the ANC leadership in 1964 and sentenced them to life imprisonment. For the next twenty years an increasingly repressive white minority state denied the most basic political rights to the majority black population.

An uprising in Soweto was defeated, as was an MK guerrilla campaign launched from surrounding states. In 1985 the government declared a state of emergency, which was followed within three weeks by thirteen terrorist bombings in major downtown areas. Reasonable people can differ on whether or not the terrorism of the ANC was justified, given the legitimacy of the goals they sought and the reprehensible nature of the government they faced. The violent campaign of the ANC in the early and mid-1980s, however, was indisputably a terrorist campaign. Just as clearly, the actions for which Mandela and others were convicted in 1964 did not constitute terrorism. Unless and until we are willing to label a group whose ends we believe to be just, a terrorist group, if they deliberately target civilians in order to achieve those ends, we are never going to be able to forge effective international co-operation against terrorism.

This same confusion between ends and means is what has given the rather silly adage that 'one man's freedom fighter is another man's terrorist' such a long life. The adage just reinforces the point that we don't like to label people whose goals we share as terrorists. Most terrorists would consider themselves freedom fighters. Bin Laden told the American people: 'We fight because we are free men who don't sleep under oppression. We want to restore freedom to our nation.'[17] Shamil Basayev said something quite similar: 'For me, it's first and foremost a struggle for freedom. If I'm not a free man, I can't live in my faith. I need to be a free man. Freedom is primary.'[18] The freedom for which they fight, however, is often an abstract concept. It means political freedom rather than conceding to others the right of freedom from fear, or freedom from random violence, as terrorists exploit civilian fear to further their ends. Whether they are fighting for freedom from repression, or freedom to impose a repressive theocracy, to suggest that 'freedom fighter' is an alternative to 'terrorist' is to confuse ends and means. As I've said, it is not the goal for which they fight that determines whether or not they are terrorists. The fact that terrorists may claim to be freedom fighters does not mean that we should concede the point to them; just as we should not concede the point that all citizens of a democracy are legitimate targets because they have the option of changing their government and have not done so, and are therefore responsible for their government's actions. This is precisely the casuistry by which bin Laden has sought to justify the targeting of American civilians. In his 'Letter to the American People' bin Laden wrote:

> The American people are the ones who choose their government by way of their own free will; a choice which stems from their agreement to its policies. Thus the American people have chosen, consented to, and affirmed their support for the Israeli oppression of the Palestinians, the occupation and usurpation of their land, and its [Israel's] continuous killing, torture, punishment and expulsion of the Palestinians. The American people have the ability and choice to refuse the policies of their government and even to change it if they want.[19]

It is often claimed, and not without reason, that history is written by the winners, so that a victorious terrorist becomes a statesman and a failed terrorist remains a terrorist. Terrorists with whom I have spoken invariably invoke Nelson Mandela and Menachem Begin as evidence that someone regarded as a terrorist today can be considered a statesman tomorrow. (In the past they also used to invoke Robert Mugabe, but less so now.) Nelson Mandela was for a long time described as a terrorist not only by the South African government but also by that of the US, as well as by many academics. As I have argued above, Mandela never in fact qualified as a terrorist. Menachem Begin, however, is a different story. Begin led Irgun from 1943 until its dissolution in 1948. The Irgun was an illegal Jewish right-wing movement made up of Revisionist Zionists. They attacked both Arabs and British in an effort to establish a Jewish state on both sides of the River Jordan. In 1938 Irgun exploded land mines in an Arab fruit market in Haifa, killing seventy-four people. More famously in 1946 they blew up the King David Hotel in Jerusalem, killing ninety-one people. In 1948 the Irgun and its offshoot the Stern Gang attacked the Arab village of Deir Yassin and killed 254 of the inhabitants. Both the Irgun and the Stern Gang were soon absorbed into the fledgling Israeli army on the expiration of the British mandate in 1948. Notwithstanding this past, Menachem Begin served as prime minister of Israel from 1977 to 1983 and shared the Nobel Peace Prize with Anwar Sadat in 1978. In truth Begin was a terrorist in the 1940s and a statesman in the 1970s. His subsequent political success does not alter the fact of his earlier terrorist actions.

So a terrorist is not a freedom fighter and a terrorist is not a guerrilla. A terrorist is a terrorist, no matter whether or not you like the goal s/he is trying to achieve, no matter whether or not you like the government s/he is trying to change.

Types of Terrorism

Terrorism is a tactic used by many different groups in many parts of the world in pursuit of many different objectives. Today the term 'terrorist' connotes the image of a radical Islamic fundamentalist from the Middle East. Thirty years ago the term conjured images of atheistic young European communists. Throughout this period terrorists around the world from Sri Lanka to Northern Ireland were also fighting for traditional goals like territorial control over a homeland. Aside from their willingness to visit violence on civilians to achieve their objectives, all these groups shared the characteristic that they were the weaker party in an asymmetrical conflict. Groups that have had the ability to launch an all-out military campaign have done so. Terrorism is the weapon of those who want to effect change, and to do so quickly, but have lacked the numbers either to prevail in a democratic system or to launch a viable military campaign.

Terrorism has not been limited to one part of the world, nor confined to one religion or political ideology. It has been practised by the right as well as by the left, by atheists, agnostics and religious millenarians, by Christians, Jews, Muslims, Hindus and members of most other religions. It has taken place in rich countries and poor, under authoritarian regimes and democratic governments. Terrorists' objectives range from Maoist revolution in Peru and Nepal to bringing about the apocalypse in Japan; from the destruction of the state of Israel to the destruction of capitalism in Europe; from the expulsion of US influence from the Middle East to the return of the Caliphate; from the expulsion of Russia from Chechnya and of Britain from Northern Ireland to creating homelands for Kurds, Tamils, Sikhs and Basques. In light of the diverse range of examples, any attempt to reduce all of them to one simplified notion of terrorism is only likely to cloud our understanding.

Social revolutionary movements, like the Italian Red Brigades, the German Red Army Faction (RAF), the Japanese Red Army and the French Action Directe, and millenarian movements, like the Japanese Aum Shinrikyo, have arisen primarily in advanced industrialized countries. Maoist movements (like the Peruvian Shining Path, the Nepalese Communist Party and the New People's Army in the Philippines) have emerged in the developing world. Radical religious movements have so far emerged primarily in the Middle East and east Asia (like Hezbollah in Lebanon and the Abu Sayyaf group in the Philippines), while ethno-nationalist movements have occurred all over the world from India to Ireland.

Since September 2001, the US administration has focused its concern with terrorism on 'terrorists with a global reach' – in other words, terrorists with the capability of hurting America. The number of terrorist groups possessing both the means and the motive to hurt the US is quite limited, though this is likely to change over time due to the increasing unpopularity of its foreign policy and the invention of technological innovations that permit weapons of greater and greater lethality to fall into the hands of smaller and smaller groups. Smaller groups are, of course, much more difficult to track than larger ones.

In spite of the dizzying array of terrorist movements, the two key variables for understanding all terrorist groups are the nature of the goals they seek and their relationship to the community they claim to represent (see Figure 1). This simple matrix enables us to organize the ever-growing and quite disparate set of terrorist movements, but it will also prove essential later in understanding how terrorists groups terminate their campaigns and how they can most effectively be countered.

NATURE OF GOALS

		Temporal	Transformational
RELATIONSHIP TO COMMUNITY	**Isolated**	GRAPO Dev Sol November 17 Real IRA	Red Brigades Red Army Faction Aum Shinrikyo Old IRA al-Qaeda?
		1	2
		3	4
	Close	PIRA ETA Hamas Shining Path PKK	al-Qaeda?

Figure 1: Goals of Terrorist Groups[20]

Goals of Terrorist Groups

The goals of all terrorist groups fall into one of two categories: temporal and transformational. By temporal I mean political goals that can be met within the current socio-political configuration. An independent homeland for Sikhs, Tamils, Chechens and Basques would qualify, as would the secession of Kashmir from India and of Northern Ireland from the United Kingdom. This is not to trivialize these aspirations nor to underestimate the difficulty of conceding them. The United States fought a bitter and bloody civil war at a cost of 600,000 lives on the issue of secession. Nevertheless, these goals could be won or lost without overthrowing the fundamental balance of power. They are also issues on which compromise could be negotiated, substituting local autonomy for complete independence, for example.

On the other hand, a transformational goal by its nature is not subject to negotiation and its satisfaction would require the complete destruction of the regional state system. The social revolutionary movements in Europe in the 1970s sought the destruction of capitalism. Similar in scale is the desire to replace the states of the contemporary Middle East with the Caliphate, the era of Islam's ascendancy from the death of Muhammed in 632 until the thirteenth century. It should of course be pointed out that the declared policy of these movements, much like the stated policy of many governments, should not always be taken at face value. An essential element in understanding these movements and effectively countering them is precisely to understand the degree of commitment to the declared goals and whether or not they might actually be motivated by more traditional political aspirations.

The second variable is the relationship of the movement to the community they claim to represent. Some movements are quite isolated from their communities. Those that are have been easiest to defeat. They have been most vulnerable to defections and internal splits and ultimately have proven easiest to counter with traditional security measures. Lacking financial support, they have often been forced to engage in criminal activity to fund their operations and this in turn exposes them to capture. Groups in this category, like the left-wing extremists November 17 in Greece or GRAPO in Spain, have been able to inflict only limited damage on their enemies.

Far more dangerous are those groups that have close ties in the community they claim to represent. This is the sea in which Mao's fish swim. In a great many instances the broader communities share the aspirations of the terrorist groups even if they don't always approve of their means of achieving these objectives. A terrorist group can survive and thrive in this kind of complicit society. While the broader population will not themselves engage in terrorism or even openly approve of it, they will not turn in the terrorists. They will look the other way and provide crucial albeit often passive support. When the authorities come looking, these terrorists are simply absorbed into the community. When the authorities respond harshly to terrorist acts, this is the community that provides willing new recruits to the movement. Groups that have a strong base of support within the community can last indefinitely, as many ethno-nationalist groups can demonstrate. These groups tend to be altogether more difficult to counter, but handled properly the community can serve as a source of restraint on the movement. Terrorist groups with support from the community can also turn into a broad-based insurrectionist movement or, given the right conditions, into political movements.

The examples in Figure 1 above are intended to be illustrative, not exhaustive. It is also not always entirely clear what precisely is the nature of the goal being pursued. In the case of Hamas, the charter of the movement and the language of the leadership is suffused with religious rhetoric, yet if one considers the actions of Hamas it is clear that the movement is motivated by the very polit-ical desire to replace the PLO as the legitimate voice of the Palestinians. Similarly with al-Qaeda, we do not yet know what is the correct weight to assign to the religious fundamentalist aspira-tions of the movement and the very political goals they often espouse. The scale of their ambitions however, be they religious or political, suggests that they belong in the revolutionary/transfor-mational camp.

Rationality of Terrorism

The enormous gap between the ends pursued and the means employed has often caused us to think of terrorists as crazies. How can killing tourists at a shrine in Luxor or airline passengers in the US possibly help the cause of Islamic fundamentalism? How can killing children in Beslan, shoppers in London or tourists in Spain advance the cause of Chechen, Irish or Basque nationalism? The willingness to commit acts that are entirely outside the accepted code of civilized conduct by randomly killing children, women, the elderly and whoever else happens to be in the wrong place at the time causes us to think that terrorists must be deranged psychopaths. Their actions seem to make no sense.

But terrorists, by and large, are not insane at all. The primary shared characteristic of terrorists is their psychological normalcy, insofar as we understand the term. On the contrary they ration-ally and carefully calibrate their tactics to exploit their enemy's weakness and ensure maximum effect. Psychological studies of

terrorists are virtually unanimous on this point.[21] The British journalist Peter Taylor remembers asking a young prisoner from Derry,
who was serving a life sentence for murder, what an IRA man was
doing reading Tolstoy and Hardy. The prisoner replied, 'Because
an IRA man's normal like everyone else.' When Taylor pointed
out that normal people did not go around killing people, the prisoner said that normal people elsewhere did not live in Northern
Ireland.[22] There are, of course, psychopaths to be found in many
terrorist groups, as in many organizations in which violence is
sanctioned. But there are not nearly as many psychopaths in terrorist groups as one might imagine. Most organizations consider
them a liability and quite deliberately try to select them out.[23] This
holds true across different types of groups from ethno-nationalists
to religious fundamentalists.

Historically, terrorists have been very conservative in their
choice of tactics. The most common terrorist act is a bombing and
it is not hard to see why. It is cheap. It is easy to get away from
the scene of the attack. Moreover, it is dramatic and often indiscriminate. The notion that terrorists are mad has been advanced by
the increasing use of suicide terrorism. But even here, from an
organizational point of view, suicide attacks are very rational,
indeed economical. In the words of Dr Ayman al-Zawahiri, bin
Laden's second in command: 'the method of martyrdom operation
is the most successful way of inflicting damage against the opponent and least costly to the mujahideen in terms of casualties'.[24] It
is also of course more effective. Different academics offer different
estimates of how much more effective, but they are all unanimous
that it is, indeed, more effective.[25]

Even if suicide terrorism makes sense from an organizational
point of view, it seems insane from an individual point of view.
Again, all the available evidence suggests that the organizations that
employ the tactic have more volunteers than they need. They deliberately do not accept volunteers they consider depressed or suicidal.
In the words of the Palestinian Fayez Jaber, an Al-Aqsa commander
who trained suicide bombers: 'There are certain criteria that we
observe. People with mental or psychological problems or personal
family problems – I cannot allow myself to end such people . . .

A person has to be a fully mature person, an adult, a sane person, and of course, not less than 18 years of age and fully aware of what he is about to carry out.'[26] Those who become martyrs appear to do so out of a combination of motives: anger, humiliation, a desire for revenge, commitment to their comrades and their cause, and a desire to attain glory. In other words, for reasons no more irrational than those of anyone prepared to give their lives for a cause.[27]

Terrorist behaviour has long appeared senseless to onlookers. The actions of the famous medieval sect the Assassins seemed so incomprehensible to others that for centuries it was believed that they were high on hashish when they undertook their suicide operations. It now appears that they were intoxicated only by their own ideology.[28]

Morality of Terrorism

Another almost universally accepted attribute of terrorists is their amorality – in the words of President Bush: 'abandoning every value except the will to power'.[29] Yet I have never met a terrorist who considered him/herself either immoral or amoral. Quite the contrary. When not acting as terrorists they practise as much or as little morality in their daily lives as most of the rest of us. Most terrorists, moreover, go to considerable lengths to justify their actions on moral grounds, both in their public pronouncements and in their internal writings.

Albert Camus in his play *Les Justes* beautifully captures the sense of morality of the nineteenth-century anarchists, the precursors to many contemporary terrorists. He describes how Kaliayev, seeing two children seated in the carriage next to his intended target, the grand duke, could not bring himself to hurl the bomb. He goes back to his comrades and explains his thinking and they accept him. Kaliayev is quite prepared to sacrifice his own life in taking someone else's. He subsequently does kill the grand duke and is executed, but he could not justify to himself killing children.[30]

Many contemporary terrorists, of course, have no trouble justifying the killing of children. There are generally a number of defences offered for the resort to terrorism. First, that it is entered into only as a last resort. Bin Laden made this claim in his 1996 fatwa, or declaration of war against America: 'why is it then the regime closed all peaceful routes and pushed the people towards armed actions?!! Which is the only choice left for them to implement righteousness and justice.'[31] This is an empirical claim. As such it can quickly be refuted by reference to the facts. Many terrorist groups do first try political action, but they have hardly exhausted the options available to them when they resort to terrorism. The only terrorist campaign that can make a remotely plausible claim to have turned to terrorism as a last resort is the ANC bombing campaign of the 1980s. Even in this instance the leadership of the organization sought to exert control over the use of violence, but, given the radicalization of the black population in the face of government repression, they were largely unable to do so.

The second common claim is that no other strategy is available. Vellupillai Prabakharan, the charismatic leader of the Tamil Tigers, put it succinctly: 'We have no other option but to fight back.'[32] One member of al-Qassam, the military wing of Hamas, told the Pakistani writer and relief worker Nasra Hassan: 'We do not have tanks or rockets, but we have something superior – our exploding human bombs. In place of a nuclear arsenal, we are proud of our arsenal of believers.'[33] If you are the twenty-five members of the Baader–Meinhof Gang in Germany and desire to overthrow the German capitalist state immediately, there are not too many options available. Ulrike Meinhof, in one of the first communiqués of the Baader–Meinhof Gang, declared that urban guerrilla warfare was 'the only revolutionary method of intervention available to what are on the whole weak revolutionary forces'.[34] The problem with this argument is that there are always other options available. If those who seek change decided to take a longer time-frame and embark on a protracted political strategy of propaganda and civil disobedience they might undermine the state. But they want immediate results. So their weakness is in relationship both to the state and to the broader population who do not share their views. If they had wider support they wouldn't need to resort to terrorism. So terrorism may well be the only option available, but only if one lacks support, wants immediate results and is prepared to murder innocents.

Thirdly, those who commit terrorist acts often argue that terrorism works. Certainly the actions of Black September Palestinians, famous for hijacking aircraft and, most notoriously, for murdering the Israeli Olympic team in Munich in 1972, brought international attention to the plight of the Palestinians just as IRA violence in Northern Ireland brought attention to the denial of civil rights to Northern Irish Catholics. But to prove that terrorism works one would have to show that terrorism achieved what the terrorists wanted and what other means could not, and this has never been done. Maybe the IRA campaign and the ensuing loss of 3,500 lives in Northern Ireland resulted in the power-sharing executive in Northern Ireland, but this executive (currently suspended) is a far cry from the Irish unity the IRA has always demanded. Moreover, it is surely reasonable to expect that the same result could have been achieved through concerted peaceful political action over the past thirty years and without any significant loss of life.

The two most common arguments put forward by contemporary Islamic fundamentalists to justify their actions are those of collective guilt and of moral equivalence. Palestinian radicals have long insisted that Israeli civilians, all of whom are obliged to serve in the country's security services, are not civilians and hence constitute legitimate targets: 'They are not innocent if they are part of the total population, which is part of the army . . . From 18 on, they are soldiers, even if they have civilian clothes.'[35] Similarly, bin Laden has argued explicitly that Americans and western citizens have the option of changing their governments and when they do not are responsible for their actions. He declared: 'The American people are the ones who pay the taxes which fund the planes that bomb us in Afghanistan, the tanks that strike and destroy our homes in Pakistan, the armies which occupy our lands in the Arabian Gulf, and the fleets which ensure the blockade of Iraq.'[36]

The final argument is the familiar teenage response, 'Everybody does it.' Our terrorism is justified because everyone else practises terrorism too. An angry Palestinian told Nasra Hassan: 'The Israelis kill our children and our women. This is war, and innocent people get hurt.'[37] Eddie Kinner, a young Protestant paramilitary in Northern Ireland, used similar language: 'As far as I was concerned, I had joined an army and we were engaged in a war. The enemy had attacked my community and I was prepared to respond in kind.'[38] In all his statements bin Laden goes into detail about the iniquities of the US, the bombing of Hiroshima and Nagasaki, the killing of Iraqi children by US sanctions and of Afghan villagers by US bombs. He and his followers believe that the US lives by force and so they must respond with force. Bin Laden declared long before 9/11: 'Through history America has not been known to differentiate between the military and the civilians, between men and women, or adults and children. Those who hurled atomic bombs and used the weapons of mass destruction against Nagasaki and Hiroshima were the Americans. Can the bombs differentiate between military and women and infants and children?'[39]

Even when arguing that it is legitimate to kill civilians and that they are only doing to their enemies what their enemies are doing to them, they continue to impose limits on the degree to which they can inflict harm on their enemies. Ramzi bin al-Shibh, one of the masterminds of the 9/11 attacks, who was arrested in Karachi, Pakistan on September 11, 2002, composed an ideological justification of the 9/11 attacks intended for internal consumption. He wrote:

> Because of Saddam and the Baath Party, America punished a whole population. Thus its bombs and its embargo killed millions of Iraqi Muslims. And because of Osama bin Laden, America surrounded Afghans and bombed them, causing the death of tens of thousands of Muslims . . . God said to assault whoever assaults you, in a like manner . . . In killing Americans who are ordinarily off limits, Muslims should not exceed four million non-combatants, or render more than ten million of them homeless. We should avoid this, to make sure the penalty is no more than reciprocal.[40]

The fact that a senior al-Qaeda operative feels justified in killing 4 million Americans and making 10 million homeless is hardly grounds for optimism, but it does demonstrate that they have a code that imposes restraints on their actions. As bin Laden has said: 'Reciprocal treatment is fair.'[41] The constant declarations of war by fatwa are another attempt to appeal to a higher authority to justify their actions.

Finally, the popularity of suicide attacks or 'martyrdom operations', as those who volunteer prefer to call them, is in itself a moral claim. Our fascination with the suicide attack is due to a number of factors – our fear of its destructiveness, our sense that it is crazy and therefore incomprehensible, and finally our discomfiture that it doesn't quite fit with our sense of terrorists as depraved. Part of the popularity of the act among terrorists is, indeed, its destructiveness, but volunteers are also attracted precisely because it is an assertion of a claim to moral superiority over the enemy.

This is most obviously the case for hunger-strikers. The tradition of inflicting harm on oneself in an effort to shame one's enemy has a long history in many cultures, particularly the Gaelic one. When ten imprisoned republican prisoners slowly starved themselves to death in 1981, they were denying the depiction of them as depraved criminals. They were in fact claiming the moral high ground. It was also an enormously effective tactic. Even if they did not thereby gain their immediate goal, political-prisoner status, they won worldwide attention and more new recruits than the movement could manage. The popular sympathy was such that one of the hunger-strikers was elected to the London parliament in a landslide.[42]

It is, of course, easier to justify killing oneself for a cause than killing oneself as a means of killing others, especially when those others are civilians going about their daily lives. Nevertheless, the scores of young men, and increasingly young women and older men, who volunteer for suicide operations do so believing that they are acting morally, selflessly giving their lives for a cause.[43] In one video, made on the eve of a suicide attack on an Israeli bus, a member of Hamas says: 'We want to make it clear to the world that the true killer is Israel because our demands are legitimate.'[44]

We have seen then that terrorists are sub-state actors who violently target non-combatants to communicate a political message to a third party. Terrorists are neither crazy nor amoral. They come from all parts of the world. They come from many walks of life. They fight for a range of different causes. Some have support from the communities from which they come, some do not. They range in size from a handful of Corsican nationalists to thousands of armed Tamils. Some are fighting for the same traditional goals that have driven wars for centuries, like control over national territory. Some are trying to overthrow the state system itself. They come from all religious traditions and from none. One thing they do have in common. They are weaker than those they oppose.

The brutality of terrorist violence and in particular the targeting of random victims in apparent disregard for all norms of civilized behaviour leaves us with a great many questions. In the chapters that follow I will explore the historical antecedents of contemporary terrorism and what we know about the underlying factors that tend to precipitate terrorism. I will investigate the motives of terrorists and will argue that in light of these motives killing oneself in order to kill others is far from irrational. I will argue that given what we know about what terrorists want and how they try to achieve it, a democratic effort to wage war on terrorism is doomed to failure.

2

Where Have Terrorists Come From?

> I, as chairman of the Palestinian Liberation Organization, hereby once more declare that I condemn terrorism in all its forms, and at the same time salute those sitting before me in this hall who, in the days when they fought to free their countries from the yoke of colonialism, were accused of terrorism by their oppressors, and who today are the faithful leaders of their peoples, stalwart champions of justice and freedom.
>
> Yassar Arafat, United Nations General Assembly,
> December 1988[1]

The three terrorists hid the 548 pounds of explosives in a thirty-six-gallon beer cask, covered it in tarpaulin and placed it in a wheelbarrow.[2] They had earlier bought the explosives in small quantities to avoid suspicion. They wheeled the barrow to the prison walls and rested it there. Following a prearranged plan, they tossed a white ball over the prison wall as a signal to the prisoners exercising inside. Then they lit the fuse and withdrew to a safe distance. The fuse spluttered and went out. One of the team came forward, lit the fuse again and retreated. Again it went out. A third time he came forward and lit the now dangerously short fuse and retreated. Yet again the fuse went out. The team decided to wheel their explosives away.

The next day the same three men, thought to have been James Murphy, Michael Barrett and Jeremiah O'Sullivan, once more wheeled the barrow to the prison wall. This time they lifted the cask from the barrow, set it against the prison wall, lit the fuse and withdrew only after establishing that the fuse was well and truly alight. The barrel exploded. The resulting hole in the prison wall was twenty feet wide at the base and sixty feet wide at the top. The prison authorities, having been tipped off about the planned rescue attempt, had removed the prisoners to cells on the opposite side of the prison. The blast was heard forty miles away.

The real impact of the blast was felt in the surrounding neighbourhood. Thousands of terrified Londoners spilled on to the streets from their ruined houses. Fires spread through the overcrowded slums. Six people were killed by the explosion, including seven-year-old Minnie Abbot and sixty-seven-year-old Martha Evans. More than a hundred people were injured, including five members of Minnie Abbot's family. Over 400 houses were damaged, many were destroyed. All army and police leave was cancelled and a nationwide call was made for volunteers to act as special constables in the emergency: 166,000 were enrolled. In the House of Lords a member declared that terror had seized society.[3] *The Times* described the explosion as 'one of the most heinous, most reckless, and most foolish outrages that are to be found in the records of crime'.[4]

This explosion at Clerkenwell Prison in London occurred on December 13, 1867. Except for the type of explosives used, gunpowder rather than fertilizer or semtex, it could have happened this week. I mention it here to illustrate the point that terrorism has been with us for some time.

In the aftermath of the 9/11 attacks, international public opinion rallied around the United States in support and to a degree that was simply unprecedented. The warmth of that reaction has certainly modulated with time. Even among the US's closest allies there has been a degree of exasperation with the American sense that terrorism was invented on September 11. Terrorism has bedevilled many European countries since the late 1960s. But it has a much longer history than the last thirty to forty years. The Zealots, the Assassins and the Thugs (the three words have entered our lexicon thanks to the role the movements played in history) have been constantly invoked as precursors to contemporary terrorism.

More recent nineteenth-century examples, like the Irish Fenians and the Russian anarchists, are also often mentioned.

Whether or not the terrorism the US faces today is new I think matters for two reasons. If it is not new, then it is less intimidating. It is less frightening to realize that the type of adversary one faces has been faced, and faced down, before. As the psychological impact of terrorism is both a key weapon for the terrorist and a key vulnerability for the victim, the fact that we have not entered an entirely new world order can be reassuring. Our ability to be resilient against terrorist threats is, in fact, a much neglected but quite crucial element of the counter-terrorist arsenal. Second, and perhaps more important, it matters because the US can learn from the experience of other countries. Many countries, including many democratic countries, have effectively countered terrorism in the past. Most learned the hard way, that is over time and through mistakes, how to develop an effective counter-terrorism strategy. All the indications are that the US government are repeating the pattern, learning from their own mistakes instead of from the mistakes of others. Later I will examine the lessons to be derived from the experiences of other countries in countering terrorism. For now I would like to make the general point that if we are ever to understand what changed on September 11 we must first understand what happened before.

I will briefly review some of these historical cases with an eye to the present in order to demonstrate that terrorism is not new and not a modern phenomenon (these examples go back to the first century after Christ); that terrorism is not now, and never has been, the sole preserve of Islam (these examples are drawn from four religions and none, Judaism, Islam, Hinduism, Christianity and atheism); and to illustrate that the mixture of religious and political motives that has marked so much of contemporary terrorism since the Iranian revolution in 1979 is not new either. The point is not to provide a history of these movements – several good ones already exist – but rather to examine them for contemporary relevance.[5]

The Ancient Trilogy

The three most important and most commonly cited historical pre-cursors to contemporary movements were all religiously inspired, throwing into question the conventional belief that the combination of terrorism and religion is a recent phenomenon. These three cases are the Sicarii or Zealots from ancient times, the Assassins from the medieval period, and the Thugs who lasted from medieval to modern times. The fact that their names have entered our every-day vocabulary is no coincidence: terrorist groups do tend to make an impression.

Their preferred weapon, the dagger, gained for the first group the name Sicarii, while their zeal in demonstrating their faith in God, for example by burning their own food supply, won them their other name, Zealots.[6] Their goal was largely a political one, to elim-inate Roman rule in Palestine. Their targets, however, extended far beyond Romans and included any local Jews willing to work with the Imperial Romans, or collaborators as they would be termed today. So, while from their perspective the targets were not random, their lists of enemies were so extensive that the killings appeared to onlookers to be indiscriminate and hence instilled widespread fear. As today's terrorists have learned, random violence has a much bigger impact than discriminate violence, because if nobody is selected then nobody is safe, and the terror inspired is more far-reaching. The Zealots' preferred tactic was to mingle in the crowds at a festival or other larger gathering, locate their opponent, pull a concealed dagger from beneath their clothes, stab their victim, and then disappear back into the crowd. Lacking a mass media to pub-licize their exploits, they certainly understood a good propaganda tactic, playing as it does on the psychology of terrorism. By acting in the midst of a large crowd they ensured that word of their action would spread. Writers of the period spoke of the widespread terror inflicted. 'The panic created was more alarming than the calamity itself; everyone, as on the battlefield, hourly expected death.'[7]

The Zealots' targets were Romans and their collaborators, loosely defined. Their tactic was stabbing in public places. Their immediate objective was to provoke conflict and their ultimate goal was the elimination of Roman rule. They did succeed, as terrorists often do, in provoking conflict but not in achieving their ultimate objectives. Their revolt was crushed after twenty-five years, but it had enormous ramifications. It contributed to the destruction of the Temple and the mass suicide at Masada. Unusually for a terrorist group they did succeed in inspiring two subsequent, but futile, insurrections against Roman rule that were brutally suppressed.

There are a number of interesting parallels to be drawn between the Zealots and contemporary terrorist movements, and not just their name. The word 'Hamas', incidentally, means 'zeal'. Most modern terrorists argue that they are acting on behalf of 'the people' and hope to inspire the people to rise up against the oppressor. The people, by and large, have proven extremely reluctant to do so. The Zealots were unusually successful in this regard. A great many later terrorist movements, from the nineteenth-century Russian anarchists to the twentieth-century European urban social revolutionaries and to the Latin American rural movements, have tried and generally failed to inspire the people to rise up behind them.

Like contemporary groups the Zealots understood the importance of publicity as what Prime Minister Thatcher called the 'oxygen' of terrorism.[8] Their political goal and international character are also characteristic of many contemporary movements. Their deliberate attempt to provoke a spiral of violence, of reprisal, and counter-reprisal, and their lack of concern for the innocents caught in the middle, is another hallmark of contemporary terrorism.

The next group, known as the Assassins, operated from the eleventh to the thirteenth centuries. Medieval times are often thought to have been marked by such brutality that terrorism is difficult to distinguish from the other forms of violence that proliferated, but this is not entirely the case. In the latter part of the Middle Ages rules of warfare began to develop, partly under the influence of the church and partly due to the crippling expense of maintaining an army. While human rights were unknown and torture was standard practice, armies were generally relatively small. A medieval army, for example, rarely comprised more than 100,000 troops, compared to 350,000 in Roman times or France's 300,000 in 1710. There were also distinct differences in the treatment of peasants and aristocrats. To give one fairly extreme example, in the Battle of Lincoln, England, in 1217 the value of ransoming captives was such that only one knight died on the winning side and two on the losing side, while about 400 were taken prisoner.

The medieval contribution to the terrorist lineage was the Assassins, who were a fanatical and murderous Shia Muslim sect active for about 200 years in the Middle East. They were inspired by the goal of purifying Islam, which had both political and religious ramifications. Like the Zealots, their preferred weapon was the knife and the method was stabbing. Their strategy was a policy of assassination and their victims were orthodox religious leaders who refused to heed their warnings. Like the Zealots, they compensated for the absence of a mass media by choosing prominent victims whom they murdered on holy days, preferably while there were many witnesses around.

Again, there are a number of similarities to contemporary groups. The Assassins too sought to address a wider audience and to generate sympathy for their cause. They demonstrated the patience and long-term planning that has marked recent radical Muslim groups. In an early version of a sleeper cell, they would send a young recruit into the house of an intended victim to develop a relationship with the victim before stabbing him in front of others. They also had an international character and moved back and forth across state lines. They did, however, go on to establish their own state, essentially a set of mountain fortresses where they trained recruits and from where they launched attacks. It was eventually sacked by Mongol and Arab armies.

The other similarity to current groups and the reason the Assassins are so often invoked today lies in the fact that, much like some contemporary terrorists, they too had a culture of the martyr, or shaheed. Having stabbed their victim they would not disappear into the crowd like the Zealots; rather, they would wait to be beaten to death by the crowd or arrested and executed. This bizarre behaviour appalled and fascinated their contemporaries, so much so that it was widely believed that they were on hashish when committing their attacks. The term Assassin is actually derived from the term for hashish-eater. Recent historiography, however, has revealed that there is no evidence that they were on hallucinogens.

The third member of the ancient terrorist trilogy is the Indian Thugi. They were an extraordinary group who operated in India for about 600 years. Their motives were religious rather than political and for this reason they do not qualify as terrorists by my definition, but I mention them here as they are widely considered terrorists and do have an interesting contemporary resonance. The Thugi were both the longest-lasting and the most destructive group, being credited by the political scientist David Rapoport with up to half a million deaths. Their victims were not chosen randomly. Instead they had very elaborate rules as to who could and could not be killed: they killed only travellers and no Europeans, and only those with whom they had developed a friendship and whom they then offered as a gift to their god. The method of killing was strangulation with a silk tie and without shedding blood, and in the most painful way possible. They were devotees of the goddess Kali and believed she was more pleased the more terror she witnessed. To compound the atrocity and enhance the psychological impact, they dismembered the corpses to prevent cremation or proper burial. They operated under very specific constraints and had rules about every aspect of their behaviour. Some contemporaries mistakenly thought they acted out of self-interest in order to steal the belongings of their victims, but in fact this was not the case at all. They were forbidden to take property without killing and burying the owner first and they were disdainful of ordinary robbers.[9] They used the booty they did acquire to pay off their sponsors, not for their own enrichment. The Thugi were, eventually, annihilated by the British in the nineteenth century.

They are relevant to us today for two reasons. They were the first precursors of state-sponsored terrorism, which in part explains their longevity. So while their own goals were religious they played into the political agendas of others. They took as loot the belongings of their victims and used this to pay princes who provided their expeditions with sanctuaries. Second, they demonstrate how knowledge of the philosophy of a group can be used against them. The British defeat of the Thugi was assisted by the knowledge that the group believed that Kali would destroy the order when its members no longer served her. Aware that some members of the brotherhood were developing an unseemly interest in booty, the British appealed to the more traditional members of the group and helped persuade them that their responsibility now was to assist Kali by becoming informers.

An awareness of the group's beliefs might also have been helpful to the Japanese authorities when they started receiving complaints about the strange behaviour and peculiar smells emanating from buildings owned by the Aum Shinrikyo cult in Japan in the early 1990s. This is the cult that released sarin gas in the Tokyo subway in March 1995. The cult's leader, Shoko Asahara, and his followers were also devotees of the goddess Kali. They too killed only travellers and did so without shedding their blood. It is, of course, easy to overdo these analogies. There are huge differences between the Thugi and the Aum Shinrikyo, but it is hard to deny that a greater knowledge of the terrorist groups, their writings and their motives can help the authorities to anticipate and prevent or pre-empt their actions.

Terror from Above: The French Revolution

We acquired names for nasty characters like thugs and assassins from early terrorist groups. We acquired the term 'terror' itself from the French revolution, but in those days it referred to terror from above, terror imposed by the state, rather than from below, from insurgents. The regime of terror in France in 1793–4 contained many of the themes that were to become familiar to succeeding generations. Fundamentally, the Terror was simply the logical application of a particular philosophy: the people had to be reborn and if some of them got in the way they were enemies of the revolution and had to be removed. In the words of Saint-Just, one of the architects: 'We want to establish an order of things such that a universal tendency towards the good is established and the factions find themselves suddenly hurled on the scaffold.'[10] The problem, of course, is with the concept of 'we'. Initially 'we' was the people, broadly defined, but the concept was progressively narrowed to become only a sub-group of the Committee of Public Safety. The narrowing of the category of those entitled to act on behalf of the people was matched by a continued widening of the range of the victims. Initially, the Terror was aimed only at aristocrats, but the category progressively expanded. In the end, only about 37 per cent of those guillotined during the reign of terror were actually aristocrats. Eventually the machine turned in on itself, and its chief architect, Robespierre, was himself guillotined. His death heralded a reaction against state terror.

A key legacy of the French revolution to contemporary terrorism has been this notion of the killers as the self-appointed guardians of the will of the people. It must be said, though, that when one has the apparatus of the state at one's disposal, as Robespierre and some more recent autocrats have, one can do a lot more damage than any latterday terrorist movement has ever managed.

The second essential legacy is the introduction of political ideology as a substitute for religion as a motivating force for terrorism. Prior to the French revolution all terrorist groups had religious motivations, though in most instances these religious motivations had political ramifications.

After the French revolution, and until the Iranian revolution in 1979, terrorist movements were motivated by political aspirations and political ideologies. These quite different ideologies were based on a number of assumptions that had been launched in the course of the French revolution. The first was the belief that radical change was possible and the goal of remaking society attainable. The second was the idea attributed to Rousseau that man is naturally good, that evil comes not from inside man but from the external structures of society. Destroy these structures and you have destroyed evil. This lent itself to a missionary role for politics, as well as to the identification of an out-group. For Robespierre it was the aristocrats, for Marx the capitalists, for Hitler the Jews, for Fanon the imperialist powers, for bin Laden the Israelis and Americans, and so on. It is not difficult to see how this new style of politics as mission could lend itself to interpretations that make the use of terrorism for ideological ends appear as a natural out-growth of the idealistic belief in man's natural goodness.

Finally, there was the doctrine of popular sovereignty as a basis for political legitimacy. Again, it is easy to see how this doctrine, which was intended to liberate the masses and inaugurate an era of harmony, might instead produce the opposite. As we have seen, the concept of 'the people' can be defined in any way at all. This means that popular sovereignty can be invoked by anyone wishing to defy a government by claiming to be a truer representative of the popular will than the established authority. This idea has been particularly useful to all kinds of contemporary terrorists, who are invariably outnumbered by their adversaries, and who claim to act in the name of the people. Most actually believe that they are doing so.

After the French revolution and the defeat of Napoleon the forces of conservatism and indeed reaction dominated European politics, but on the ground nationalism, liberalism and republicanism were gaining adherents. Secret societies and conspiratorial student groups proliferated in European coffee houses culminating in the year of revolutions of 1848. These revolutions, which occurred in capital cities all over Europe, were an ignominious failure.

Marx and Bakunin

Two nineteenth-century thinkers, Marx and Bakunin, have been linked closely to terrorism, one more legitimately than the other. Marx was denounced as a terrorist because of his support for the Paris Commune in 1871, but he did not consider himself a sup-porter of terrorism at all. He dismissed Bakunin's idea of a peasant revolution as 'schoolboy's asininity'. Marx saw the Commune as the first stage of a workers' state, a radically democratic govern-ment, and an authentic representation of the French proletariat. He worried that terrorism might pose a premature threat to the state before the workers were ready to take it over. He objected to the efforts to destroy the state, arguing instead that the goal of the organized urban proletariat should be to master the apparatus of the state.

Marx's two daughters, Jenny and Laura, were ardent supporters of the Fenians, who had carried out the Clerkenwell explosion, but Marx himself was not. While he shared the Fenian view of the injustice of British rule in Ireland, he had his eyes firmly fixed on the goal of proletarian revolution. He wrote to his close collaborator Friedrich Engels the day after the explosion: 'The last exploit of the Fenians in Clerkenwell was a very stupid thing. The London masses who have shown great sympathy for Ireland will be made wild by it and driven into the arms of the government party. One cannot expect the London proletarians to allow themselves to be blown up in honour of Fenian emissaries.'[11] Engels replied on 19 December: 'The stupid affair in Clerkenwell was obviously the work of a few specialized fanatics . . . In particular, there has been a lot of bluster in America about this blowing up and arson business, and then a few asses come and instigate such nonsense. Moreover these cannibals are generally the greatest cowards . . . and then the idea of liberating Ireland by setting a London tailor's shop on fire.'[12]

Engels's family, like Marx's, was more sympathetic. Engels's common-law wife, Lizzy Burns, was a staunch supporter of the Fenians. Their home in England was a hotbed of Fenian activity and provided shelter to members on the run. It was even decorated in the Fenian colours of green and black. Later Engels was outraged by the Fenian campaign of the 1880s in which bystanders were again killed. He argued that even revolutionaries must behave like soldiers and kill only those actually fighting against them.

Marx's nemesis Mikhail Bakunin was in many ways the prototype of the modern social revolutionary terrorist and was the most influential of the nineteenth-century thinkers on terrorism. An aristocrat bored with debate, he wanted immediate action. His goal was to seize power quickly with a small group of elite co-conspirators and unleash a mass revolt against property and authority. He travelled indefatigably around Europe to any place experiencing civil disturbance and tried to mobilize a revolution. His critics said of him that his revolutionary fervour never flagged, his plotting never ceased, and his rebellions never succeeded. He believed that violence could generate immediate justice by sweeping away the oppressive institutions of the state. So you had in Bakunin the completion of the transition from the old-style insurrectionist with an emphasis on mass violence to the advocate of violent terrorism by small groups claiming to represent the masses.[13]

Irish Nationalists

Two late-nineteenth-century terrorist groups are worth mentioning as precursors to contemporary terrorism, the Irish nationalists and the Russian anarchists. The Irish Republican Brotherhood (IRB), the forerunner of the contemporary IRA, was a secret society dedicated to achieving an independent Ireland by force. There was a significant degree of support for this aspiration in Ireland, though most of the politically aware population favoured the peaceful policies of the Irish Home Rule Party, which sought to achieve these ends through parliamentary action. The IRB, like the Jacobins before them, claimed an exclusive right to decide what was best for the Irish people, though this did not actually make them terrorists. They were so convinced that the people would follow their lead that they actually preferred the old-fashioned tactic of open insurrection. In fact, their one effort at open insurrection in the Fenian Rising of 1867 was an unmitigated disaster, not least because almost nobody rose up to join them. The event was hardly noticed in Britain.

Among those who had fought with the Fenians in 1867 were Irish Americans who were recruited at the end of the American Civil War to deploy their military training on behalf of Ireland. Some who did not return to Ireland launched a number of Quixotic attempts to invade Canada from the US. Their plan was to seize Canada's transportation network and force Britain to exchange Ireland's freedom for possession of the Province of Canada.

In Britain the group were widely denounced as terrorists, though they were often given credit for the actions of several more radical offshoots that launched a bombing campaign in England in the 1880s. One such group was the Clan na Gael (Irish Family), which was actually funded by Irish immigrants living in the US. This is the first known instance of a pattern that was to become quite common a century later. Members of diaspora communities, feeling out of place in their new homes, develop a powerful affinity for their homeland and finance movements for radical change back home. Simplicity of interpretation tends to increase with distance from the conflict. The Fenian campaign was unsuccessful not least due to a reluctance to cause civilian casualties, and without deaths they couldn't attract attention.

One act of violence did gain a lot of attention. Known as the Phoenix Park murders, an offshoot of the IRB murdered two leading representatives of British rule in Ireland. In 1882 a new chief secretary, Lord Frederick Cavendish, arrived in Dublin. On the evening of his arrival in May, while walking with his under secretary T. H. Burke, he was attacked and stabbed to death by a group calling themselves the Invincibles. This action really belongs in the tradition of the Sicarii and the Assassins, a precise action against carefully chosen targets. The reputation of the Irish separatists for terrorism, then, is somewhat misplaced, though it is easy to see where it came from. While the actual actions of these groups were fairly minor their rhetoric was extremely bloodthirsty. On paper they loudly called for all kinds of acts of aggression, but on the ground they never quite managed to pull them off. Jeremiah O'Donovan Rossa, one the great Fenian heroes and a prominent figure in republican mythology to this day, once actually produced a scheme for spraying the House of Commons with a lethal gas, probably the first recorded terrorist plan to deploy chemical weapons. In the event the man proved squeamish and never quite managed to launch even a minor bombing campaign.

Russian Anarchists

The other groups regarded as the precursors to contemporary terrorism are the Russian anarchists of the late nineteenth century.

The best known were the Narodnaya Volya (People's Will), who operated in Russia from 1878 to 1883. The group's philosophy was a kind of idealistic anarchism that required the destruction of the existing order as a prelude to a new and better society. Like other terrorist groups and other revolutionaries from Marx on, the Narodnaya Volya tended to be vague about the details of this new world. They spent far more of their energy attacking the iniquities of the present system than describing the virtues of the one with which they would like to replace it. This trait can also be found in most terrorist groups today.

Like Bakunin, Narodnaya Volya believed in immediate action; they argued that a single act of destruction could achieve more than debates and publications ever could. They believed that the assassination of a few government officials would ignite revolution across the land. Their actions therefore were precise and concentrated on killing a few key government players, most notably the tsar. They did succeed, in fact, in killing Tsar Alexander II in 1881. Far from a revolution being ignited, the peasantry did not react at all, urban public opinion was horrified, and the radical cause lost support.

Credited with creating the notion of propaganda by deed, the Russian anarchists in fact produced more propaganda than deeds. This was true even of more extreme groups like the Russian Socialist Revolutionary Party, whose members carefully sought to avoid the deaths of innocents and constrained themselves within clearly defined limits. They believed, for example, that terrorism was justified only when the perpetrator was prepared to sacrifice his own life to atone for his actions. The government's response was much less restrained and dealt effectively with these groups through brutal repression. That these groups were fighting for many rights we take for granted today does not make them early democrats. Their fatal weakness, and one shared with their twentieth-century successors, was their tendency to arrogate to themselves the right to decide what was good for the people. Their failure was in part due to the fact that their elitist self-confidence blinded them both to the degree of their isolation from the people and to the strength of their opponents. Nevertheless, their methods revealed a strong sense of moral responsibility that was not always reciprocated by the governments they opposed.

Curiously enough, Lenin, who was to prove such an inspiration for the social revolutionary terrorist movements of the late twentieth century, was critical of the Russian anarchists, whom he considered misguided zealots. (When Lenin was seventeen, his elder brother Alexander was convicted of attempting to assassinate the Tsar and was hanged in St Petersburg.) He believed that he had a more efficacious way of overthrowing the system. Rather than hurling bombs at ministers, Lenin advocated the creation of a revolutionary elite dedicated to one simple goal, the seizure of power. Far from being isolated from those around them, Lenin's cadre of revolutionaries exploited popular grievances as a means of consolidating their support. It did not matter to Lenin that the complaints might be from nationalists, aspiring landowners or others unsympathetic to his cause. What did matter to the ultimate pragmatist was that animosity towards the authorities made them potentially sympathetic to subversives, whose political powerlessness left them free to make empty promises. Lenin's key contribution to terrorist strategy, therefore, lay in recognizing the importance of exploiting every fragment of local alienation for its own ends. It is very clear from reading bin Laden's public statements that he has taken this lesson to heart. He criticizes the US for everything from support for Israel to the deployment of troops in Saudi Arabia, to its refusal to sign up to the international criminal court, to profiteering by the Halliburton Corporation.[14]

There were a number of other anarchist groups operating in Europe and the US at the same time. Between them they managed some significant assassinations, including the prime minister of Spain in 1892; the Empress Elizabeth of Austria in 1898; King Umberto of Italy in 1900 and President McKinley in 1901.[15] These actions provided an early spur to international co-operation against terrorism. Then, as now, initiatives on the counter-terrorism front were usually driven by an atrocity. When international co-operation to combat crime was formalized in extradition treaties in the early nineteenth century, the principle of non-intervention was enshrined in the treaties by means of a clause excluding political offenders from the scope of extradition. But an attempt on the life of Napoleon III in 1855 led to a modification of the political-exception clause so as to make the murder of a head of state or his family an extra-ditable offence. Then in the 1890s Britain decided to extradite a French anarchist wanted for the bombing of a French café in which two civilians died. The court ruled that, as anarchists did not believe in government, they could not avail themselves of the political-exclusion clause in extradition treaties.

Compared to the levels of violence practised by twentieth-century terrorists, these nineteenth-century precursors seem anaemic indeed. The two world wars of the last century did a great deal to eliminate the distinction between combatant and non-combatant by legitimating the deliberate massacre of civilians, even by the good guys. Disregard for this distinction is, as I pointed out earlier, a defining characteristic of terrorism. In the twentieth century, nation states mobilized their power to kill people from other countries for political reasons. Examples from the Second World War would include the London blitz, the siege of Leningrad, the bombing of Dresden, not to mention the bombing of Hiroshima and Nagasaki. In each case the motives of the killers were political, the victims were random civilians, and the message was aimed at a wider audience, whether it was the general public, the armed forces, the government or the leader of the country concerned. Indeed, in the first half of the twentieth century some governments mobilized their power to murder their own people, not just foreigners – the most egregious cases being Stalin and Hitler. The point here is that the greater brutality of terrorists reflects a greater brutality in political life generally. The nineteenth-century terrorists were more restrained and more discriminating than their twentieth-century successors. Their abandonment of the combatant–non-combatant distinction, however, occurred after the distinction had been profoundly challenged by the conduct of states during the world wars.

The deliberate targeting of civilians, even if it has a great many precedents, remains difficult to understand. The act of deliberately blowing up a school or a government or corporate office building, to say nothing of killing fellow passengers on a bus or subway, is a more personalized act than dropping a bomb from an aircraft at 30,000 feet in time of war. We find the latter much easier to understand. We see it as a matter of discipline, training and commitment to a righteous cause articulated by a representative government. An act of terrorism is much harder to comprehend. There is no doubt that the Fenians betrayed an extraordinary disregard for human life when they set alight almost 550 pounds of gunpowder a few yards from a densely populated area. I believe it is fair to assume that had they known that their explosion would kill six women and children and destroy hundreds of homes they would have devised a different rescue effort. Had many contemporary terrorists anticipated that their plan would cause only six fatalities they also would have devised a different plan, one designed to inflict more harm. What causes people to be so immune to the suffering their actions cause, and what do they hope to achieve by inflicting this suffering? These are the questions to which we will now turn.

3

What Causes Terrorism?

Thinking people, when disaster strikes, make it their priority to
look for its causes, in order to prevent it happening again.

Osama bin Laden, October 2004[1]

I still remember those distressing scenes: blood, torn limbs,
women and children massacred. All over the place, houses were
being destroyed and tower blocks were collapsing, crushing their
residents, while bombs rained down mercilessly on our homes.

Osama bin Laden, October 2004[2]

Ahmed Omar Saeed Sheikh, better known as Omar Sheikh, seems
an unlikely terrorist. Born in London, he enjoyed a comfortable
upbringing. His father, a Pakistani businessman, sent him to the
expensive private Forest School where he was a contemporary of
the English cricket captain Nasser Hussain. His economics tutor at
Forest School said of him: 'The chap we knew was a good all-
round, solid and very supportive pupil . . . he was in the premier
league of students . . . He was a nice bloke and very respectful.'[3]
Another of his superiors said of him: 'He was a very nice guy, well
mannered and educated.'[4] Sheikh passed four A-levels with good
grades and was admitted to the prestigious London School of
Economics to read applied mathematics, statistical theory, economics and social psychology.

Aside from his evident intellect and charm Sheikh was a compassionate young man. In 1992 a man waiting for a train at Leytonstone
tube station in east London lost his balance and fell on to the
tracks. Sheikh, who was then eighteen, witnessed the incident.

Ignoring the danger from a train pulling into the station, he jumped down on to the tracks and saved the man. He later received a commendation from the London Underground for this selfless act of bravery.[5]

When Sheikh matured from charming schoolboy to committed terrorist he did not lose this compassionate side. An Indian newspaper acquired a copy of the diary Sheikh kept during his time in prison. While on a mission to trap and kidnap foreign visitors in India, one of his colleagues moved out of their shared apartment. Sheikh wrote:

> He left. I had the room to myself. Now, since I had been in India, the sight of emaciated beggars everywhere particularly around the Markaz had posed a serious dilemma for me. I had never seen so much poverty first hand in my life before. But I soon realized that superficial help was only perpetuating the problem – most of the money they received was spent on cigarettes or charas. But they were genuinely needy people. Anyway, that night I decided that since I had the room to myself, I would offer to share it with an old one-legged man who sat outside the Markaz. I went and brought the old man to the room. We had dinner.[6]

In the same diary Sheikh details how he befriended travelling westerners and then kidnapped them, chaining them to furniture at gunpoint and holding them hostage.

In July 2002 Omar Sheikh was convicted of kidnapping and murdering the *Wall Street Journal* reporter Daniel Pearl. Sheikh pleaded not guilty to the Pearl charges but in one of his court appearances shouted to reporters that he was responsible for other celebrated terrorist atrocities, including the bombing of the Kashmir parliament in October 2001, the attack on the Indian parliament two months later and the attack on the American Cultural Center in Calcutta in January 2001.

It is simply baffling that someone with a background no different from many others, and a great deal more privileged than most, should choose to become a terrorist. In attempting to understand the causes of terrorism one must look for explanations at the level of the individual, like Omar Sheikh. But that is not enough.

Explanations are found at national and transnational levels too. In short, the emergence of terrorism requires a lethal cocktail with three ingredients: a disaffected individual, an enabling group and a legitimizing ideology.

In the wake of the September 11 attacks Americans flocked to their bookstores to buy copies of the Koran, and books about Islam enjoyed unprecedented popularity. Bin Laden himself noted the phenomenon. He told some friends: 'I heard someone on Islamic radio who owns a school in America say: "We don't have time to keep up with the demands of those who are asking about Islamic books to learn about Islam." '[7] Americans were trying to understand the causes of what had happened. Presidential adviser Karl Rove was wrong to criticize this effort to understand. Rove told the New York Conservative Party: 'Conservatives saw what happened to us on 9/11 and said: we will defeat our enemies. Liberals saw what happened to us and said: we must understand our enemies.'[8] Indeed, it reflects one of the strongest elements in the American counter-terrorist arsenal – the public's desire to understand, which does not mean to sympathize, or empathize with, the causes of the terrible violence wreaked upon their country. This understanding is the first step towards formulating an effective counter-terrorist strategy.

Any effort to understand immediately brings one to an examination of causes. Of course there is no single cause of terrorism any more than there is a single cause of killing. People kill for many different reasons. A soldier kills because he is trained to do so. An inebriated driver kills because he has diminished control, a psychopath because he is crazy, a battered woman because she is frightened, a teenager in a fight because he is angry, and so on. We do not expect a single explanation as to why people kill – we know that each situation is different. So we should not expect a single reason why people carry out acts of terrorism.

If there is one single explanation it is that terrorism is a tactic and people use it because they think that, at some level, it works. But this is almost a truism and does not get us much closer to understanding the causes of terrorism. There are at least two reasons why it is very difficult to come up with a convincing explanation for terrorism. The first is that there are so many terrorists. The second is that there are so few. As mentioned earlier, terrorism is a tactic employed by many different groups in many different parts of the world in pursuit of many different objectives. It occurs in democracies, autocracies and, most often, in transitional states. It would be exceedingly difficult, for example, to come up with a single explanation for the behaviour of a Saudi cleric, a German university student, a Peruvian peasant, a Chechen soldier, a Japanese scientist and an Indian factory worker. On the other hand, there are actually very few terrorists. If Islam causes terrorism, with 1.2 billion Muslims in the world and, at most, a few thousand Islamic terrorists, why are there not more? If the social revolutionary movements in Europe in the 1970s were caused by the alienation of the disaffected youth, why were there not more terrorists? Alienation was widespread among European and American youth, but for all their notoriety there were not that many members of the Red Army Faction, Action Directe, the CCC and the Red Brigades in Germany, France, Belgium and Italy respectively.

Rather than imposing an explanation derived from one's own political predilections or worldview on terrorist movements the world over, my work has been dedicated to examining each of these groups to try to understand each one in its own context and then to see if there are any general conclusions that can be drawn to guide policymaking. Trying to understand is not simply the self-indulgence of the academic, it is also essential for policy. If one believes terrorism to be caused by poverty, for example, dispatching the military to defeat it will not solve the problem. Conversely, if one believes terrorism to be the work of maniacal religious fanatics, all the best social programmes in the world won't reduce the threat. Or as Joseph Stycos put it: 'If theory without policy is for academics, then policy without theory is for gamblers.'

There are a number of different levels, from very narrow to very broad, at which the underlying causes of terrorism can be sought. The level of the individual terrorist, of the terrorist organization and of the sponsoring state all suggest causes. At the level of society, socio-economic factors like poverty and inequality reveal causes; while at the transnational level causes can be found in religion and globalization. Many of these causes are interconnected. Terrorists fight for very different reasons. Some want a change in the political structure, like ethno-nationalist groups. Some want to bring about a revolution and introduce a new world order, like the social revolutionary movements. Some want to roll back the clock to an earlier halcyon era, like Islamic fundamentalists, and some, like the right-wing Italian movements in Italy or the Protestant terrorist groups in Northern Ireland, want to defend the status quo. What they share is a willingness to kill innocent civilians in order to achieve their objectives. The explanations for their actions are likely to be as diverse as the individuals involved in other forms of murder.

Individual-level Explanations

Instinctively we all first seek explanation at the level of the individual. Why does an individual decide to join a terrorist organization, to stay in one, to lead one or to leave one? Why does a human being decide to kill others he does not know in furtherance of an objective unlikely to be realized in his lifetime, and in so doing place himself outside the law and dramatically increase the likelihood that he will be killed or imprisoned and his family put at risk? In the most extreme cases, why does someone kill himself as a means of killing others in furtherance of an abstract cause? The most obvious explanation, and the most common, is that he is, simply, crazy. But terrorists, as I have said, by and large are not crazy at all. Psychological studies of terrorists are virtually unanimous on this point. Interviews with current and former terrorists as well as imprisoned terrorists confirm that their one shared characteristic is their normalcy, insofar as we understand the term. Attempts to produce a terrorist profile have invariably failed. Some are introverted, some extroverted; some loud, some shy; some confident, some nervous.

Simplicity, Identification and Revenge

From the vast literature on psychology a few points can be extracted.[9] Three in particular stand out. Terrorists see the world in Manichaean terms, that is in black and white; they identify with others; and they desire revenge. They have a highly oversimplified view of the world in which good is pitted against evil and in which their adversaries are to blame for all their woes. They tend to act, not out of a desire for personal gratification but on behalf of a group with which they identify (though the two motives can of course coexist). Islamic terrorists, for example, will regularly invoke the suffering of Palestinian and other Muslims. In one of many such statements, Osama bin Laden argued: 'But when the victim starts to take revenge for those innocent children in Palestine, Iraq, southern Sudan, Somalia, Kashmir and the Philippines, the ruler's ulema [Islamic leaders] and the hypocrites come to defend the clear blasphemy.'[10]

The identification with others and the desire for revenge commonly emerges in conversations with both rank-and-file terrorists and their leaders. The German militant Michael 'Bommi' Baumann, in his book *How It All Began*, writes that it was the unprovoked killing by the German police of a student demonstrator against the shah of Iran that turned him into a terrorist. Italian and German activists told similar tales to the Italian sociologist Donatella Della Porta. Members of the Finucane family described to the British reporter Kevin Toolis how they were radicalized by the experience of being driven from their home by Protestant mobs. And Protestant paramilitaries told the BBC's Peter Taylor of being radicalized by the sight of neighbours injured by IRA bombs.[11]

Omar Sheikh wrote in his confession that during his time as a student at the London School of Economics in 1992 'Bosnia Week' was observed and a number of documentary movies were shown. He wrote that one film, *The Death of a Nation*, which depicted Bosnian Muslims being murdered by Serbs 'shook my heart' and launched his political awakening and subsequent radicalization. He helped organize a student conference on Bosnia and then began fundraising for a convoy of relief materials for Bosnia. Soon he was making contact with Islamic militants.

Terrorist group leaders have told similar stories of being radicalized by identifying with the suffering of others. Renato Curcio, the intellectual leader of the Italian left-wing social revolutionary group the Red Brigades, says that he was converted to violence in reaction to an incident in which the police fired on farm workers, killing two and injuring several children among many others. Vellupillai Prabakharan, the poorly educated leader of the Sri Lankan nationalist group the Tamil Tigers, said: 'It is the plight of the Tamil people that compelled me to take up arms. I felt outrage at the inhuman atrocities perpetrated against an innocent people. The ruthless manner in which our people were murdered, massacred, maimed . . .'[12] Abimael Guzman, the academic leader of Peru's Maoist Shining Path, spoke in a similar vein: 'I'd say that what has most influenced me to take up politics has been the struggle of the people. I saw the fighting spirit of the people during the uprising in Arequipa in 1950 – how the masses fought with uncontrollable fury in response to the barbarous slaughter of the youth.'[13] Each of these men led very different types of terrorist movements pursuing very different political objectives in very different parts of the world, yet all speak in very similar terms about how they were radicalized by their sense of identification with others.

The power of the desire to avenge is discussed more fully in the next chapter. Terrorists invariably cast their actions in terms of revenge. Osama bin Laden's speeches, for example, are suffused with such language. Just a couple of weeks after September 11 he told Al-Jazeera television: 'Here is America struck by God Almighty in one of its vital organs, so that its greatest buildings are destroyed. Grace and gratitude to God. America has been filled with horror from north to south and east to west, and thanks be to God that what America is tasting now is only a copy of what we have tasted. Our Islamic nation has been tasting the same for more than eighty years, humiliation and disgrace, its sons killed and their blood spilled, its Holy Places [Mecca and Medina in Saudi Arabia] desecrated.'[14]

The two biggest gaps in how terrorists see themselves and how they are seen by others are precisely on the points of being altruistic versus being self-serving, and being defenders versus being aggressors. Terrorists see themselves as heroically working for the

benefit of others, not for themselves. In this way they regard themselves as morally distinguishable from criminals out for their own
selfish gain. Bin Laden once described how the idea of blowing up
the twin American towers came to him:

> God knows that the plan of striking the towers had not occurred to us,
> but the idea came to me when things went just too far with the
> American–Israeli alliance's oppression and atrocities against our people
> in Palestine and Lebanon. The events that made a direct impression on
> me were during and after 1982, when America allowed the Israelis to
> invade Lebanon with the help of its third [6th] fleet. They started
> bombing, killing and wounding many, while others fled in terror . . .
> It was like a crocodile devouring a child, who could do nothing but
> scream. Does a crocodile understand anything other than weapons?
> The whole world heard and saw what happened, but did nothing. In
> those critical moments, many ideas raged inside me, ideas difficult to
> describe, but they unleashed a powerful urge to reject injustice and a
> strong determination to punish the oppressors. As I looked at those
> destroyed towers in Lebanon it occurred to me to punish the oppres-
> sor in kind by destroying towers in America, so that it would have a
> taste of its own medicine and would be prevented from killing our
> women and children.[15]

Addressing a joint session of Congress on September 20, 2001,
President Bush gave a rather different version of the forces driving
al-Qaeda: 'They stand against us because we stand in their way.
We're not deceived by their pretences to piety. We have seen their
kind before. They're the heirs of all the murderous ideologies of
the twentieth century. By sacrificing human life to serve their
radical visions, by abandoning every value except the will to power,
they follow in the path of fascism, Nazism and totalitarianism.'[16]

We see them as violating all moral codes in pursuit of power and
domination. They see themselves as defending the weak against the
strong and punishing the strong for their violation of all moral
codes. From a counter-terrorism point of view the distinction is
important. If one is trying to affect the incentive structure that
causes someone to join or to leave a movement, knowing why they
join in the first place is essential. Bin Laden, for example, scoffed
at American efforts to put a price on his head. He told Al-Jazeera

that his followers 'left the world and came to these mountains and land, leaving their families, fathers and mothers. They left their universities and came here under shelling, American missiles and attacks. Some were killed . . . These men left the world and came for the jihad. America, however, which worships money, believes that people here are of this [same] calibre. I swear that we have not had the need to change a single man from his position even after these reports [that the US was offering a $5 million reward for information leading to his arrest].'[17]

If terrorists are engaged in self-gratifying behaviour, it is more likely to be a desire for significance, for glory, than for material gain. Terrorists, just like most other individuals, are likely to have a mix of motives – so the desire for revenge and significance and the sense of responsibility for the broader community as well as the relationship to the group's ideology are mixed up to different degrees in different individuals.

Defenders vs Aggressors

Sociologist Mark Juergensmeyer asked Dr Abdul Aziz Rantisi, one of the founders of Hamas (assassinated by Israel in April 2004), in what way he thought Hamas was misunderstood. He said, 'You think we are the aggressors. That is the number-one misunderstanding. We are not: we are the victims.'[18] Bin Laden, characteristically, phrased it more dramatically: 'The truth is the whole Muslim world is the victim of international terrorism, engineered by America and the United Nations.'[19] A member of the IRA explained to Kevin Toolis why he joined the terrorist movement: 'I knew that the IRA were our defenders, looking after our interests, fighting for our rights. There was a great sense of anger.'[20] On another occasion bin Laden used a homely analogy to explain his followers' behaviour: 'Let us look at a chicken, for example. If an armed person was to enter the chicken's home with the aim of inflicting harm on it, the chicken would automatically fight back.'[21] Seeing oneself as a victim who is fighting defensively, of course, makes it altogether easier to justify one's actions.

Leaders and Followers

An individual seeking revenge and identifying with others does not become a terrorist in a vacuum. For someone who objects to injustice, identifies with the disadvantaged and wants to help them, becoming a social worker is a more typical career path. It requires a charismatic leader or a functioning organization to mix these feelings with the desire for revenge and turn them into action.

In terrorist organizations, as in most others, the leaders tend to be different from the followers. They often, for example, come from higher educational and socio-economic backgrounds than the followers. In attempting to understand terrorist organizations therefore it is important to recognize that the motives driving the leaders of organizations are often distinguishable from those of the followers. The role of the leader is crucial in turning the eager volunteers into an organized force. The leader not only arranges training but provides an ideology, identifies the enemy and articulates a strategy. In some cases the leader becomes the personification of the group or ideology. Some leaders have almost godlike status among their followers, such as Osama bin Laden of al-Qaeda, Vellupillai Prabakharan of the Sri Lankan Tamil Tigers, and Shoko Asahara of Aum Shinrikyo. Some organizations create a cult of personality around their leaders, like Abimael Guzman of the Shining Path or Abdullah Ocalan, founder and leader of the Kurdish Workers' Party, the PKK, in Turkey.

This can represent real vulnerability for the movement as the removal of the leader can do irreparable damage to the organization. Cool organizational thinker that he is, Osama bin Laden is well aware of this vulnerability and has gone to great lengths to point out that his demise will not weaken his movement. He claims that the US and Saudi Arabia have been trying to assassinate him since 1990 but have failed because only Allah can decide when he should die, so he has no fear of death. 'Being killed for Allah's cause is a great honour achieved only by those who are the elite of the nation. We love this kind of death for Allah's cause as much as you like to live. We have nothing to fear for it is something to wish for.'[22] Other terrorist groups have a collective leadership, like the Army Council of the IRA, or otherwise play down the importance of individual leaders. The motivations of these individuals are often different from those of the rank and file of the movements. Some Palestinian families, for example, have pointed out that it is not the sons of the leaders who are volunteering for suicide missions.

The leaders of terrorist movements tend to be older as well as more highly educated and from a higher socio-economic background than their followers, no matter what part of the world they come from. Latin American terrorist leaders have been consistently older than their followers. The doyen of the group, Pedro Antonio Marín, better known as Manuel Marulanda, leader of Colombia's FARC, was born in 1928. Brazil's Carlos Marighella, author of *The Mini-manual of the Urban Guerrilla*, the most prominent terrorist manual before al-Qaeda's own, was fifty-eight at the time of his violent death. Abimael Guzman, the leader of the Shining Path, was also aged fifty-eight at the time of his arrest in 1992. Raúl Sendic, leader of the Uruguayan Tupamaros, was forty-two when he launched his movement. Mario Santucho, leader of the Argentine ERP (People's Revolutionary Army) was forty at the time of his violent death. Guzman an academic, Sendic a lawyer and Santucho an economist also had considerably more education than most of their followers.

Leaders of the European movements were younger than the Latin American leaders but still older than their followers and consistently middle and upper-middle class. Most of the leaders of Italy's Red Brigades were college professors in their thirties. Among the leadership of the German Baader–Meinhof Gang, Baader was the son of an historian, while Meinhof was a journalist and the daughter of an art historian; Horst Mahler was a lawyer and the son of a dentist; Suzanne Albrecht was the daughter of a wealthy lawyer, and Holger Meins was the son of a business executive. Most were university dropouts. The pattern of middle-aged leaders and younger followers is found in different types of terrorist movements throughout the world. In Japan, Shoko Asahara, leader of Aum Shinrikyo, was born in 1955. Vellupillai Prabakharan, leader of the Tamil Tigers, was born in 1954. Abdullah Ocalan of the PKK was born in 1948.

In general, therefore, leaders of terrorist movements are older and have more education and higher socio-economic status than the people they lead. This is less true of Islamist groups, which appear to recruit successfully from all sections of society. Osama bin Laden has the most famous and most unusual profile. A multi-millionaire who studied economics in Jeddah, he was born in 1957. His second in command, Ayman al-Zawahiri, is a doctor who was born in 1951. Mohammad Atta, the leader of the 9/11 team, was the son of an Egyptian lawyer and had earned a PhD in urban planning. George Habash, leader of the Popular Front for the Liberation of Palestine, the PLFP, was also a medical doctor, born in 1926. Abdul Aziz Rantisi, one of the founders of Hamas and another doctor, was fifty-six when he was killed by the Israelis. Sheikh Ahmed Yassin, the spiritual leader of Hamas, trained as a teacher. He was sixty-eight when he was killed by the Israelis. The PLO's Yasser Arafat was a graduate engineer and died at the age of seventy-five. Unlike these leaders, Hassan Nasrallah, the leader of Hezbollah, was born into a modest home in 1960. He was the eldest of nine children and his father was a grocer.

Marc Sageman studied the biographies of 172 members of al-Qaeda and found that two-thirds were middle or upper class and that 60 per cent had gone to college; several had doctorates.[23] Their average age was twenty-six. Similarly, Gilles Keppel studied 300 Islamic militants in Egypt and found that they too were more highly educated and of a higher socio-economic status than most terrorists.[24] Similarly Peter Bergen's examination of the backgrounds of seventy-five terrorists responsible for some of the most damaging attacks found that 53 per cent had attended college while two had doctorates from western universities and two others were working on PhDs.[25] Every terrorist army has need of footsoldiers and cannon fodder, but Islamist groups have successfully recruited a cadre of more educated followers. Men like Omar Sheikh and Mohammad Atta are required for the kind of international operations that necessitate international travel and functioning in different societies. Moreover, increased reliance on the internet, essential for secure transnational communication, requires operatives with some technological facility.

Terrorist Organizations

Not all terrorist groups are the same. The two key differences mentioned in the last chapter, the nature of the goals sought and the relationship to the broader community, have significant psychological implications too. Jerrold Post has made the point that there are real psychological differences between those who are carrying on the work of their parents, that is the ethno-nationalist groups like the ETA, the IRA, the LTTE and the PKK, and those who are trying to destroy the world of their parents, the social revolutionary groups like the RAF and Red Brigades.[26] Nationalist groups see themselves as occupying a place in their group's historical struggle. Social revolutionary groups completely reject the past. In her seminal book *Hitler's Children*, Jillian Becker describes the members of the Baader–Meinhof Gang, the precursor to the RAF, as 'children without fathers'.[27]

In looking back at their life as terrorists many activists speak of the intense feeling of camaraderie within the group. Jerrold Post, after interviewing thirty-five imprisoned Middle East terrorists, recounts the process by which 'an overarching sense of the collective consumes the individual'.[28] Italian and German militants describe a similar process by which the ties to the small collective become stronger as ties to all others become weaker. Former members all attest to the powerful emotional draw to their comrades in arms.[29] One Italian activist put it this way: 'We shared the idea that the armed struggle, besides its historical necessity, was also an occasion to build human relations which had to be, I don't know how to say, absolute, based on the readiness to die, the opposite of everyday life, of the individualization of a capitalist society.'[30]

It should come as no surprise that ethno-nationalist terrorist groups are those that have tended to last the longest, not least because they have close ties to their communities. Psychologically this means that membership in the group does not cut you off from a broader population that can serve as a counterweight to the mores of the movement. Conversely, groups that are isolated from the community, like most social revolutionary groups and millenarian cults, tend to have no external source of information or security, nor any perspective with which to question the dictates of the movement. Members of these isolated groups create a subjective reality which they inhabit and which their isolation prevents being subject to rational tests. Contemporary Islamist groups seem to be able to combine the transformational aspirations of the social revolutionaries with the community ties of the ethno-nationalist groups. It is a very powerful combination.

Most psychologists agree that group, organizational and social psychology are more helpful than individual psychology in explaining terrorist behaviour. Oliver and Steinberg in describing the streets of the West Bank and Gaza, and Kevin Toolis in his depiction of the streets of Belfast, provide riveting accounts of the cultures that make joining a terrorist movement the most natural thing in the world for a young man to do.[31] They describe whole societies collectively engaged in protest and providing encouragement and support for those who take up arms. They describe young men getting together with their friends and deciding to fight for the cause. This social setting can motivate even the most introverted and independent individuals. Eamon Collins was an unusually ruthless and cold-blooded killer, who plotted the assassination of men with whom he worked. Even he describes being caught up in the popular demonstrations in favour of the H Block prisoners that finally led him into the arms of the IRA.[32]

Aspects of what I call a 'complicit surround' that are conducive to terrorism are cultures in which violence is condoned, even glorified. This is more often the case in societies in which there is a history of violence in the region. Another essential ingredient is a religion or ideology that makes sense of violence and legitimates its use, whether it be the Maoism of the Shining Path and the Nepalese Communist Party or the nationalism of the Basques, the Kurds and the Chechens, the Marxism–Leninism of the RAF and the Red Brigades, or the Islamic fundamentalism of al-Qaeda, Algeria's GIA and Egypt's al-Gama'a al-Islamiyya. Practical possibilities can be provided by an available enemy against whom to organize; whether it be American soldiers in Baghdad, or British soldiers in Belfast, or Jewish settlers in the Gaza Strip, they are available as targets. A sense of injustice can provide a personal incentive to act. An individual is more likely to do so if he sees empirical evidence of injustice as well as evidence that the identified enemy is to blame.

State-level Explanations

States are accustomed to dealing with other states, so it is attractive for them to see terrorism as a threat from another state, or as caused by the nature of another. There are fairly clear-cut policy implications to this perspective. If one sees terrorism as being caused by the behaviour of an adversarial state, the traditional methods of conducting relations with adversaries will be invoked. Since time immemorial the armed forces have been the means of conducting inter-state behaviour. But an examination of known terrorist cases suggests quite powerfully that neither the nature of the state nor the sponsorship of a state is a cause of terrorism.

The idea that democracy is the best antidote to terrorism has been enjoying widespread acceptance recently. But as with most one-dimensional solutions this one is too simplistic. The truth is that terrorism has occurred in democracies the world over. It has occurred in mature democracies like Britain, France, Germany, India, Israel, Italy, Japan and Sri Lanka, as well as in new, fragile or partial democracies like Colombia, Peru, Russia, Turkey and Venezuela. Terrorism is employed by minorities. (If they were not in a minority they would not need to resort to terrorism.) To be a permanent minority within a democracy can be a frustrating position and unless democracies can demonstrate that they not only provide a non-violent means of expressing dissent, but also offer a non-violent means of redressing the grievances of minorities, they are unlikely to be an acceptable substitute. The leader of the Tamil Tigers could have been speaking for many ethnic minorities when he put it this way: 'The Tamil people have been expressing their grievances in parliament for more than three decades. Their voices went unheard like cries in the wilderness. In Sri Lanka there is no parliamentary democracy where our people could effectively represent their aspirations. What passes as parliament in Sri Lanka is an authoritarian rule founded on the tyranny of the majority.'[33]

Terrorist movements have often emerged in democracies when those trying to change the current system realize that they do not have the numbers required to prevail in a democracy. What's more, many of the hallmarks of democracies, like freedom of movement and freedom of association as well as protections for privacy and personal rights, made them convenient operating grounds for terrorism.

State Sponsorship

I have argued that, by definition, terrorism is the behaviour of sub-state groups. This view is not universally shared. The idea that terrorism was fundamentally a question of state behaviour has long dominated American discourse on the subject. In the 1980s when terrorism was high on the list of the public's priorities it was seen as another front in the Cold War. The prototypical terrorist was a communist funded by and dictated to by Moscow, while Colonel Qadaffi was the *bête noire* of the Middle East. In April 1986, ten days after the bombing of a Berlin discotheque in which two American servicemen were killed, the US bombed Libya's capital Tripoli in retaliation, killing at least a hundred people. In a familiar pattern most of America's allies were outraged; some refused even to allow use of their airspace by US bombers, but Britain, under Prime Minister Thatcher, permitted the planes to take off from military bases in the UK.

Cast in terms of state sponsorship of terrorism, it is hard to see how any self-respecting state could engage in the crime. Perceived however as the use of terrorism as an instrument of foreign policy, the same actions can be seen to have many advantages for many states and not to have been the sole preserve of international pariahs. If a state is opposed by a much stronger one, its government out of self-interest will be creative and avoid a head-on clash they would inevitably lose. State sponsorship of terrorism has had relatively low risk because it is so difficult to prove and it may serve to achieve a state's foreign-policy objectives. If it does not, it is easily deniable. Moreover, the primacy placed on human life by western democracies leaves them very vulnerable to attack through their individual citizens because there are so many of them in so many places. So state sponsorship is often low cost, easy to deny and difficult to prove, and it has a potential for a high pay-off. It should come as no surprise that relatively weak states resort to the tactic against their more powerful enemies.

It is often in fact a political judgement as to who is or is not a state sponsor of terrorism and who does or does not use terrorism as an instrument of their foreign policy. In the 1970s the USSR and Cuba topped the American public's list of state sponsors of terrorism. In the 1980s it was Iran and Libya. In the 1990s Iraq and Syria. Yet if you were to ask people in other countries, even in allied countries, you would find the US high on most lists, and if you were to ask people in countries hostile to America you would find the US at the top of their lists. The examples invoked in support of the contention that the US has sponsored terrorism would include the Contras in Nicaragua, the mujahideen in Afghanistan and local groups trying to overthrow Castro in Cuba and Allende in Chile. An examination of these cases reveals that the US had very good reasons to object to the governments of Chile, Cuba and Nicaragua. Their ideological orientation was inimical to its own, so it supported local groups who used whatever means were available to try to bring them down. To have engaged in open warfare against these governments, which were allied to America's enemy the Soviet Union, would have provoked international uproar.

These are very much the same type of justifications that state sponsors of terrorism in the Middle East would use. They perceive the existence of the state of Israel as inimical to their interest. They cannot directly and openly fight it, so they do so surreptitiously. The only real difference between their position and America's is that if the US had chosen to fight openly it could be confident of winning, but it was not prepared to pay the price. These countries believe that they cannot defeat Israel militarily (they have tried and failed many times), so they fight it in other ways. Moreover, given the nature of the US's economic and political power, it has many more options at its disposal in terms of isolating these governments than most state sponsors of terrorism have had. So in some ways they have a better case than the US did for using terrorism as an instrument of their foreign policy. I make this point not to indict American foreign policy but only to underscore that not only the bad guys use terrorism as an instrument of their foreign policy. Sometimes the good guys do too. So sometimes weak states use terrorism because they believe that they have no other effective means available to them and sometimes strong states do it because they do not want to display their strength openly. In every instance, the sponsoring state is capitalizing on the availability of pre-existing terrorist movements, not creating them.

States have not just sponsored terrorism as a means of conducting foreign policy, they have done so for domestic reasons too. The two most persistent and generous state sponsors of terrorism have been Iran and South Africa (though the latter never made it on to the US State Department's list of state sponsors). Iran sponsored terrorism as a means of exporting revolution, while South Africa did so as a means of preventing the importation of revolution from abroad.

Iran has generally been seen as the most active state sponsor of terrorism, driven by a desire to export the Iranian revolution, to undermine unfriendly regimes, and to remove what supreme leader Khomeini referred to as the 'cancerous tumour' that is Israel. As soon as the Ayatollah Khomeini came to power in 1979 he set about trying to export his brand of fundamentalist Islamic revolution by backing radical groups throughout the Middle East, especially in Kuwait, Saudi Arabia and Bahrain, as well as Shiite groups in Iraq and terrorist groups in Egypt. At one point, after the death of 260 Iranians in Mecca in the course of a riot during the hajj or pilgrimage, Iran publicly called for the overthrow of the Saudi ruling family. Iran continues the policy of supporting Hezbollah in Lebanon and Palestinian rejectionist groups like Hamas, Palestinian Islamic Jihad and the Popular Front for the Liberation of Palestine-General Command by providing funding, safe havens, training and weapons. The US government has also accused Iran of encouraging Lebanese and Palestinian groups to co-ordinate their anti-Israel activities.[34] Suspicions abound that Iran has tolerated an al-Qaeda presence in, or at a minimum transit through, its territory and has helped to facilitate the operations of some sections of the anti-American insurgency in Iraq.

South Africa is never counted among the ranks of state sponsors of terrorism yet it was quite a successful one for a time, and had a deliberate and sophisticated policy. Finding itself surrounded by unfriendly front-line states in the wake of the wave of independence in southern Africa in the 1960s and 1970s, the Pretoria government undertook a policy of supporting terrorist movements in those neighbouring states. These movements were hostile to the new post-independence governments. Pretoria supported them as a means of perpetuating the dependence of the front-line states on the more powerful South African economy, of destabilizing unfriendly regimes, but most importantly to discourage and prevent support for the ANC. The policy was clearly dictated by domestic needs. South African support for Renamo, a brutal terrorist organization in Mozambique, is a case of a government supporting one terrorist organization outside the country as a way of undermining what it perceived to be another terrorist organization, the ANC, within its own country. It was a creative strategy and eventually Prime Minister Samora Machel approached the South African government offering a deal: you stop supporting Renamo and we'll stop sup- porting the ANC. They signed a non-aggression pact, the Nkomati Accord in 1984. (Ironically Prime Minister Machel's widow later became Nelson Mandela's wife.)

South Africa followed a similar strategy in the other former Portuguese colony, Angola. South Africa supported UNITA against the government of Jonas Savimbi. Ultimately, as a part of the American-sponsored Namibian peace settlement, South Africa ceased its support of UNITA in return for Angola closing down ANC training camps and expelling its members.

Supporting terrorist movements was just one piece of the South African strategy. The government also used more conventional military attacks against ANC targets in the front-line states – that is, Angola, Zambia, Zimbabwe, Mozambique and Tanzania – and actually invaded Angola at one point. Attacks were launched as far north as the ANC headquarters in Lusaka, Zambia. For all South Africa's military predominance, and for all the government's willingness to use it against the ANC, and against neighbouring states which supported them, the government eventually realized that the threat was political not military, and could not be won with military force. The white minority regime ultimately ceded power to the 'terrorist' ANC.

There can be no doubt that having a state sponsor strengthens terrorist movements. It is hard to see how Hezbollah could ever have developed into the powerful and sophisticated terrorist movement it became without the generous and persistent support of the state of Iran. The existence of safe training grounds in the Bekaa Valley of Lebanon protected by Syria greatly augmented the military skills of a range of terrorist movements and helped them to develop relationships with one another. Osama bin Laden understood the value of having space within which to train and organize, first in the Sudan and later, when exiled from the Sudan under US pressure, in Afghanistan. As the subsequent history of Afghanistan has demonstrated, however, having a state sponsor is not enough. Having a generous sponsor can make terrorist movements more lethal by facilitating training and providing weapons, but ultimately a large part of terrorism's appeal lies in its affordability. Terrorists can survive without state sponsorship. The US attack on Afghanistan destroyed al-Qaeda's base of operations, but it has not destroyed al-Qaeda. Generous state sponsors strengthen pre-existing terrorist movements. They are not a cause of terrorism.

President Bush made his position on this point very clear in the aftermath of September 11. He declared: 'Every nation in every region now has a decision to make. Either you are with us or you are with the terrorists. From this day forward, any nation that continues to harbour or support terrorism will be regarded by the United States as a hostile regime.'[35] As it has turned out over the past few years, however, many countries including America's allies have unwittingly harboured terrorists. Moreover, the history of state-sponsored terrorism suggests that relationships between terrorist movements and their state sponsors are far from uniform. In some instances states provide direction, in some they provide support, in some they simply turn a blind eye to the activities of resident groups and in others they are unaware of the activities of terrorists in their midst.[36]

If a government assumes that state sponsorship is a basic cause of terrorism then that government is likely to be drawn into wars against other states, as the US has been in Afghanistan and Iraq. The history of terrorism suggests that waging war against states will not eliminate terrorism.

Societal-level Explanations

While terrorism can and does occur in both rich and poor countries, it is more likely to occur in developing countries and especially in countries experiencing rapid modernization. Changing economic conditions are conducive to instability, and traditional means of making sense of the world, like religion or local power structures, are challenged by the scale of the change. In the face of sweeping socio-economic changes the promulgation of a particularist ideology which explains what is happening, which provides something constant to hold on to and which values the identity being challenged is likely to be well received. On a more practical level, two of the most commonly shared characteristics of terrorists, their gender and their youth, are very often in ample supply in transitional societies or societies feeling the effects of rapid modernization. Modernizing societies experience a disproportionate growth in the youth population. If the structures are not in place to absorb these young men into the workforce they are likely to have time to contemplate the disadvantages of their position and to be available to be mobilized behind a cause to change the situation.

The relationship between poverty and terrorism has long been debated, with one side pointing to the impoverished refugee camps of the Middle East as spawning grounds for terrorists and the other pointing to the relative affluence of many individual terrorists like Mohammad Atta, leader of the 9/11 attacks, and especially to the personal wealth of Osama bin Laden. Both are right, but neither tells the whole story. The few academic investigations of the links between terrorism and poverty have concluded that they are, at best, indirect.[37] One of the most popular explanations for terrorism is poverty and inequality, that people are driven to terrorism by economic deprivation and that therefore the best response is to improve economic conditions in affected regions. Again this is not entirely true. If there were a direct link between poverty, inequality and terrorism, the areas with the highest rates of poverty and inequality would have the highest rates of terrorism, but they do not. If there were a direct link between poverty and terrorism, Africa, the poorest continent on the planet, would be awash in terrorism. It is not. If terrorism was caused by inequality, countries in Africa and Latin America with the highest rates of inequality would have the highest rates of terrorism, but they do not.[38] Conservative opponents of this liberal view point to the wealth of individual terrorists as proof positive that there is no relationship between poverty, inequality and terrorism. Indeed, many nationalist terrorist movements have been formed among ethnic groups who are relatively well off, like the Tamils in Sri Lanka, the Sikhs in India, the Basques in Spain and the Catholics in Ireland. The relationship once again is more complicated than either of these positions suggests.

What appears to drive some people to violence is not their absolute levels of poverty but rather their position relative to others.[39] Northern Irish Catholics did not compare themselves to southern Irish Catholics, who enjoyed a much less generous social welfare system at the time the civil rights movement emerged; rather they compared themselves to Northern Irish Protestants. Impoverished Palestinians are comparing themselves not to other impoverished Arabs in Egypt, Jordan or elsewhere, but to the much wealthier Israeli settlers. With global mass communications and American TV shows broadcasting American affluence around the world, it cannot be difficult to mobilize a sense of resentment of American wealth. Proximity to the other is no longer a requirement. Previously one compared oneself to others near by, but the contrast between American wealth and Arab poverty is now being broadcast daily into people's tiny homes. The very poorest people, preoccupied with survival, do not have the means even of realizing the extent of their relative deprivation.

Rather than being a cause of terrorism, poverty and inequality are risk factors that increase the likelihood of terrorism. Moreover, once terrorism has broken out, poverty and inequality increase the likelihood that it will acquire adherents. Individuals may not be driven to terrorism by poverty and inequality, but the alienation that these conditions breed may lead others to support them. Experience indicates that it is less people's objective condition that drives them to action than their position relative to others. This concept was termed 'relative deprivation' by Ted Robert Gurr in his seminal work *Why Men Rebel*, published in 1970. The essence of the concept is well known to every parent who tries to ensure tranquillity at home by treating and being seen to treat all children equally.[40]

With the impact of globalization and especially global media and communications, the relative economic inequalities of the world are increasingly known. They become known both to those who experience them and to those recruited to empathize with them. A young British cricket player may not therefore have to endure poverty himself to feel outraged at the poverty of Palestinians in refugee camps. The occupant of the camps can be persuaded to blame the satellite-TV-owning Israeli settlers a few miles away for his relative poverty. That said, poverty and relative deprivation are far more widespread than terrorism, so this does not tell the whole story.

Part of the success of many Islamist groups and especially of well-established groups like Hamas and Hezbollah has been based on their understanding of the recruitment potential of social services to alleviate socio-economic conditions. These groups painstakingly built up their support in the region by attending to the social needs of their potential recruits far more effectively than the governments did. They established hospitals, schools and orphanages. The Islamic Group (al-Gama'a al-Islamiyya) in Egypt adopted a similar strategy with similar success. High unemployment rates, ranging from 11 per cent in Egypt to 18 per cent in Lebanon, to 50 per cent in Gaza and the West Bank, ensure continued economic privation.[41] These rates also raise another risk factor for terrorism, the existence of large numbers of unemployed young men. The demographics of many modernizing societies result in a population shift leading to a disproportionate increase in the number of young people and the inability of the economy to integrate them. The proportion of the population under fifteen years of age in the Palestinian Territory is 46 per cent; it is 42 per cent in Iraq, 37 per cent in Saudi Arabia and Jordan and 36 per cent in Egypt, as compared to 21 per cent in the US and 18 per cent in the UK.[42] These developments are not unique to the Middle East. The ranks of the Shining Path in Peru, for example, were swelled by young men from the indigenous population. They were the first in their families to go to college. They received an education and the heightened expectations that accompany education but were unable to find employment. In this way well-meaning reforms on the part of the government backfired, producing unintended consequences. The Peruvian government created universities in the remote countryside, such as Ayacucho, in order to bring education to the local populations. It was through the university that Abimael Guzman recruited followers to his Maoist interpretation of the reason for their problems. This case speaks to the importance of thinking through the implications of social reform policies. It is not enough to provide education if you do not provide the means to employ those you have educated. The same risk factor is very much in evidence in the Middle East and north Africa. In countries like Egypt and Algeria only about half of university graduates are able to find jobs and even fewer are able to find jobs commensurate with their expectations. Similarly, in the period leading up to the first intifada, the number of men with twelve or more years of education doubled while their real wages dropped 30 per cent and their unemployment rates soared.[43]

Different terrorist groups have tended to attract people from different socio-economic backgrounds. Between 50 and 70 per cent of the members of the Latin American urban terrorist groups were students. Japanese and European social revolutionary movements in the 1970s were predominantly populated by middle-class dropouts. By contrast, large-scale ethno-nationalist movements have generally been more working class, like the IRA, the FARC, the LTTE and the PKK. In the Middle East, in the past at any rate, the footsoldiers have tended to be poor while the leadership, as in most political organizations, tends to come from the middle class. More recently ideology appears to trump class as recruits are drawn from around the world. Many of these recruits, whether home grown, as in the case of the British suicide bombers, or members of the diaspora, as in the case of the Spanish bombers, are by no means destitute. On the contrary they are often quite highly educated, though underemployed, and have attained at least a minimal technical competence as the transnational networks rely so heavily on the internet to communicate.

Bin Laden was asked to explain the apparent incongruity of a man of his wealth and background fighting on the front lines:

> 'We believe that livelihoods are preordained. So no matter how much pressure America puts on the regime in Riyadh to freeze our assets and to forbid people from contributing to this great cause, we shall still have Allah to take care of us; livelihood is sent by Allah; we shall not want.'
> He also dismissed the notion that there were any economic explanations for the surge of Islamic radicalism: 'They claim that this blessed awakening and the people reverting to Islam are due to economic factors. This is not so. It is rather a grace from Allah, a desire to embrace the religion of Allah. And this is not surprising. When the holy war called, thousands of young men from the Arab Peninsula and other countries answered the call and they came from wealthy backgrounds.'[44]

The trial transcripts of those accused in the bombing of the US embassies in Nairobi and Dar-es-Salaam reveal that not all the members of al-Qaeda were as otherworldly as their leader. Jamal Ahmad al-Fadl went into intricate detail in his testimony about the salaries paid to different members and the resentment bred by the apparent inequities in salaries.[45] Another defendant, L'Houssaine Kherchtou, described how he began to resent al-Qaeda when the organization refused to pay $500 for his wife's medical expenses. He found this particularly unfair as the organization was prepared to send a group of Egyptians to Yemen for a month with all expenses paid in order to renew their passports.[46]

Examining economic causes of terrorism leads one back to the same conclusion: it's complicated. Terrorism has occurred in both rich and poor countries but most often in developing countries and in societies characterized by rapid modernization. Swift socio-economic changes are conducive to instability and tend to erode traditional forms of social control. These situations are then open to exploitation by militants offering to make sense of such changes, to blame others for the dislocations and humiliations involved, and to offer a means of redress. Only a tiny percentage of the population needs to be persuaded by the militants in order to lead to the creation of a terrorist movement. Whether this small group remains small and isolated or grows into a broadly based movement will depend on a range of factors, from the response of the authorities to the extent of the social dislocation being experienced, as well as the success of the militant leadership in integrating their message with historical, cultural or religious traditions. The mix of factors will differ in every case, and each case has to be understood within its own context if it is ever to be effectively countered.

Transnational-level Explanations

Globalization

Globalization is sometimes offered as both a cure and a cause of terrorism. Again, it is neither and both. Countries that have benefited most from globalization and those that have benefited least have not produced significant terrorist movements.[47] It is often argued that the most open or the most globalized countries are most vulnerable to terrorism in that their permeable borders and technological developments are so easy for terrorists to exploit. Yet the countries that have topped the globalization index in recent years, Ireland, Singapore and Switzerland, have not experienced terrorism. On the other hand, India, Indonesia and Egypt, which along with Iran occupy the bottom of the globalization index, have indeed experienced terrorism.[48] For many of the weak globalizers, the advantages have not been shared and the result has often been an increase in structural inequalities along with a sense of humiliation as traditional cultures are seen being diluted by foreign influences. Abu Shanab, a leader of Hamas, was expressing a widely held view when he told interviewer Jessica Stern: 'Globalization is just a new colonial system. It is America's attempt to dominate the rest of the world economically rather than militarily. It will worsen the gap between rich and poor. America is trying to spread its consumer culture. These values are not good for human beings . . . It leads to disaster for communities.'[49]

The ideology of militant Islamist movements is, of course, radically anti-globalization. They want to remove external influence and return to the rule of traditional Islamic law, called sharia. These are the very groups, however, which have most creatively exploited the attributes of globalization to their own advantage. While articulating a vision of a pre-modern future they seek to achieve it by ultra-modern means. They have created the first truly global terrorist network and have done so by exploiting the very attributes of globalization that they condemn. They rely on the internet, for example, to communicate, to recruit, to mobilize and to organize and even to fundraise. They seem quite untroubled by the inconsistency.

Religion

In recent years religions, and particularly Islam, have been widely seen as a cause, indeed the cause, of terrorism. As with all single explanations this one is oversimplified. As pointed out in Chapter Two, most religious traditions have produced terrorist groups, and many terrorists have been atheists, so the notion that Islam and terrorism are inextricably linked is simply wrong. As Muslims constitute about a fifth of the world's population, form a majority in forty-five countries ranging from Africa to south-east Asia, and exist in significant and growing numbers in the US, Europe and the former Soviet Union, it is well worth remembering how large and how disparate a religion Islam is.

Nevertheless there has been an extraordinary growth in the number of terrorist groups with religious motives over the past thirty years. In 1968, of the eleven known terrorist groups none had any kind of religious affiliation. By the mid-1990s, of the fifty known groups about a dozen had religious motivations.[50] In 2004, of seventy-seven terrorist groups designated or listed by the US Department of State, forty appear to have some mixture of religious and political motives.[51] Historically, terrorist groups with a mixture of religious and political motives have shared two characteristics. They have been more transnational than groups with purely secular motives, and they have exercised less restraint. Religious boundaries have never conformed to political borders, so religious groups have always managed to operate across borders – which has made them more difficult to contain.

Even more damaging is their relative lack of restraint. A great many terrorist groups have controlled their behaviour and the extent of the casualties they have been prepared to inflict out of a desire not to alienate their core constituency. The IRA, for example, planted a bomb outside Harrods and killed six people in December 1983. They could just as easily have planted that bomb in the Harrods Food Court on the first day of the after-Christmas sale and thereby killed many hundreds of people. They chose not to do so, largely out of a fear of alienating their core constituency, the Catholic population of Northern Ireland. Indeed, an analysis of the pattern of IRA violence reveals a chronic concern on their part to tailor their targeting strategies in such a way as to inflict harm, gain attention and raise the costs for Britain of its presence in Northern Ireland, but not to alienate the Catholic population of the province. One sees this in the move away from indiscriminate bombing towards more defined military targets, or financial targets timed to avoid civilian casualties, such as the Bishopsgate bomb in the City of London in 1993 that killed one and did at least £350 million worth of damage. The considerations for religious groups can be different. If one's audience is God, one does not need to worry about alienating him. Those with religious motives have defined their religious directives in such a way as to justify their actions. These groups have therefore tended towards inflicting mass casualties, as the only constraint is their own capabilities.

Religious terrorists are not all the same – far from it. Religion can play different roles in different terrorist groups. For many

groups religion is just a badge of ethnic identity. It serves to solid-
ify alliances and divisions, to identify enemies and friends. In this
way religion has made several conflicts more intractable, but the
underlying conflict has little to do with religion. In the Northern
Irish conflict, for example, mavericks on the loyalist side like the
Reverend Ian Paisley have sought to cast the antagonism in doctrinal terms, and on the republican side local Catholic priests have
often reflected the republican instincts of the communities that
produced them. The leadership of both churches, however, has
invariably counselled non-violence, and there is no doctrinal
dispute involved. The goals of both sides are entirely political.
Religion just sharpens the differences.

In other cases religion appears to provide the objective for the
terrorist group, but it is usually very difficult to separate religious
from political motives, and both are usually operating inextricably
together. Yigal Amir, the man who assassinated the Israeli prime
minister Yitzhak Rabin in November 1995, offered this explanation: 'I have no regrets. I acted alone and on orders from God.'[52]
On the face of it he would appear to have been motivated exclusively by religion. But his act was calculated to achieve a political
objective, the destruction of the Arab–Israeli peace process, even if
it was also motivated by a desire to fulfil what he perceived to be a
divine command. Jewish groups use the Torah to justify not giving
up Judaea and Samaria. Islamic groups use the Koran to stake their
claim to the same territory. But it is not clear that the political can
be separated from the religious in these instances.

Even the case of the Aum Shinrikyo group, the Japanese cult that
released sarin gas on the Tokyo subway in March 1995 ostensibly
in an effort to bring about the apocalypse, is not a clear-cut case of
religiously driven terrorism. They too had political aspirations and
turned to terrorism only once those had been thwarted. The
organization put up twenty-four members in the 1989 parliamentary elections, but none was elected. Moreover, their actual attack
was precipitated not by any religious doctrine but rather by the
paranoid fear that the police were closing in on them.[53]

To this day we do not know quite how much weight Osama bin
Laden attributes to his religious and his political goals. The manner

in which he has altered the listing of his various aspirations in his various statements suggests that the political is primary and religion a tool. But we do not know that for sure and he would certainly deny it. Bin Laden has long listed the American presence in Saudi Arabia as the primary offence. When asked by Peter Arnett whether an end to the American presence in Saudi Arabia would lead to an end to his call for jihad against the US, bin Laden replied: 'The cause of the reaction must be sought and the act that has triggered this reaction must be eliminated. The act came as a result of the US aggressive policy towards the entire Muslim world and not just towards the Arabian Peninsula. So if the cause that has called for this act comes to an end, this act in turn will come to an end. So the defensive jihad against the US does not stop with its withdrawal from the Arabian Peninsula, but rather it must desist from aggressive intervention against Muslims in the whole world.'[54]

Evidently he has no interest in attempting to convert Americans or others; he wants the west to remove itself from the Muslim world, broadly defined so that it can return to the days of the Caliphate and the law of sharia. We may never know whether bin Laden would be satisfied with assuming control of one country, most likely Saudi Arabia, and trying to impose an Islamist state there. Interestingly enough, when this hypothetical was put to him and he was asked what would happen to the price of oil if an Islamic state were to be established in Saudi Arabia, he replied like the student of economics he once was: 'As for oil, it is a commodity that will be subject to the price of the market according to supply and demand. We believe that the current prices are not realistic due to the Saudi regime playing the role of a US agent and the pressures exercised by the US on the Saudi regime to increase production and flooding the market that caused a sharp decrease in oil prices.'[55]

For many groups religion plays a role not unlike that of a political ideology, like Maoism for the Shining Path or Marxism–Leninism for the social revolutionary movements. It provides a unifying, all-encompassing philosophy or belief system that legitimates and elevates their actions. The number of Maoist and

Marxist–Leninist groups, however, has declined in the course of the past thirty to forty years, while the number of religiously motivated groups has increased dramatically.

The evolution of a philosophical justification for radical Islamism began with the founding of the Muslim Brotherhood in 1920. The most influential of the thinkers were the Egyptian Sayyid Qutb and the Pakistani Abul A'la Mawdudi. Three political events were enormously influential in making these fundamentalist views popular beyond an isolated number of marginalized intellectual extremists. The three events were the Iranian revolution and the wars in Lebanon and Afghanistan.

The revolution in Iran in 1978–9 overthrew the shah, who was much despised and very closely identified with the west, and established a Muslim Shiite state under the radical cleric Ayatollah Khomeini. The success of the revolution proved inspirational to other groups and provoked a wave of Shiite militancy throughout the Middle East. The new Iranian leaders were only too delighted to export their revolution and provide material as well as moral encouragement to those in other countries seeking to emulate their success. Moreover, the revolution gained widespread admiration throughout the Muslim world for the manner in which the new regime humiliated the United States by seizing the US embassy, holding the staff hostage for over a year, and forcing the US to negotiate a settlement.

Second was the war in Lebanon where Iranian-inspired Shiite terrorists, especially from Hezbollah, again enjoyed considerable success against American and Israeli forces. Hezbollah was, of course, enormously assisted by the $60–$80 million a year provided by Iran. Hezbollah became famous for three terrorist tactics in the 1980s. First was hijacking, with the most celebrated case being the protracted media extravaganza surrounding the hijacking of TWA flight 847. In this case a US serviceman was brutally killed and the US was perceived as giving in to the terrorists by pressuring Israel to release hundreds of prisoners in return for the freeing of the hostages. The second tactic was kidnapping of high-profile western targets, with significant repercussions for domestic US policy once it was learned that US officials negotiated an arms-for-hostages deal with Iran. The third tactic, and the one with the longest shelf life, was suicide bombings. The most successful example of this tactic occurred on October 23, 1983. A suicide car bomb exploded outside the US Marine barracks near Beirut airport and killed 241 American soldiers serving as peacekeepers in Lebanon. That same evening another bomber drove to the French headquarters and killed fifty-eight French soldiers. The American and French forces promptly withdrew from the country.

The Iranian revolution had occurred on President Carter's watch and he was widely perceived as being weak, and soft on terrorism. Ronald Reagan, by contrast, was elected, in large part, because he articulated a vision of a strong and powerful America. Yet he too withdrew in the face of attack. This exploded the myth for many in the Middle East that there was any essential difference between Democrats and Republicans in the US. Both were paper tigers. To this day, Osama bin Laden repeatedly invokes the American withdrawal from Lebanon after the attack on the Marines as evidence of American cowardice and unwillingness to fight. In his 1996 Declaration of War, he responded to a quote from the 'crusading' American defense secretary William Perry, who said that 'the explosion at Riyadh and al-Khobar had taught him one lesson: that is not to withdraw when attacked by cowardly terrorists', by declaring, 'We say to the defense secretary that his talk can induce a grieving mother to laughter and shows the fears . . . Where was this false courage of yours when the explosion in Beirut took place in 1983? You were turned into scattered bits and pieces at that time; 241 mainly Marine soldiers were killed. And where was this courage of yours when two explosions made you leave Aden in less than twenty-four hours [the attack on the USS *Cole* in October 2000]?'[56] The withdrawal from Lebanon provided example number two of how a superpower can be humiliated by a determined and much weaker adversary prepared to use violence against it.

The third and, I believe, most important political event leading to the escalation of Islamic fundamentalist terrorism was the war against the Soviet Union in Afghanistan. This war demonstrated to Islamists not only that a superpower could be forced to withdraw peacekeepers, as in Lebanon, but that a superpower could actually be defeated by motivated, armed mujahideen. The Soviet Union invaded Afghanistan in 1979, fearing that a surge in Islamic fundamentalism there inspired by the Iranian revolution would spread to the neighbouring Soviet republics of Uzbekistan, Tajikistan and Turkmenistan. Ten years later, after the deaths of 1 to 1.5 million Afghans and 15,000 Soviet troops, and the creation of 5 million Afghan refugees, the Soviets withdrew. Afghanistan proved to be a training ground for Islamic militants who were recruited from across the Middle East to come to the country, to train and to fight. In the course of the decade fighting the Soviets they acquired ideological unity, international connections and experience in warfare and in the use of sophisticated weaponry (often provided by the US to help defeat the Soviet Union). At the end of the war the mujahideen, hardened and radicalized by the experience, returned to their home countries, joined pre-existing terrorist groups and radicalized them. The Afghan experience demonstrated to them that they could bring down a superpower. The sole remaining superpower was the United States. Returning to their home countries, they encountered American influence everywhere and often faced harsh repression from secular Muslim governments anxious to preserve stability. They blamed the United States for propping up many of these governments and despised the governments for selling out the cause of Islam, as they saw it.

The two main branches of Islam, Sunni and Shia, both experienced fundamentalist revivals among intellectuals in the twentieth century. These three political events ensured that the writings of intellectuals and extremist thinkers like the Sunni Sayyid Qutb, in his treatise *Milestones*, and the Shia participants in the Al-Dawa movement, did not remain marginalized but rather received extensive circulation when embraced by militant leaders. The combination of a philosophical justification for terrorism with empirical evidence of its success proved lethal.

The interplay of religion and politics is an essential part of Islam, which does not recognize the compartmentalization of society into public and private realms. There has never been an Islamic equivalent of the Reformation leading to the legal or constitutional separation between religion and state. Rather, Muslims are called upon to bring the behaviour of the wider world into conformity with the religious teaching and moral precepts of the Koran (God's written revelations through Muhammad) and hadith (the divinely inspired traditions of Muhammad's sayings and practices).

Fundamentalists have a fairly simple and powerful message. The problems Muslims face are due to the pervasiveness of foreign ideologies, be they capitalist or communist, which have displaced the much nobler cultural values and philosophy of Islam. Muslims will be able to develop their own modern civilization and address the social, economic, political and moral problems they face only if they reject these alien influences and embrace sharia. The fundamentalist appeal, therefore, is to blame the social and economic problems of the region on corrupt, secular leaders and the nefarious external forces which support them. The political symbol of the failure of their leadership is the existence of the state of Israel in their midst; the social symbol of failure is the spread of western culture unaccompanied by a western standard of living. Fundamentalist leaders have therefore successfully linked economic privation with religious decline.

Islamic fundamentalists differ from Muslim traditionalists in their emphasis on the state as the means for religious reform. Their immediate goal, therefore, is to capture the state. By invoking Islam's glorious past they both dramatize the humiliation of the present situation and hold out a vision for a proud future. Moreover, the teachings of fundamentalists like Qutb promise that ultimate victory is assured. Qutb concedes that there will be defeats along the way but asserts that victory is not in doubt.

We in the west have long recognized that democracy can facilitate terrorism by protecting the freedom of speech, of movement and of association of its residents. We do not, however, consider democracy a cause of terrorism. Quite the contrary. (To a degree that I find overly optimistic, we often tend to think of it as a cure.) Religion too facilitates terrorism. It does so not just among those who live together in the slums and refugee camps of the Middle East; more dangerously it does so across borders. Earlier I mentioned the capacity to identify with others, a capacity many terrorists share, though it is by no means unique to them. It has long been recognized that a capacity to identify and empathize is a human trait but one which is held to a different degree towards different groups. We identify most closely with our families, then our neighbours and our professional colleagues, our town, state, country, in ever widening and weakening circles. Does anyone doubt that the west's dilatory response to the Rwandan atrocity was in large part due to the failure to identify with the victims? Had they been closer, whiter, more like us, would we have delayed so long? I doubt it. Or why did the terrorist campaign of the IRA get such coverage in the US in the course of the thirty-year conflict that claimed 3,500 lives, when the terrorist campaigns of the Shining Path that claimed 69,000 lives in ten years and of the PKK that claimed 35,000 over twenty years got so much less attention? I expect it was because Americans could identify with the white and English-speaking residents of Northern Ireland more than with Peruvians, Kurds and Turks.

Part of the power of fundamentalist Islam is precisely to be able to cause a young educated Briton to identify, not with his neighbours, teammates or schoolfriends, but with Palestinians in a country he's never seen. In a video made by the two British jihadists Omar Khan Sharif and Assaf Mohammed Hanif, on the eve of their martyrdom operation in Gaza in 2003, they argued, 'But Muslims are being killed every day.' They identified with other Muslims first and foremost. Similarly, it appears to have been religion which caused the twenty-two-year-old, college-educated, cricket-playing, Mercedes-driving young Briton Shehzad Tanweer from the suburbs of Leeds to identify not with his fellow Britons but with Muslims across the world, and plant a bomb in the London Underground. The successful promulgation of their unique brand of extremist Islam has proven enormously useful to the leaders of the Islamist global networks. The existence of the internet has of course helped the development of this virtual community. Religion can serve as a link between the personal and the political. Interviews with terrorists often reveal their sense of frustration bred of failure. Religion provides them with a means of dealing with these personal issues in a way that addresses their particular inadequacies by making them part of a more powerful movement and promising ultimate victory.

Religion cannot, therefore, be said to have caused terrorism; but Islamic fundamentalists have provided a justification for the use of terrorism in the interests of achieving a greater good. The economic and social failures of many Muslim countries have produced adherents willing to embrace the method as a means of redressing humiliations, improving economic and social conditions and effecting change. In this way, religion interacts with social, economic and political factors and contributes to the creation of a culture of violence. It makes recruitment, mobilization and retention easier for the leaders of these groups. Religious groups can have more staying power because they have an ideology that legitimates their actions and gives each individual a role.

Religion is never the sole cause of terrorism; rather religious motivations are interwoven with economic and political factors. Yet religion cannot be reduced to social and economic factors. It is a powerful force in itself. Religion serves to incite, to mobilize and to legitimize terrorist actions. Moreover, religion's preoccupation with fundamental notions of good and evil tends to ensure that movements with religious motives are much less prone to compromise. Islamic fundamentalists tend to see the world in terms of an enduring and cosmic struggle between good and evil. Religiously motivated terrorist groups, therefore, tend to be more fanatical, more willing to inflict mass casualties and better able to ensure unassailable commitment from their adherents. As such they are much less susceptible to conventional responses like deterrence or negotiation. So while religion is only a cause of terrorism in combination with other social and political factors, it does make terrorist groups more absolutist, more transnational and more dangerous.

The two most common explanations of terrorism are that it is the work either of crazy individuals or of war-mongering states; however, the best explanations are not at these levels at all but at the level of the societies that produce them. Terrorism needs a sense of alienation from the status quo and a desire to change it. Terrorism needs conditions in which people feel unfairly treated, and leaders to make sense of these conditions, to organize a group and make it effective. Terrorism needs an all-encompassing philosophy, a religion or secular ideology, to legitimize violence, to win recruits to the cause and to mobilize them for action. Terrorism, to survive and thrive, needs a complicit society, a societal surround sympathetic to its aspirations if not necessarily to its actions.

In light of these requirements one can see why diaspora communities have become such fertile recruiting grounds for Islamic fundamentalists. Removed from the sureties of their own culture, feeling disaffected because marginalized and undervalued in their new one, immigrants are vulnerable to the appeals of radical clerics attacking the inequities of the society from which they are disaffected and offering an alternative community. But recruits are not just found among the physically displaced. Militant leaders and the organizations they lead are more likely to find followers in situations in which economic developments and rapid change are increasing inequalities and disrupting traditional structures, when expectations are being raised and not met, where feelings of frustration and humiliation are widespread among underemployed youth. These leaders are more likely to be successful in winning recruits if they can construct an ideology that is rooted in religious or historical traditions and thereby legitimizes and even glorifies their actions and offers a path to a different future.

In short then, broad social, economic and cultural factors may be the underlying causes or rather the risk factors that make a society more or less susceptible to the appeal of terrorist groups. But they are not the cause. The cause lies in the complex interplay between these broad factors and the actions, beliefs and political aspirations of a small group of people, the founders, leaders and members of the terrorist groups, and the complicity of the community from which they come. Terrorism is caused by the complex interplay of forces operating at three different levels – of personal disaffection, an enabling group and a legitimizing ideology. Quite how this mix will play out will depend on the context in which they interact.

An understanding of the risk factors that tend to precipitate the resort to terrorism doesn't really help us understand what terrorists are trying to achieve by acting in this way. If one accepts, as I have argued, that their action is purposive and not simply the behaviour of deranged psychopaths or provoked by a desire to lash out against all enemies, then one must ask, what are they fighting for? What motivates them? What are they trying to attain? What do they want? These are the questions which we will consider next.

4

The Three Rs: Revenge, Renown, Reaction

If we are mark'd to die, we are enow
To do our country loss . . .

                             I am not covetous for gold,
Nor care I who doth feed upon my cost;
It yearns me not if men my garments wear;
Such outward things dwell not in my desires.
But if it be a sin to covet honour,
I am the most offending soul alive . . .
We would not die in that man's company
That fears his fellowship to die with us . . .

                                then shall our names,
Familiar in his mouth as household words,
Harry the king, Bedford and Exeter,
Warwick and Talbot, Salisbury and Gloucester,
Be in their flowing cups freshly remember'd.
This story shall the good man teach his son;
And Crispin Crispian shall ne'er go by,
From this day to the ending of the world,
But we in it shall be remembered;
We few, we happy few, we band of brothers;
For he today that sheds his blood with me
Shall be my brother.

                        William Shakespeare, *Henry V*, IV, iii

Nine-year-old Dermot Finucane sat on the stairs with his brothers, who were aged eleven and twelve. He remembers the fear etched on his parents' faces and audible in their muffled voices as they looked out from their bedroom window. 'You would be sitting there terrified, not making a sound; you were like a mouse, just listening.' The children carried hammers, hatchets and the poker from the fireplace to defend themselves when the mob outside broke down the door to their house to burn them out. They were a Catholic family living in a fine five-bedroom house on a mixed street. Their Protestant neighbours wanted them out. Two other brothers, John and Pat, who were sixteen and eighteen at the time, were not able to get back to the house to help them. The policemen outside watching the mob burn and loot the 'Catholic' houses were not about to interfere. Dermot recalls: 'The thing I most clearly remember is that the adults were terrified and as a child you picked that up. I can remember thinking we were going to be killed soon, our area would be overrun by hostile Indians.' They were not killed, but they lost their house, and their dad and eldest brother lost their jobs, having been threatened with death if they showed up for work. The family's fortunes plummeted. The parents and eight children squatted in a two-bedroom flat in the Catholic part of town.

Dermot was ten when his brother John joined the IRA. His younger brother Seamus explained: 'We were all proud of John. There was a sense of adventure about people taking up the gun and the bomb at that time. Yes, it was exciting at times. You got satisfaction out of it.' Immediately the rest of the family became suspect. Their house was regularly raided by soldiers. Dermot estimated that this happened more than a hundred times. His father would make tea for the raiding soldiers to try to show that they were a respectable family and in the vain hope that they would not then beat his children. The children reacted differently. Martin, two years older than Dermot, recalls the raids: 'I remember them telling my father what to do. It was my father's house, it was my mother's house. But they were telling them what to do and going about our house as if they owned it, searching it, looking at personal things and private things. I began to hate them.' Martin never joined the IRA. Instead, unable to handle the constant harassment on account of his brother, he fled the country. His sister Rosie fled too. It wasn't long before their brother Seamus was caught up in the excitement. At the age of fifteen he was picked up by the

British army and interned without trial for over a year. In the internment camp it was the regular army visits with dogs that scared him the most. 'It was frightening, they had the dogs in and big batons, and if you moved when you were not supposed to they just clipped you with them.' When he emerged he was more committed than ever to the IRA.

Dermot was eleven when his brother John died. What Dermot remembered most was the funeral: 'The crowds were massive . . . My elder brothers told me that it was the biggest funeral up until that time to leave Andersonstown. I remember being very proud that John was getting a military funeral.' The brothers describe the way the entire community was united against the enemy. In Dermot's words: 'The whole area was against them, so I was against them. It was a community thing.' Martin agreed: 'You just got involved because you were caught up in it.'

When Dermot was seventeen the army raided the house again. He assumed that they had come for his brother Martin, so he turned to him and said, 'They are here again for you.' But this time they had come for Dermot. 'I got a bit of a beating . . . and after that I just collapsed. I would have told them anything, signed anything. But luckily I didn't know anything.' The day after he was released his father died of a heart attack. The family blamed his premature death on the strain of the Troubles. Dermot decided it was time to join the IRA. He had difficulty doing so at first as he didn't know who to talk to or how to join. Having been accepted into the IRA, he had to undergo training. He made an excuse to his mother to explain his four-day absence but when he returned he was proud as punch. 'We got a big buzz out of the arms training. I came back with my chest sticking out – Big Man. I should have had a sticker printed on my forehead, "Top Man Now". It gave you a lift and a sense of achievement.' Once he was a member of the movement, he thought, 'In three years' time I will be dead so I am going to do my damnedest to hurt those who have hurt my family, my community.'

When Dermot was twenty he was charged with murder, only to be released in the absence of any evidence against him. A year later he was convicted of terrorist offences and sentenced to eighteen years in prison. At the age of twenty-three he escaped. He fled to the Republic of Ireland, where he lived on the run for four years before being caught. He successfully fought extradition proceedings brought against him and was freed in Dublin in 1991. By then his eldest brother Pat, a prominent solicitor, had been assassinated in his home in front of his wife and three children in an apparent act of collusion between Protestant paramilitaries and the security services that is being investigated to this day.

The story of the radicalization of Dermot Finucane contains many of the themes found in the stories of other terrorists in other parts of the world. In particular, the sense of being part of a larger community and the desire for revenge are ever present when terrorists explain their motivations. For Dermot the glory of a big funeral was matched by the glory of being listed on a 'wanted' poster. When looking at a poster of three of the most wanted men in Ulster he remembers thinking, 'That's what you want, you want to inflict so much damage on the enemy they want you badly. There is no point doing it Mickey Mouse style; I was always putting myself on the front line . . . I wanted the honour of doing it.' The honour and glory of the battle is another constant theme in the conversations of terrorists everywhere from Andersonstown to Afghanistan.

Another constant theme among terrorists is confidence in victory, the belief that through their violence the enemy will react. Dermot Finucane, looking at Northern Ireland during the mid-1990s, insisted, 'Britain is finished in Ireland. It's over. It's all a question of when, when do they decide to pull out.' Looking back on his career as a terrorist Dermot says, 'Militarily and politically, I have inflicted damage and I am glad. I am glad I have been a thorn in their side. I did set out to fight them and I fought them.' When asked to specify how much damage he had inflicted, he was vague: 'Let's just say it is in double figures.'[1]

Primary and Secondary Motives

There has been a vigorous debate on the question of whether or not terrorism works. I must confess to finding this entire argument quite pointless. You cannot know whether or not it works until you know what it is terrorists are trying to achieve. Those who argue, for example, that the establishment of the power-sharing executive in Northern Ireland has rewarded the terrorism of the IRA are quite wrong.[2] The IRA did not wage a terrorist campaign to share power with Protestants in Northern Ireland. Quite the contrary: the IRA and the republican community from which they come have always refused to participate in the running of the province, as to do so would be to concede the legitimacy of its existence. The IRA campaign was fought to bring about a united Ireland, which they have not succeeded in achieving.

Alan Dershowitz's provocative argument in his book *Why Terrorism Works* is based almost entirely on his interpretation of the Palestinian case.[3] He argues that the Palestinians' terrorist tactics have brought more attention and sympathy for their cause than those with better national claims who have not resorted to terrorism, like the Tibetans and Armenians. If the goal of terrorism is attention and sympathy, then Dershowitz might be right in the Palestinian case, though hardly in many others. If the goal is a national territory commensurate with their nationalist aspiration then the Palestinians, like the Tibetans and the Armenians, have a long way to go.

I believe that all terrorist movements have two kinds of goals: short-term organizational objectives and long-term political objectives requiring significant political change. This distinction is crucial to understanding their actions and places the current debate on whether or not terrorism works in a very different light.

The enormous distance between the means employed and the ends pursued often causes us to think that terrorists are just crazies, but, as I have argued, they are not, by and large, crazy at all. How, for example, can murdering bond traders in New York, dancers in Bali or random people en route to work in London and Madrid possibly hasten the return of the Caliphate? How can murdering Olympic athletes possibly advance the cause of impoverished Palestinians? Hannah Arendt once wrote that 'Violence being instrumental by nature is rational to the extent that it is effective in reaching the end that must justify it.'[4]

If one keeps in mind the ultimate objective of the terrorists, the violence may indeed appear to be irrational, but it is important to remember that along with the primary, or long-term, motivations driving terrorist action there are often secondary or more immediate objectives to be pursued. It must be said that the record of terrorists in obtaining these second-tier objectives is much better than their record in achieving the fundamental political change they generally seek.

The long-term objectives differ across different types of groups. Ethno-nationalist groups are looking for traditional territorial gains like independence and secession. (Examples include the PLO in Palestine, the PKK in Turkey, the LTTE in Sri Lanka and the IRA and ETA in Europe.) Social revolutionary groups are seeking to overthrow capitalism (examples include the Red Brigades in Italy, the RAF in Germany, Action Directe in France and the CCC in Belgium). Maoist groups – like the Shining Path in Peru and the Communist Party of Nepal – seek to remake society. Some religious sects such as Aum Shinrikyo in Japan seek to bring about the millennium; fundamentalist groups seek to replace secular law with religious law. There are enormous similarities within these types of groups but very significant differences among them, although some movements, like Hamas and Hezbollah, appear to be hybrids and some groups evolve from one kind to another, like the transformation of the isolated 'old' IRA into the pragmatic and more broad-based Provisional IRA. In every instance they are driven by an ideal.

Those who argue that terrorism works are often confusing these primary and secondary motives of terrorism. Unlike the primary objectives, the more immediate or secondary motives for specific acts are often shared across all types of terrorist movement. There are a number of secondary motives. We will now examine the most important of these.

Revenge

The desire of individual terrorists for revenge has been mentioned already. It serves as a powerful motive across all kinds of terrorist organizations. A captive on hijacked TWA flight 847, for example, could not understand why a hijacker kept running up and down the aisle with a grenade and shouting the name of her home state, 'New Jersey! New Jersey!' The terrorist remembered, though the passenger certainly did not, that it was the USS *New Jersey* which had fired on Shiite sites in Lebanon. The desire for revenge explains why so many attacks take place on the anniversary of earlier actions. The Oklahoma City bombing, for example, occurred on the anniversary of the storming of the Branch Davidian compound in Waco, Texas. Colonel Qadaffi, the Libyan head of state, used to mark the anniversary of the 1986 US bombing of Tripoli by providing funding to terrorist groups.

Publicity

Since the days of the Zealots, terrorists have understood the value of publicity. Terrorists, especially those operating in democracies, have been singularly successful in achieving this objective. Even before the most recent terrorist spectaculars, an estimated 500 million people watched the abduction and murder of the Israeli Olympic team in Munich in 1972. More recently, the Tupac Amaru, a small group unknown outside Peru, where they were overshadowed by the much larger Shining Path movement, became virtually a household name throughout much of the industrialized world after they took over the Japanese embassy in Lima and held hostage members of the political, military and diplomatic elite. No spectacular, however, quite compares with the image of aircraft crashing into the Twin Towers and the subsequent collapse of those bastions of American capitalism. Celebrating this case of propaganda by deed, bin Laden said to a colleague: 'Those young men [inaudible] said in deeds, in New York and Washington, speeches that overshadowed all other speeches made everywhere else in the world. The speeches are understood by both Arabs and non-Arabs, even by Chinese. It completely dominated the media.'[5]

Specific Concessions

Sometimes the terrorist act is carried out in an attempt to procure specific concessions. Most often the concession sought is the release of comrades imprisoned either by the country in which the incident occurs or by an ally of that country. In one of the most dramatic instances, Lebanese hijackers agreed to release 145 passengers on board TWA flight 847 in return for Israel's agreement, under intense pressure from the US, to release 766 detained Lebanese. In another case, in December 1999, the Indian authorities agreed to negotiate with the al-Qaeda-affiliated group Harakut-ul-Mujahideen (HUM) in return for the release of 154 passengers on board an Indian Airlines airbus, flight IC-814. India released three imprisoned Islamic fundamentalists, including the British-educated Omar Sheikh who was subsequently convicted in the abduction and murder of the *Wall Street Journal* reporter Daniel Pearl. In another case, in 1974, the Japanese Red Army seized the French embassy in The Hague and held nine hostages including the French ambassador, until they were exchanged for one of the group's imprisoned leaders, Yoshiaki Yamada.

This strategy does not always work. The US government's refusal to negotiate with Black September terrorists led to the assassination of Ambassador Cleo Noel, Deputy Chief of Mission George Curtis Moore and a Belgian diplomat named Guy Eid in Khartoum in 1973.[6] Similarly, Pakistan's refusal to negotiate with the HUM in an earlier effort to secure the release of Omar Sheikh and Maulana Masood Azhar led to the deaths of five kidnapped western tourists. While the US government and many other governments have official policies of no concessions to terrorists, terrorists have often, in fact, achieved their limited objectives in these circumstances.

More recently hostages have been seized in an attempt to secure a commitment from the victim's government to withdraw troops from Iraq. Japanese, Romanian and Bulgarian hostages have been taken in an effort to force such withdrawal. In the case of the Philippines, fifty-one medics, engineers and soldiers were brought home in July 2004 in response to the kidnapping of a truck driver.

Causing Disorder

Very often terrorists act with the intention of undermining the legitimacy of the state by demonstrating that it cannot protect its citizens. Generally, they try to make themselves seem more trouble than they are worth in the hope that this will encourage capitulation to their broader objectives. The IRA in Northern Ireland, for example, frequently said that their immediate goal was to make Northern Ireland ungovernable. Terence, better known as 'Cheeky', Clarke, who was subsequently to become Gerry Adams's chief of security and who spent twenty-one years in prison for terrorist offences, told journalist Peter Taylor: 'The more you hurt them, I thought, the more fed up they'll get and want to get out. At that time there were British politicians saying, "Why are we there? Why are our boys dying?" '[7]

Provoking Repression

Very often the goal of a particular action is to provoke the government to retaliate forcibly. The hope is that in so doing the government will alienate the public and thereby force recruits into the arms of the movement. This tactic, of course, lends itself to a vicious cycle of violence that has rarely brought the ultimate objective any closer. The most articulate spokesman of this tactic was the nineteenth-century Russian populist Sergey Nechayev, who in his famous handbook *Cathechism of the Revolutionist* advocated violent attacks to force the government into repression, to deny it legitimacy and to radicalize the masses. The Spanish group ETA discussed the theory behind this tactic at their Fourth Assembly held in 1965 and formally adopted it at their Fifth Assembly. In the 1980s a prominent leader of the ETA who went by the *nom de guerre* 'Antxon' complained that the Spanish authorities were becoming too professional and discriminating in their responses to ETA action.[8]

Organizational Dynamics

Occasionally the terrorist action has little to do with external factors and everything to do with the internal dynamics of the group.

A particular action may be decided upon as a test of loyalty, to enforce obedience to a code, to initiate newcomers or to demonstrate the prowess of a particular leader or faction of the group. The action is then undertaken much like a new management strategy, with the goal of enhancing the internal effectiveness of the organization. On other occasions the intensity of the internal dynamics is such that the actions undermine the group. One of the more extreme examples took place in the mountains of central Japan in 1972 when fourteen members of the United Red Army were brutally killed by their peers as part of a re-education process.

A Show of Strength

Often, after the capture of a leader or after a particularly damaging government action, a group will carry out another terrorist attack in an effort to demonstrate to the public at large, to the government and, most importantly, to their own supporters that they are still a force to be reckoned with.

After the arrest of her husband Renato Curcio, a founder of the Red Brigades, the young Mara Cagol came into her own. A talented musician and practising Catholic, she grew up in a conservative, supportive and solidly middle-class family. When she wasn't performing in concerts and competing in national competitions with her favourite instrument, the classical guitar, she enjoyed many activities such as tennis and skiing. She was also a deeply caring young woman and at the age of twenty spent long hours comforting the sick and volunteering in hospices. She was enormously popular among the elderly patients, who called her 'la Margherita'. Cagol went to college and obtained a PhD in sociology.

When Curcio and several of the other leaders of the Red Brigades were captured in 1974, Cagol took over, determined to demonstrate that the organization had not been decapitated. She not only organized and sustained the movement through its first crisis but also managed to rescue her husband from prison in February 1975. She died that June in a gun battle with the Carabinieri.

Revenge, Renown, Reaction

All of these secondary or more immediate motives can be sub-sumed under the three motivations: revenge, renown, reaction. If we ask ourselves whether Mohammad Sidique Khan, Shehzad Tanweer, Hasib Hussain or Germaine Lindsay, the four young men who blew themselves and fifty-two others up in London on July 7, 2005, honestly thought that by placing bombs on the London Underground they were really going to hasten the return of the Caliphate, the answer must be no. But if we wonder whether by placing these bombs they expected to get revenge, renown and reaction, the answer must be that they probably did. If they did, they were certainly correct. By inflicting suffering, they had pre-sumably decided, they were simply causing the British public to reap what they had sown in the Muslim world. They undoubtedly got renown – the bombing managed even to sideline the much anticipated G8 summit. The names and photos of the four suspects are familiar all over the world. The reaction they got may have dis-appointed them. Rather than resorting to the language and actions of warfare, even of a crusade, the British prime minister spoke instead of police work, crime scenes and criminal investigation. There were no official attempts to denounce Muslims, though there appears to have been an increase in hate crimes and petty dis-crimination against British Muslims. As a result of the bombings, there has also been increasing pressure on the UK to withdraw from the wildly unpopular Iraq war, but this has been countered by a reluctance to appear to give in to terrorism.

In analysing both the words and the actions of terrorist move-ments over the years it seems quite clear to me that they pursue these two sets of long- and short-term motivations simultaneously. Moreover, it is also apparent that the more philosophical or polit-ical aspirations are of greater interest to the leadership of the movements, while the followers tend to be attracted by the more near-term appeal of revenge, renown and reaction. Terrorist groups have been singularly unsuccessful in delivering the political change they seek, but they have enjoyed considerable success in achieving their near-term aims. It is this success which appeals to disaffected youth with time on their hands who seek a means of rapid redress.

This distinction between the interests of leaders and of followers is evident across all kinds of terrorist groups. In 1971, the IRA's political cover, Sinn Fein, held a party conference (Árd Fhéis) and approved political plans for a New Ireland (Éire Nua). What they envisioned, once they had achieved Irish unification, were four regional parliaments. To the man in the street, however, this did not resonate. 'Cheeky' Clarke explained: 'I was politically naive. I thought I was doing the right thing because it was for my people . . . I hadn't a political thought in my head other than that I knew what we were doing was right because it was to get the Brits out of Ireland.'[9] Another member of the IRA, Raymond Gilmore, who was subsequently to become a notorious informant, was sworn in nine years later in 1980. He describes how he was required by the IRA's education officer to study the IRA's 'Green Book' in a school building in the evenings before being allowed to join.[10]

A member of al-Qaeda told a very similar story. In his trial for terrorist conspiracy in the federal district court in Manhattan, Ali Muhammad told the judge that 'The objective [was] . . . just to attack any western target in the Middle East, to force the government of the Western countries just to pull out from the Middle East.'[11] Young European social revolutionaries often felt the same way. One German militant explained: 'Most of the comrades of my group called themselves "anarcho-trade unionists" and so did I, although I did not really understand what it meant.'[12]

Primary Motivations

Generally ethno-nationalist terrorist movements, those with political aspirations that could be realized without overthrowing the current order, have been much more definite in spelling out their objectives, though generally vague on the details of a post-conflict society. Most of these groups suggest that in the new order present inequities will be redressed, but few offer details on how this might be accomplished. Some adopt the language of socialism or Marxism, but all are primarily driven by nationalist aspirations. Euzkadi Ta Askatasuna, or Basque Fatherland and Liberty (ETA), was founded in 1959 with the aim of establishing an independent Basque home-land in the northern Spanish provinces of Vizcaya, Guipúzcoa, Álava and Navarra and the south-western French departments of Labourd, Basse-Navarra and Soule.

The Kurdistan Workers' Party (PKK) founded in 1974 is pri-marily composed of Turkish Kurds whose goal is to establish an independent democratic Kurdish state. The Irish Republican Army (IRA) want a united thirty-two-county island of Ireland. The Liberation Tigers of Tamil Eelam (LTTE), better known as the Tamil Tigers, was founded in 1976 with the goal of establish-ing an independent Tamil state.

Maoist groups like the Shining Path in Peru, the Communist Party of Nepal and the Communist Party of the Philippines, better known as the New People's Army, seek to overthrow the state and replace it with a proletarian dictatorship. Each of these groups were based initially in the countryside, in keeping with Maoist dogma. In Colombia, in the words of a terrorist spokesman, 'The FARC's goal is to be the government. The FARC wants to become a new government to offer the Colombian people the possibility of a worthy life. The FARC wants to begin to build socialism in Colombia.'[13] The FARC appears to combine a rural insurgency with a social revolutionary leadership.

There are also a large number of smaller, more urban Marxist–Leninist groups like the MRTA in Peru, GRAPO in Spain, November 17 in Greece and Dev Sol in Turkey. These contem-porary groups are of a similar ilk to the social revolutionary move-ments that proliferated in the 1970s, like the Japanese Red Army, the RAF in Germany, the Red Brigades in Italy and so on. They seek to overthrow the institutions of the state and replace them with an ill-defined but perfect classless society.

Terrorist groups do not remain static. They often split in response to peace overtures as the more extreme elements reject the compromise of the leaders. Examples include the Continuity IRA and Real IRA, who split from the Provisional IRA in response to the peace process in Northern Ireland. The Palestinian movement over the years has split and split again on issues of personality, tactics and strategy, leading to a whole array of movements with compatible but not identical aspirations.

In the case of Chechnya, what started out as a number of nationalist groups seeking independence from Russia have become infiltrated by Islamists and are turning what was a more narrowly focused nationalist terrorist campaign into a front in the more broad-based conflict between Islamists and the west. There are three main Chechen groups today. The Riyadus-Salikhin Reconnaissance and Sabotage Battalion of Chechen Martyrs (RSRSBCM) is led by Shamil Basayev. The Special Purpose Islamic Regiment (SPIR) was led by Movzar Barayev until he was killed in the seizure of the Dubrovka Theatre in Moscow in October 2002. The Islamic International Peacekeeping Brigade (IIPB) is jointly led by the Chechen Basayev and an Arab mujahideen leader, currently Abu al-Walid.

The Harakut ul-Mujahideen (HUM) in Pakistan is another case of a group with a primarily territorial objective – liberating Kashmir from India – joining forces with radical Islamist groups. The HUM signed bin Laden's 1998 fatwa against the west and their members are now an essential part of the al-Qaeda front.

Few terrorist movements have been as consistent and coherent in spelling out their objectives as Hezbollah. Their programme stipulates:

> Let us put it truthfully: the sons of Hezbollah know who are their major enemies in the Middle East – the Phalanges, Israel, France, and the United States. The sons of our *umma* [community of Muslims] are now in a state of growing confrontation with them and will remain so until the realization of the following three objectives:
> a) to expel the Americans, the French, and their allies definitely from Lebanon, putting an end to any colonialist entity on our land;
> b) to submit the Phalanges to a just power and bring them all to justice for the crimes they have perpetuated against Muslims and Christians;
> c) to permit all the sons of our people to determine their future and to choose in all liberty the form of government they desire. We

> call upon all of them to pick the option of Islamic government,
> which alone is capable of guaranteeing justice and liberty for all.
> Only an Islamic regime can stop any further tentative attempts at
> imperialistic infiltration.

These are Lebanon's objectives; those are its enemies. As for our
friends, they are all the world's oppressed peoples.

This document goes on to reveal that the moderation implied by
the objectives does not run very deep. Of Israel, Hezbollah's programme states:

> We see in Israel the vanguard of the United States in our Islamic
> world . . . our primary assumption in our fight against Israel states that
> the Zionist entity has been aggressive from its inception, and built on
> lands wrested from their owners, at the expense of the rights of the
> Muslim people. Therefore our struggle will end only when this entity
> is obliterated. We recognized no treaty with it, no ceasefire and no
> peace agreements, whether separate or consolidated.[14]

Osama bin Laden has been less consistently coherent in his artic-
ulation of the objectives he is trying to achieve. In his 1998 fatwa
against Jews and Crusaders, he listed three 'facts': American occupation of Saudi Arabia, American sanctions against Iraq, and
American support for Israel, as a clear declaration of war against
Allah. When asked, however, whether he would call off his jihad
against the US if the US were to withdraw from Arabia, bin Laden
replied that he would not stop until the US ceased all aggressive
actions against Muslims everywhere.[15] Later in the same interview
he refers to bringing an end not just to occupation but to 'western
and American influence on our countries'. On other occasions bin
Laden articulates an even more ambitious agenda, the restoration
of the Caliphate. This would require the elimination of current
political boundaries throughout the Middle East and beyond and a
return, in essence, to the Middle Ages. Bin Laden, for all his carefully choreographed statements and his colourful descriptions of
the iniquities of the west, has completely failed to articulate a positive political alternative. Like other revolutionaries before him,
therefore, he appears to be more enamoured of the revolution itself
than of the new world it would herald.

One of the very striking and quite surprising aspects of most terrorist movements is how little of their attention is devoted to describing the new world they intend to create. They are happy to provide the outlines of their future world like rule by sharia law or national independence, but they are very short on detail. They are not unique in this. Readers of Marx have invariably been disappointed by the absence of a coherent picture of the new world. In all his voluminous writing Marx devotes only a paragraph in *The German Ideology* to a description of the future, and it is simply a future in which workers have time to explore their hobbies: 'While in a communist society, where nobody has an exclusive sphere of activity but each can become accomplished in any branch he wishes, society regulates the general production and thus makes it possible for me to do one thing today and another tomorrow, to hunt in the morning, fish in the afternoon, rear cattle in the evening, criticize after dinner, just as I have a mind, without ever becoming hunter, fisherman, herdsman or critic.'[16] Terrorist leaders today also appear altogether more interested in the process by which the present system is destroyed than in the functioning of the new system. By contrast, Martin Luther King eloquently described his vision of the new America he sought to bring about through his non-violence campaign of civil disobedience, most famously in his 'I have a dream' speech at the 1963 March on Washington. Possessing a vision of the future may well serve to constrain one's behaviour in the present. Certainly igniting a race war would be unlikely to bring about a peaceful, equitable multiracial democracy. But if one does not have a coherent vision of the future, one's means are more likely to be determined not by the needs of the society one is trying to create but rather by the iniquities of the society one is trying to destroy.

This inattention to the details of the future world they are trying to create holds true across the leaderships of very different terrorist movements. When asked by Peter Arnett of CNN in March 1997 what kind of society would be created if the Islamic movement were to take over Arabia, Osama bin Laden was extremely vague. He replied:

> We are confident, with the permission of God, praise and glory be to him, that Muslims will be victorious in the Arabian Peninsula and that

God's religion, praise and glory be to him, will prevail in this peninsula. It is a great pride and a big hope that the revelation unto
Muhammad, peace be upon him, will be resorted to for ruling. When
we used to follow Muhammad's revelation, peace be unto him, we
were in great happiness and great dignity, to God belong credit and
praise.[17]

Abimael Guzman, leader of the Maoist Shining Path, was
equally vague in describing what his new, perfect society would
actually be like. He went into enormous detail about the process
of getting there and, like bin Laden, spent most of his time casti-
gating his enemies and detailing the injustices of the past and the
present, with only the vaguest notion of what the future for which
his followers were expending such a sacrifice would bring. He
responded to a sympathetic question about life after the triumph of
the revolution with these words:

We have not studied this question sufficiently, because it involves problems that will pose themselves in the future. We have general guide-
lines, but we agree with what Lenin said: You want to know what war
is like? Wage it. And let us have inexhaustible confidence in the international proletariat, in the oppressed nations, in the people of the
worlds; and most particularly in the communists, in the parties and
organizations, whatever their level of development. Holding fast to our
ideology, Marxism–Leninism–Maoism, we will advance, even if we
begin by feeling our way in the dark, finding temporary solutions for
certain situations for brief periods of time, until we find the definitive
one. As Lenin taught us, no revolution can be planned out completely
ahead of time.[18]

Paul Reyes, a member of the Secretariat of Colombia's FARC
and a spokesman for the organization, was likewise remarkably
vague when asked by a sympathetic Cuban reporter what the ruling
programme of the FARC would be. He said:

I must admit that we have yet to define this aspect. However, we have
thought about it to some extent. We start out based on the idea that
the type of government that should be installed in Colombia must be
in accordance with the country's situation and in accordance with the
world's technical and scientific development. We are aware that

Colombia is an immensely wealthy country, a country which can feed itself and finance itself and a country which cannot be blocked completely. We are also aware that imperialism and foreign financial capital will exert pressure, they will always exert pressure, and we know this. Likewise, we believe that the socialist model we should implement in Colombia is a socialism for Colombians.[19]

The charismatic leader of the Tamil Tigers, Vellupillai Prabakharan, was only a little more specific in answer to a question posed by an Indian reporter. She asked: 'If and when Eelam is achieved, what sort of a nation do you conceive it to be?' He responded:

Tamil Eelam will be a socialist state. By socialism I mean an egalitarian society where human freedom and individual liberties will be guaranteed, where all forms of oppression and exploitation will be abolished. It will be a free society where our people will have maximum opportunity to develop their economy and promote their culture. Tamil Eelam will be a neutral state, committed to non-alignment and friendly to India, respecting her regional policies, particularly the policy of making the Indian Ocean a zone of peace.[20]

The Chechen leader, Shamil Basayev, was asked a similar question by a Russian journalist who wanted to know who would rule Chechnya when the Russians left. He replied: 'First thing that comes to mind are the words "power to the people". I have never sought power and I have never fought for power. I have always fought for justice and justice has been my only goal.'[21]

Here we see the leaders of five of the bloodiest terrorist movements in the world whose campaigns have cost tens of thousands of lives over many years and several continents in pursuit of religious, secular, Maoist and nationalist objectives, and none of them is able to describe the society he is trying to create.

These very vague notions of the future world are hardly enough to motivate followers to lay down their lives for the cause. By contrast with these occasional references to the future and even more occasional details about what it would actually look like, all of their statements and interviews are full of invective about the evils of their enemies. It is not so much a vision of a new world, therefore, that drives even the leaders of these groups but rather their outrage at the injustices of the present one. What appears to drive most terrorists, therefore, is not the desire or expectation of achieving the primary political objective articulated by their leaders but rather the desire for, and reasonable expectation of achieving, revenge, renown and reaction. This holds true whether the terrorists are members of nationalist, right-wing, Marxist–Leninist, Maoist, millenarian or Islamist terrorist groups.

The Three Rs: Revenge

The most powerful theme in any conversation with terrorists past or present, leader or follower, religious or secular, left wing or right wing, male or female, young or old, is revenge. It is not the objective severity of the grievance any more than it is the objective severity of poverty that drives terrorists, but a desire for revenge is ubiquitous among them.

Suhail al-Hindi, elder brother of the Palestinian suicide bomber Abu-Surur, captured the power of revenge in his entry in the martyr book compiled after his brother's death:

> That day he was born for revenge . . . revenge for me and my country and my people and the honor of the umma. Revenge for Majdal from which my parents were forced to flee, despite their passionate love of their soil, despite their sweat and blood, despite their huge love of its soil. Yes, he will take revenge, he will take revenge, he will take revenge, Allah permitting. And at the moment of this cry, the soldiers of Zion were breaking into houses, searching for cells of fedayeen belonging to the Liberation army or other groups as was their wont during that long period during the history of Palestine. At the moment they entered, upon hearing the voice of Mohammad of al-Qassam, they looked into the face of the newborn and asked his mother, What is his name? And she replied in the voice of revenge, 'Mohammad'.[22]

Before his own death on a suicide mission, Abu-Surur approached the mother of a friend who had blown himself up and assured her: 'I will kill everybody who killed your son.'[23] A video he made on the eve of his death makes clear that he and his fellow suicide bombers saw themselves as avenging the deaths of those who had gone before them.

The thirst for revenge pervades the posters, songs and popular culture of the intifada as well as the official communiqués. Posters of martyrs declare: 'The right of revenge is ours.' Popular songs ask: 'The scoundrels have taken Palestine – who will bring revenge?' Popular poetry and ubiquitous graffiti call for vengeance. In a communiqué issued on June 4, 1994, the Qassam Battalion announced the group's responsibility for a revenge attack shortly after the Hebron Massacre: 'To the leadership of Israel: You turned Eid al-Fitr into a black day so we swore to turn your independence holiday into Hell. This is our first reply to the Hebron slaughter.'[24]

The ideologically inspired social revolutionary movements were also driven in large part by a desire for revenge. The people they chose to murder were usually held up as symbols of the corrupt capitalist system they wished to replace, but the lengthy and often turgid communiqués they delivered to the media after most of their atrocities usually spelled out more banal explanations for the selection of particular targets. After the attempted assassination in July 1990 of Hans Neusel, a senior official in the German Ministry of the Interior, the RAF issued a communiqué saying that they were punishing him for his crimes – that is, his work co-ordinating European counter-terrorist efforts.[25] Similarly GRAPO, the Spanish group, issued a communiqué a day after they murdered Dr José Ramón Muñoz in 1990. He was murdered in revenge for his role in force-feeding prisoners. The communiqué declared: 'the socio-fascist government swine have not shrunk from applying any means to undermine the prisoners' will to resist, including force-feeding to make them abandon the struggle for their just demand.'[26]

The powerful appeal of revenge is equally strong among ethno-nationalist movements like the IRA. The ranks of the IRA swelled after events like 'Bloody Sunday' in January 1972 when British paratroopers shot dead thirteen Catholic civil rights marchers. Far from taking all-comers, the IRA sought to ensure that recruits were not volunteering on a whim. Raymond McCartney, who later spent fifty-three days on hunger strike while serving a life sentence for murder, remembers the devastation in his family when one of his cousins was killed on Bloody Sunday. His elder brother, however, advised him not to act precipitately, but to think it over: 'I should take time to make up my mind so that no one could ever accuse me of letting emotions cloud my judgement, so no one could say "you're joining the IRA just because of Bloody Sunday."' He waited a few months and then approached a senior IRA member to tell him that he was thinking of joining. Even then he was sent away, given some books to read, and told to think through his decision. Only then was he permitted to begin the process of joining.[27]

The desire for revenge does not end with the decision to join a terrorist movement. On the contrary, once a person becomes involved in violence the grievances to be avenged multiply and the opportunities and means for vengeance expand dramatically. In Northern Ireland IRA members sought vengeance against the British army for events like Bloody Sunday and the introduction of internment. They avenged the ill treatment of prisoners by murdering prison officers and wreaked vengeance on the Protestant community for burning them from their homes.

The attacks on the Protestant community had the effect of spawning more terrorist organizations seeking revenge. A month after the introduction of internment without trial the IRA expanded their attacks beyond 'economic' targets. They bombed a pub in the Protestant Shankill Road, killing two. The Protestant terrorist group the UVF retaliated by bombing a 'Catholic' pub. Fifteen people were killed, including the owner's wife and child who lived upstairs. One week later the IRA took revenge by bombing a 'Protestant' furniture shop. Two adults and two toddlers were killed. Several of those who arrived on the scene soon joined loyalist terrorist groups. One, Eddie Kinner, explained:

'If somebody had handed me a bomb to plant anywhere you want in the Falls [a Catholic area] I would have done it . . . I was angry and wanted to do just as much damage to the community responsible for those actions. My mentality then would have been, whenever they blow up a location in the Shankill, killing one or two people, I would want to blow up somewhere in the Falls killing double. Doing twice the amount of damage that they were doing in my community.' When it was pointed out to him that it was not the Catholic community but the IRA who planted the bomb he replied: 'I think you're right about that, but that's not how I saw it then. I would have linked it into other events that were taking place and would have seen it as not necessarily the Catholic community carrying it out but it being done on their behalf. So they were part of it.'[28]

Individual sectarian killings were one of the most gruesome aspects of the Northern Irish conflict as each side tried to take revenge against the other. These tit-for-tat murders were entirely anathema to the political ideology of the organizations that carried them out. Similarly, just as large-scale events like Bloody Sunday swelled the ranks of the IRA, large-scale IRA atrocities like Bloody Friday, when the IRA planted twenty-two bombs in the centre of Belfast, swelled the ranks of Protestant paramilitary organizations. In carrying out these atrocities the perpetrators were not seeking to bring about either a united Ireland or a loyalist Ulster, they just wanted revenge.

In Italy too the dynamics of violence were driven not just by conflict between the left and the state but by violence between the left and the right-wing militant groups. Just as Catholics and Protestants became abstract, depersonalized enemies to one another in Northern Ireland, left and right became abstract, depersonalized enemies to one another in Italy. One militant right-wing radical explained his involvement in political violence as part of a spiral of revenge: 'There had been violence against my brother, and I felt a sense of injustice that pushed me to get involved, as he was, in politics. My first attitude was one of retaliation: my mother's car had been burned, and I burned other cars. I returned to others the blows my brother had received. It grew year after year. Violence produced violence.'[29] The story on the left was quite similar. 'If you see black [the fascist colour] shoot at once, that was the slogan . . . there was a manhunt, without any pity, it was a hunt against the fascists that then had repercussions for us, because there was a spiral of revenge.'[30]

In the narrow confines of Northern Ireland the defended community is small, and the names of the victims and sometimes the victims themselves are known to their murderers. In Italy the stage was larger and the arguments different, but the dynamic was very similar. Vengeance, however, can be sought with equal fervour on behalf of a much larger group such as the world's Muslims. Nowhere is the power of revenge more vividly portrayed than in the writings of Osama bin Laden, which are suffused with its language. In appealing to the American people over the heads of their leaders in October 2004 bin Laden declared: 'Just as you lay waste to our nation so shall we lay waste to yours.'[31] In some cases the act for which he seeks vengeance is quite specific, like Israel's assassination of Hamas leader Ahmed Yassin: 'The act that horrified the world; that is the killing of the old, handicapped sheikh Ahmed Yassin, may God have mercy on him . . . We pledge to God that we will punish America for him, God willing.'[32] More often it is revenge for a long train of abuses by the US and its allies:

> The youths hold you responsible for all of the killings and evictions of the Muslims and the violation of the Holy Places, carried out by your Zionist brothers in Lebanon; you openly supplied them with arms and finance. More than 600,000 Iraqi children have died due to lack of food and medicine and as a result of the unjustifiable aggression [sanctions] imposed on Iraq and its nation. The children of Iraq are our children . . . Our youths know that the humiliation suffered by Muslims as a result of the occupation of their Holy Places cannot be kicked and removed except by explosions and jihad.[33]

In the infamous 'Dinner Party Tape', in which bin Laden is shown discussing the September 11 attacks with a coterie of supporters, one described learning of the attacks. 'I was sitting with the Sheikh [bin Laden] in a room, then I left to go to another room where there was a TV set. The TV broadcast the big event. The screen was showing an Egyptian family in their living room, they exploded with joy. Do you know when there is a soccer game and your team wins? It was the same expression of joy. There was a sub-title that read: In revenge for the children of Al-Aqsa Usama bin Laden executes an operation against America.'[34]

Once the US invaded Afghanistan there were, of course, many more actions to be avenged. In November 2001 bin Laden railed against the injustice of the attack on Afghanistan:

The entire west, with the exception of a few countries, supports this unfair, barbaric campaign, although there is no evidence of the involvement of the people of Afghanistan in what happened in America. The people of Afghanistan had nothing to do with this matter. The campaign, however, continues to unjustly annihilate the villagers and civilians, children, women and innocent people.[35]

The next month, in an interview on Al-Jazeera, he spoke even more vehemently:

America bears an unspeakable crusader grudge against Islam. Those who lived these months under continuous bombardment by the various kinds of US aircraft are well aware of this. Many villages were wiped out without any guilt. Millions of people were made homeless during this very cold weather. Those oppressed men, women, and children now live in tents in Pakistan. They committed no [crime].[36]

The Iraq war provided a great many more grievances to be avenged. Hesmat Abdul Rahman, a Jordanian mother, described how her twenty-five-year-old son, Zaid Horani, became angrier and angrier as he watched television images of the American invasion of Iraq. He and his friends became so angry that they decided, 'Let's do jihad,' and went off to the local mosque. Horani is now on trial for establishing a recruitment network for Jordanian jihadists.[37]

The ongoing conflict between Israel and the Palestinians provides an endlessly renewable stream of recruits mobilized by a desire for revenge for new Israeli atrocities. In the minds of those seeking vengeance, these new atrocities are all mixed in with received wisdom about earlier Israeli actions. One incarcerated Islamist declared:

You Israelis are Nazis in your souls and in your conduct. In your occupation you never distinguish between men and women, or between old people and children. You adopted methods of collective punishment, you uprooted people from their homeland and from their homes and chased them into exile. You fired live ammunition at women and children. You smashed the skulls of defenseless civilians. You set up detention camps for thousands of people in sub-human conditions. You destroyed homes and turned children into orphans. You prevented people from making a living, you stole their property, you trampled on their honor. Given that kind of conduct, there is no choice but to strike at you without mercy in every possible way.[38]

In Europe, too, members of social revolutionary groups describe themselves as being radicalized by encounters with an 'unfair' state. One young militant looking back remembered it this way: 'We reacted with stones against those who had guns and . . . clubs. This difference was for me a justification: it legitimized the defensive use of violence.'[39] In both Italy and Germany the death of activists at the hands either of the police or of their enemies on the right had a dramatic radicalizing effect. A former Italian activist remembered: 'the deaths . . . were the moment when rage and the desire to rebel came to possess all of us . . . Those deaths gave us a strange feeling, almost as if it were not possible to go back any more.'[40]

A desire for revenge, therefore, can get people to join a terrorist movement in the first place, but once they are involved it keeps them there as the conflict provides so many other grievances to be avenged and so many opportunities to seek vengeance. Exacting vengeance, especially on behalf of others, is seen as morally defensible, especially by Islamist groups. Bin Laden put it this way:

> What terrorism are they speaking about at a time when the Islamic nation has been slaughtered for tens of years without hearing their voices and without seeing any action by them? But when the victim starts to take revenge for these innocent children in Palestine, Iraq, southern Sudan, Somalia, Kashmir, and the Philippines . . . the hypocrites defend the clear blasphemy.[41]

From a counter-terrorist point of view there is a limit to what can be done to deny terrorists the revenge they seek. There is little correlation between the nature of the grievance and the vehemence of the desire for revenge. Certainly there are many ethnic groups, like the Tibetans and Armenians, the Scots and the Welsh, with at least as strong a claim to nationhood as those like Basques, Northern Irish Catholics, Kashmiris, Tamils, Kurds, Chechens and Palestinians who use terrorism in revenge for the denial of their own nationhood. Once engaged in a campaign against terrorism, however, a state can take care to avoid providing excuses for those wishing to use violence, to avoid committing acts that serve to strengthen the appeal of the extremists. Renown, on the other hand, is different. Unlike revenge, which terrorists take for themselves, renown has to be given by others, by a complicit community or by the adversary.

The Three Rs: Renown

From the earliest terrorist movements, publicity has been a central objective of terrorism. Publicity serves to bring attention to the cause and to spread the fear instilled by terrorism. It was the desire for publicity that ensured that the ancient Zealots and the medieval Assassins chose to carry out their attacks in front of large crowds. More recently terrorists have favoured bombings as their tactic of choice. There are a variety of reasons for this: bombs are relatively cheap and easy to use and the terrorist can easily escape the scene, if he or she wants to, but they also make very good television. Renown, however, implies more than simple publicity. It also implies glory. Terrorists seek both individual glory and glory for the cause in an effort to redress the humiliation they perceive themselves as having suffered. For the leaders this glory comes on the national or, increasingly, global stage. For the followers, glory in the community from which they come suffices. Second only to revenge, therefore, terrorists want renown.

The fact that terrorists have been extremely successful in gaining publicity has led some to conclude, rather simplistically, that terrorism works. If the goal of terrorism were simply publicity, one could conclude that it does work, but one could also devise a ready means of defeating it: deny it publicity. The sensitivity of al-Qaeda to publicity was spelled out in an article in the movement's online magazine *Al-Ansar*, by Abu Ubeid al-Qurashi, a leading member of the group. He wrote that the Palestinian murder of the Israeli Olympic team at the 1972 Munich Olympics:

> was the greatest media victory, and the first true proclamation to the entire world of the first of the Palestinian resistance movements . . .

In truth, the Munich operation was a great propaganda strike. Four thousand journalists and radio personnel and two thousand commentators and television technicians were there to cover the Olympic Games; suddenly, they were broadcasting the suffering of the Palestinian people. Thus, 900 million people in 100 countries were witness to the operation by means of television screens. This meant that at least a quarter of the world knew what was going on at Munich; after this, they could no longer ignore the Palestinian tragedy.

The September 11 [operation] was an even greater propaganda coup. It may be said that it broke a record in propaganda dissemination.[42]

He was of course right about that. The depiction of the collapsing towers and the destruction in New York and Washington made Osama bin Laden and the al-Qaeda movement he led household names all over the world and broke all records.

There have been any number of lesser examples of terrorists gaining attention, though rarely sympathy, for their cause through terrorist atrocities. IRA bomb attacks in both Britain and Northern Ireland have won widespread recognition for their aspirations. The kidnap and subsequent murder of the former prime minister and elder statesman Aldo Moro by the Italian Red Brigades in 1978 received extensive coverage. The release of sarin gas on the Tokyo subway by the Japanese Aum Shinrikyo cult brought international notoriety to a group largely unknown even inside Japan. The siege of a school in Beslan by Chechen rebels brought the issue of Chechnya to the world's televisions. The larger the number of casualties, the more innovative the tactic, the greater the symbolic significance of the target, the more heinous the crime, the more publicity accrues to the perpetrators.

The timing of bin Laden's October 2004 'Message to America' was clearly intended to gain maximum publicity, designed as it was to appear right before the American election. This video also reveals the desire for more than publicity. Gone was the Kalashnikov and the rugged mountainous terrain; instead bin Laden was seated behind a desk, playing the part of a statesman and addressing the American people over the heads of their leaders.

Abimael Guzman was known to his followers in the Shining Path as Chairman Gonzalo. He placed himself among the pantheon of communist revolutionaries with his programme known as 'Gonzalo Thought.' He described it as follows:

> It is the application of Marxism–Leninism–Maoism to the Peruvian revolution that has produced Gonzalo Thought. Gonzalo Thought has been forged in the class struggle of our people, mainly the proletariat, in the incessant struggles of the peasantry, and in the larger framework of the world revolution, in the midst of these earthshaking battles, applying as faithfully as possible the universal truths to the concrete conditions of our country.[43]

Guzman evidently saw himself and sought to be seen as a world-historical figure through his leadership of the Peruvian peasantry of the Ayacucho region.

Other terrorists too have delighted in the attention their global exploits have brought them. When he was captured in Pakistan, Ramzi Yousef, subsequently convicted for his role in the 1993 attack on the World Trade Center, had a large collection of newspaper clippings about his exploits. Similarly, the infamous Carlos 'The Jackal', among whose more famous exploits was his kidnapping of the OPEC oil ministers in Vienna in 1973, also carefully cut out newspaper articles about himself. He once declared to a colleague: 'The more I'm talked about the more dangerous I appear. That's all the better for me.'[44]

Mere membership of a terrorist group also brings a degree of glory to the rank and file. This is true across different kinds of terrorist groups. A nationalist member of Fatah reported: 'After recruitment, my social status was greatly enhanced. I got a lot of respect from my acquaintances, and from the young people in the village.'[45] Another said: 'Recruits were treated with great respect. A youngster who belonged to Hamas or Fatah was regarded more highly than one who didn't belong to a group, and got better treatment than unaffiliated kids.'[46] This recognition is more than mere deference to those who wield a gun and implies a respect for those fighting for a just cause. IRA member Shane Paul O'Doherty, who was sentenced to thirty life sentences for his bombing campaign in England, later described how he felt when waging his war against Britain: 'I was no longer an insignificant teenager. I became heroic overnight. I felt almost drunk with power.'[47]

The organizations understand this and treat their 'patriot dead', as the IRA calls them, or their 'martyrs', as Islamic fundamentalists call them, with great respect. The likenesses and names of those who have died for the cause are to be found in the streets of Gaza, the West Bank, Derry and Belfast. Moreover the status of the families of those who have died for the cause, whether in Gaza, Belfast or Sri Lanka, is enhanced. One Islamist prisoner explained:

> Families of terrorists who are wounded, killed or captured enjoyed a great deal of economic aid and attention. And that strengthened popular support for the attacks. Perpetrators of armed attacks were seen as heroes, their families got a great deal of material assistance, including the construction of new homes to replace those destroyed by the Israeli authorities as punishment for terrorist acts.[48]

Shane O'Doherty described how, at the age of sixteen, he threw nail bombs at British soldiers and almost hoped that he would be shot dead, 'fantasizing that his sacrifice would inspire a mural or, better yet, a song', ensuring his immortality.[49]

Many terrorist groups engage in complex rituals to convey a sense of glory to their followers. Members eagerly participate. Frankie Ryan was to die in 1991 while planting an IRA bomb in St Albans, England. The bomb was meant to have exploded while members of a military band were playing to a civilian audience in the town's civic centre. Before going on the operation Frankie bought the tricolour that was to wrap his coffin. The funerals of fallen soldiers are another way in which significance and glory are conveyed to members of terrorist groups by the organization. Military escorts, flag-draped coffins, rifle volleys and patriotic speeches over the grave are ways of bestowing glory on someone who might easily be perceived as an ignominious murderer. The glorification of those who die for the cause occurs in all terrorist movements. In bin Laden's words: 'Being killed for Allah's cause is a great honour achieved only by those who are the elite of the nation. We love this kind of death for Allah's cause as much as you like to live.'[50]

Many terrorist leaders delight in their status of being most wanted. This too invests them with glory. When an Indian journalist asked Prabakharan what it felt like to be the most wanted man in Sri Lanka, he answered by invoking a terrorist leader from across the world: 'An Irish leader once remarked that when the British indict a person as a terrorist it implied that he was a true Irish patriot. Similarly when the Sri Lanka government refers to me as the most wanted man it means that I am a true Tamil patriot. Hence I feel proud to be indicted as a wanted man.'[51] A Russian journalist prefaced a question to Shamil Basayev by referring to him as 'the second most wanted terrorist in the world'. Basayev replied: 'First of all I'm not the second. And secondly, I'm not wanted. I myself am trying to find these terrorists. I'm looking for them in all of Russia. And I'll keep on looking and I'll keep on finding them. And I'll keep on punishing them. So don't tell me they're trying to find me. I'm trying to find them.'[52] Abimael Guzman was also asked such a question: how does it feel to be the man most wanted by the repressive forces of the government? He replied in terms similar to those of his counterparts in other countries: 'It feels like you're doing your job and working hard at it.'[53] For his part, bin Laden delighted in the popularity of the September 11 attacks. In a statement two months after 9/11 he referred to public opinion polls: 'Polls show that the vast majority of the sons of the Islamic world were happy about these strikes because they believe that the strikes were a reaction to the huge criminality practised by Israel and the United States in Palestine and other Muslim countries.'[54] In one of his odder comments, bin Laden seemed almost peeved when he complained about American hypocrisy in calling militant Muslims terrorists while receiving the Irish republican leader Gerry Adams at the White House.[55]

Humiliation

The powerful appeal of renown, that is both publicity and glory, is clearly related to the fact that terrorists are attempting to redress the humiliation they see themselves as having suffered. Sometimes this is a personal experience of humiliation. Eamon Collins, who was to become a cold-blooded member of the IRA, before he betrayed them and was assassinated, wrote of one of the turning points in his decision to join the IRA. He was visiting the hunger-striker

Raymond McCreesh, a neighbourhood friend, in prison when he gave another prisoner some cigarettes . A 'screw', that is a prison officer, 'yelled at me that if I was caught doing that again I'd never be allowed back in. I had to swallow his dressing-down, feeling humiliated in front of Raymond. At that moment I thought that if I had a gun I would shoot the bastard, and I left the prison an angry man.'[56] There is no doubt that several people can have the same experience and not all will consider it humiliating. The number of prison visitors to have been humiliated I expect is significantly larger than the number of terrorists worldwide. Nevertheless, the experience of humiliation is a constant refrain among members of terrorist organizations.

The experience of humiliation occurs at several levels. In many cases individuals have felt personally humiliated. Communities also feel collective humiliation, as Palestinians passing through check-points in and out of Israel commonly do. In Northern Ireland the marches by Protestant members of the Orange Order in full regalia through Catholic areas in Northern Ireland were invariably per-ceived by the Catholic residents as designed to assert Protestant ascendancy and to remind Catholics that their forefathers had lost historical encounters like the Battle of the Boyne in 1691. More broadly, Bernard Lewis has written of the broad-based sense of humiliation among Muslims who have witnessed the relative polit-ical, economic and cultural decline of Islam in the face of western advancement.[57]

The desire for glory as well as publicity can, I think, be under-stood against this background of a pervasive sense of humiliation. The evident pleasure of so many people at the events of September 11 must be seen in this light. It was not pleasure that individual human beings were massacred, but pleasure that the mighty and arrogant US had been brought down by one of their own, a David and Goliath story, redressing the humiliation of always being on the receiving end of US influence. Bin Laden made this plain in an angry interview on Al-Jazeera in late 2001. 'These blessed attacks . . . clearly showed that this arrogant and supercilious power, the *hubal* [a pagan idol defeated by Muslims] of the age, America, is fragile and, thanks to Almighty God, collapsed so quickly despite having great economic power . . . They struck the largest military power deep in the heart, thanks to God the Almighty. This is clear proof that this international, usurious, damnable economy – which America uses along with its military power to impose infidelity and humiliation on weak people – can easily collapse.'[58]

Bin Laden's statements and interviews constantly reassert his desire to redress Muslim humiliation. Declaring to his followers 'Death is better than life in humiliation,' bin Laden calls on his Muslim brothers 'to expel the enemy, humiliated and defeated, out of the sanctuaries of Islam'.[59] This theme is repeated by his followers. In a pre-attack video, one of the 9/11 hijackers, Ahmad al-Haznawi al-Ghamidi, declared: 'The time of humiliation is over. It is time to kill the Americans in their own backyard, among their sons, and near their forces and intelligence.'[60]

The philosopher of radical Islamists Sayyid Qutb, in his influential book *Milestones*, explained that Muslims could not submit to anyone but Allah: 'By its very nature Islam liberates human beings everywhere from servitude to anyone other than Allah.'[61] Bin Laden has clearly adopted this position, hence the emphasis on Muslim humiliation, his insistence on the equivalence in value of western lives and Muslim lives and his contention that he has as much right to possess weapons of mass destruction, or anything else, as the west has. He asked: 'Which religion considers your killed ones innocent and our killed ones worthless?'[62] On nuclear weapons, he said: 'We congratulated the Pakistani people when they achieved this nuclear weapon and we consider it the right of all Muslims to do so.'[63]

In his statements bin Laden often addresses particular American leaders, for example quoting the American defense secretary in the 1996 fatwa. In another statement in April 2004 he offers European countries a reconciliation initiative to start 'when their last soldier leaves our country', meaning Iraq. He gives them three months to consider the offer. Again, he seems to insist on equal standing with European leaders. Clearly he sees himself and wants to be seen as an interlocutor with the political leaders of the west. He appears oblivious to the western view that it is their election that has given western leaders their legitimacy.

In one of his earliest public political pronouncements, his open letters to the Saudi leadership, bin Laden expressed anger at the embarrassing performance of their country in the Iraq war, in spite of all the money spent on weaponry.[64] He saw the stationing of American troops in Saudi Arabia as humiliating. He called these troops 'the latest and greatest of these aggressions' in his 1996 fatwa. His 1998 fatwa was even clearer on this: 'For over seven years the United States has been occupying the lands of Islam in the holiest of places, the Arabian Peninsula, plundering its riches, dictating to its rulers, humiliating its people, terrorizing its neighbours, and turning its bases in the peninsula into a spearhead through which to fight the neighbouring Muslim peoples.'[65]

He apparently sees the current conflict between al-Qaeda and the west as a means of addressing this humiliation and reasserting Islam's role. Just as historians have long said that Japan became a great power by defeating a great power, Russia in 1905, so in the war against the Soviets in Afghanistan bin Laden declared: 'The myth of the super-power was destroyed not only in my mind but in the mind of all Muslims.'[66] He appears to believe that he can repeat the same victory against the United States. Al-Qaeda statements have cast the conflict in such world-historical terms: 'Al-Qaeda's and the Taliban's resistance to the crusader campaign . . . will doubtless go down in history as a model of war between unequal sides.'[67]

Bin Laden believes, like Franz Fanon before him, that the process of fighting in itself is good for those who practise it: 'the effect of jihad has been great not only at the [regional] level of the Islamic movement but also at the [global] level of the Muslim nation in the whole world. The spirit of power, dignity and confidence in religion and the power of God has grown in our sons and brothers.'[68] Through fighting they will acquire renown and thereby redress Muslim humiliation.

The Three Rs: Reaction

Terrorists, no matter what their ultimate objectives, are invariably action-oriented people operating in an action-orientated in-group.

It is through action that they communicate to the world. This phenomenon has been called 'propaganda by deed'. Action demonstrates their existence and their strength. In taking action, therefore, they want to elicit a reaction.

Terrorists often have wildly optimistic expectations of the reactions their action will elicit: American and Israeli withdrawal from the Middle East, British withdrawal from Northern Ireland, the collapse of capitalism. There are several revealing accounts of the first meeting between British politicians and leaders of the IRA in July 1972, including Martin McGuinness and a very young Gerry Adams, who was released from Long Kesh internment camp for the occasion.[69] The British officials were stunned by the expectations of their interlocutors whom they considered, at best, young hooligans. The IRA representatives insisted upon an immediate declaration from Britain of its intent to withdraw from Northern Ireland and for the withdrawal to be complete by January 1, 1975.[70] In the 1970s former members of European social revolutionary movements similarly remember celebrating the imminent collapse of the capitalist states in which they lived.[71] For radical Islamists their faith that Allah is on their side best explains their optimism. In the words of Taliban leader Mullah Mohammad Omar, 'America is very strong. Even if it were twice as strong or twice that, it could not be strong enough to defeat us. We are confident that no one can harm us if God is with us.'[72] This optimism is reinforced by the group members, who create their own reality. The more isolated from their society they become, the more these optimistic fantasies go unchallenged.

It appears that terrorists rarely have a very coherent idea of what kinds of reaction they will get. They often expect complete capitulation. Bin Laden and other terrorist leaders constantly invoke the US departure from Lebanon and Somalia after the deaths of American servicemen as evidence of American cowardice and corruption. They seem to infer that after they have killed more Americans in other places, the US will again simply withdraw. On other occasions terrorists clearly hope to provoke a forcible response from their adversaries. By provoking democratic governments into draconian repression they can demonstrate to the world that the governments really are the fascists they believe them to be. Moreover the experience of state repression will bring new recruits into the fold. This approach has been advocated by theorists from Nechayev to Marighella and self-consciously practised by groups as different as the nationalist ETA and the social revolutionary Red Brigades.

It is often thought that bin Laden was deliberately trying to provoke a war between Islam and the west by launching the 9/11 attacks. He hoped that the US would respond militarily and that the Islamic world would then unite against it. It is also perfectly possible that he was simply trying to provoke any reaction, and either withdrawal or repression, capitulation or crusade, served his purpose. In a famous essay bin Laden's second in command, Ayman al-Zawahiri, explained why he thought it necessary to attack the United States:

> The masters in Washington and Tel Aviv are using the regimes [such as Saudi Arabia, Egypt and Jordan] to protect their interests and to fight the battle against the Muslims on their behalf. If the shrapnel from the battle reaches their homes and bodies, they will trade accusations with their agents about who is responsible for this. In that case, they will face one of two bitter choices: Either personally wage battle against the Muslims, which means the battle will turn into clear-cut jihad against infidels, or they reconsider their plans after acknowledging the failure of the brutal and violent confrontation against Muslims. Therefore we must move the battle to the enemy's grounds to burn the hands of those who ignite fire in our countries.[73]

So long as there was a reaction, therefore, the terrorist purpose was served.

Not reacting is hardly an option for a democratic country with a free press. The actions of the terrorists and the spectacular nature of their attacks are designed to provide good television coverage. The media then becomes a tool for terrorists in the desire to spread fear. Though it should be said that the media rarely encourage sympathy or understanding of terrorists, they do publicize their actions, and thereby serve their purpose. The public are frightened and insist on action to ensure their security. It is part of the power of terrorism that the fear it spreads, thanks to the random selection of victims, tends to be out of all proportion to the actual threat posed. In an attempt to ensure the safety of their citizens and to demonstrate their competence, governments invariably react strongly, and often forcibly. Moreover, if governments do not act, they not only jeopardize their own political survival but they run the risk that terrorists will feel compelled to commit ever larger atrocities in order to elicit a reaction.

Al-Qaeda's Abu Ubeid al-Qurashi declared triumphantly: 'The Western propaganda machine's size did not keep it from being defeated by Sheikh Osama with what resembled a judo move. The aggressive Westerners became accustomed to observing the tragedies of others – but on September 11 the opposite happened.'[74] It is one of the many ironies of the current threat from radical Islamic movements that while they castigate the depravity of globalization they exploit its innovations for their purposes. They exploit the western media and modern high-tech means of communication. They insist upon a confrontation with the west and refuse to allow themselves to be ignored. The release of audio- and video-tapes threatening the security of their adversaries, and the bombings in various parts of the world, all serve to magnify the threat they pose. As the first purpose of any government is to defend its citizens, governments are compelled to react. The competitive nature of western democracies and the short-term thinking that is encouraged by the electoral cycle combine to ensure that governments react forcefully and quickly. Speed and force are both critical elements in a successful military campaign; it is far less clear that they are necessary ingredients of a successful counter-terrorism policy.

Terrorists rarely have territory under their control. They have no structures to which they can point. Their clandestine existence means that the only way they can demonstrate their existence is to act. In so doing they communicate both with their adversaries and with their supporters and their followers throughout the world. By reacting, governments communicate for them too. By bombing their training camps or labelling them public enemy number one, governments also demonstrate the existence and the strength of their terrorist adversaries. Any government that refused to react, however, would soon be dismissed as weak. President Jimmy Carter failed to win re-election in 1980 in large part because he was perceived as weak when confronted by terrorist aggression. He sought to address underlying conditions that he thought spawned terrorism and he failed in the effort to rescue the Americans held hostage in Tehran. In South America civilian governments were replaced by the military when they were seen as weak in the face of terrorism. In Uruguay the terrorism of the Tupamaros was cited as justification of a military coup against a democratic government in 1973. In Brazil the terrorism of the Action for National Liberation, the ALN, was used to justify the transformation of a moderate military regime into a repressive military dictatorship. In both Brazil and Uruguay the brutal behaviour of the military state succeeded in destroying the terrorist movements, but the costs were far higher than any democracy could pay. Part of the genius of terrorism, therefore, is that it elicits a reaction that furthers the interests of the terrorists more often than those of their victims.

What terrorists want then is revenge, renown and reaction. They need only rely on themselves to get revenge. They take it; it is not given to them. The desire for revenge can get an individual involved in terrorism to begin with and can also keep him in a terrorist organization because of the growing number of issues to be avenged and the increased opportunities to claim it. Terrorists also want renown, and they cannot get this for themselves. It must be given to them by their community and by their adversaries. The desire for renown, over simple publicity, speaks to the desire to redress the perceived sense of humiliation at the hands of the enemy and is linked to the conviction most terrorists have that they are acting morally and on behalf of others. Finally, terrorists want to elicit a reaction to their action. A reaction demonstrates their strength and communicates their message. The bigger the reaction, the more successful they have been, so terrorists rely entirely on their adversary for reaction. Terrorists appear more interested in the scale of the reaction than the details. They can countenance opposite reactions, from capitulation to widespread repression, and be almost equally pleased. By focusing on these more immediate objectives rather than the underlying political change that terror-ists seek, we can get a much clearer picture of the situation we face today. Suicide bombings or martyrdom operations are not so difficult to understand and the futility of waging a war on terror is exposed.

5

Why Do Terrorists Kill Themselves?

Dulce et decorum est pro patria mori.

Horace, 65 BC[1]

Whole regiments melted in a few minutes, but others took their place, only to perish in the same way. 'It is a battle of madmen in the midst of a volcanic eruption' was the description of a staff captain . . . they fought in tunnels, screaming with the lust of butchery.

New York Times, 1916[2]

On July 7, 2005 the thirty-year-old Mohammad Sidique Khan travelled from his home in Leeds to London with three friends. Khan was the father of a fourteen-month-old daughter, Maryam, and worked as a mentor for elementary-school children with learning disabilities. He was a well-respected teacher and a committed advocate for the children he taught. One of his pupils said of him: 'He seemed a really kind man, he taught the really bad kids and everyone seemed to like him.'[3] Khan was born in Leeds to parents who had come from Pakistan. He was raised in Beeston and attended university in Leeds, where he met his Indian wife, Hasina Patel. His mother-in-law was also a dedicated educator and had received an award at a royal ceremony for her work as a teacher specializing in bilingual studies.

Travelling with Khan was the twenty-two-year-old Shehzad Tanweer. The younger man was social and sporty. He loved cricket and martial arts and enjoyed driving his father's Mercedes. He studied sports science at Leeds Metropolitan University and in his bedroom at his family's house he displayed the trophies he had won at school for athletics. Born in Bradford, he moved to Leeds at the age of two with his parents and three siblings. His father was a successful small businessman who had been born in Pakistan. The family had no financial worries and his parents were loving and supportive. A friend described him as 'not interested in politics' and added: 'He is sound as a pound.'[4]

Khan and Tanweer went by train to London with two friends the day after the city had been selected by the International Olympics Committee to host the 2012 Olympics. The attention of the news media, however, had moved to Scotland, where the G8 summit was taking place. The four friends arrived together at King's Cross station and then separated to go on four different tube lines. Khan entered the third carriage of a train bound for Liverpool Street. Tanweer took the second carriage on a Circle line train. At 8.50 they blew up themselves and everything around them. Together with their two colleagues they killed fifty-six people, including themselves, and injured 700 in the first suicide attack in Europe. A group calling itself al-Qaeda Europe claimed responsibility for the attack.

Suicide Terrorism

Few terrorist tactics have elicited as powerful a sense of horror as the increasingly popular tactic of suicide bombing. That someone would willingly strap an explosive belt around his body and blow up himself and those around him, or deliberately blow up an aircraft in which he is travelling, is deeply troubling. That a woman or a parent would do so is even more unfathomable. It is all the more troubling because it is so effective. The September 11 attacks, which necessitated the deaths of the perpetrators, killed almost ten times as many people as previous terrorist spectaculars. The tactic is not only growing in popularity, it is also growing in geographic reach. From 1981 to 1999 suicide attacks took place in seven countries. Since 2000 they have taken place in about twenty. The year 2005 witnessed escalation in suicide terrorism in a number of other dimensions too, including the appearance in London of a British-born team, the emergence in Iraq of a Belgian-born woman, and in Jordan of a husband-and-wife team acting in the name of the Iraq arm of al-Qaeda.

Suicide terrorism is so difficult to comprehend that it reinforces the view that terrorists are crazy. Moreover, the act is deeply unsettling as it suggests a degree of fanatical commitment to a cause with which we feel quite unfamiliar. It is further unsettling because there are so few obvious counter-measures. No threats of punishment are likely to influence someone who is willing to kill himself. The American public has grown familiar with the concept of deterrence. This is the edifice upon which US national security has rested since 1945. By threatening massive retaliation against its enemies the US deterred hostile action against it. This policy of deterrence served to defend it against the armed might of the Soviet Union, yet it is rendered toothless in the face of small groups of fanatics willing to kill themselves. Finally, suicide terrorism is unsettling to us because it does not quite fit the popular image of terrorists as self-serving evildoers. In willingly taking their own lives, terrorists are staking a claim to moral superiority that is quite incompatible with our notion of their moral depravity.

If one accepts the perspective on terrorism that I have been presenting, however, one sees that there is nothing fundamentally different about suicide terrorism. Suicide terrorism today is simply the tactic of choice among many terrorist groups, much as hijacking was in the 1970s. I have argued that terrorists are motivated both by long-term political objectives and by short-term immediate objectives and that the most powerful of these are the three Rs of revenge, renown and reaction. Suicide terrorism has been growing in popularity precisely because it has proven to be an effective means of exacting revenge, attaining renown and eliciting a reaction. As with terrorists generally, the necessary components for suicide operations are a disaffected individual, a supportive community and a legitimizing ideology.

I will demonstrate in this chapter that, like other forms of terrorism, martyrdom operations, as the practitioners prefer to call them, are not new, nor are they a uniquely Islamic phenomenon, or even a particularly religious one. Moreover, I will argue that in killing themselves in order to kill others they are behaving in a way that is entirely consistent with the behaviour of soldiers throughout the ages. Military historians have long ago convinced us that what drove young men over the trenches and out of the foxholes was fierce loyalty to their small band of brothers. This may appear surprising, as we tend to think of suicide attacks as individual actions, but in fact there has been no recorded case of a terrorist simply deciding to become a martyr, finding the explosives and making a plan. Instead, in every known martyrdom operation, the group plays an essential role in planning the terrorist attack and in training, sustaining and supervising the volunteer. The average martyrdom operation requires a supporting cast of about ten others. In societies the world over we reserve our highest honours for those who have given their lives for their country. Public squares everywhere are filled with monuments to those who have been victorious in battle. Suicide terrorists seek honours like these and their handlers make sure that they get them.

Historical Precedents

As with terrorism generally, the practice of suicide terrorism is not new. The most frequently cited precursors to contemporary suicide terrorists are the Jewish Sicarii in the first century and the Islamic Assassins in medieval times. Both showed complete disregard for their own lives, and the Assassins in particular had a culture of martyrdom reminiscent of the culture one finds today in the Gaza Strip. The difference between them and those we know today is that for these earlier groups who murdered by stabbing their victims it was not necessary to kill themselves in order to kill their victim. Psychologists like Ariel Merari insist that this difference is essential. Merari argues that a commitment to undertake an operation with a very small chance of success is psychologically quite different from undertaking an operation that requires one's own mortality, from which there is no possibility of escape.[5] By this thinking, the ancient groups would have more in common with contemporary terrorist operations like the Lod Airport attack carried out in 1972 by the Japanese terrorist group the JRA – more in common, indeed, with the willingness of soldiers to climb out of the trenches at the Somme, when there was very little chance, but still the theoretical possibility, of survival. Psychologists are no doubt correct in making this distinction, but for our purposes it is not relevant because the motivating factors were, I believe, the same. (In the case of the attack on the Lod Airport in Tel Aviv, in which three terrorists massacred twenty-five people and injured seventy-six in a gun and grenade attack, the terrorists did not expect to survive. Two were killed, including the husband of the group's leader, Fusako Shigenobu, but one, Kozo Okamoto, survived and was sentenced to life in prison.)

Less well known are the historical cases in which anti-colonial campaigns by Muslims in India, Indonesia and the Philippines deployed the suicide tactic against militarily superior European and American colonial powers.[6] There were significant similarities between these campaigns in Malabar, Atjeh and the Philippines. In each case the shaheed (martyr) or *juramentado* (one who took the oath) as the Spanish called them, would prepare by engaging in certain religious rites and prayers, then dress in white uncut cloth, the uniform of hajj or pilgrimage and of the burial shroud, before flinging himself on the enemy. More significantly, in each case a heroic literature emerged with songs and poems glorifying martyrdom. Individual sacrifices were vividly memorialized and the divine rewards for martyrdom widely promulgated. Volunteers were generally very young, though occasionally very old, and all were impoverished. At the time both Dutch psychiatrists and British administrators independently concluded that suicide terrorists were not suffering from any particular psychological disorder. It is taking years for contemporary observers to relearn the lesson. The cases are also instructive in that neither the British, the French nor the Spanish authorities succeeded in defeating the tactic, whether by improved police work or by military reprisal. These campaigns ended only when the broader political climate changed.

While religion provided the legitimizing ideology for these earlier groups which deployed suicide terrorists, this has not always been the case. For the Turkish PKK Marxism–Leninism was the ideology and for the Tamil Tigers and several Palestinian groups it was nationalism.

The PKK carried out fifteen suicide attacks in a three-year period from 1996 to 1999. Most of these attacks were directed against police and military targets rather then randomly on civilians, and most were carried out by women. The PKK's use of suicide operations speaks to the normalcy of the tactic. The tactic was adopted in a deliberate attempt to escalate pressure on the government in the wake of the capture of the movement's leader, Abdullah Ocalan. Ocalan asked his followers to use suicide operations in a futile bid to secure his release from prison. When the tactic failed he called it off. In this instance there was no broad-based effort to support the martyrs, nor did a culture of heroism emerge around them. Rather, a few long-serving members of the organization resorted briefly to the tactic in the face of the disastrous capture of their leader. While the tactic did not achieve its object in securing Ocalan's release, which was a fairly fanciful aspiration to begin with, the use of the tactic was also not very effective. Each attack resulted in the deaths on average of fewer than two victims, which by the standards of suicide terrorism is very anaemic indeed.

The Tamil Tigers have been altogether more serious and effective in their use of suicide terrorism. Alone of terrorist groups, the LTTE have assassinated two heads of state, Prime Minister Rajiv Gandhi of India in 1991 and President Ranasinghe Premadasa of Sri Lanka in 1993. The current President of Sri Lanka, Chandrika Kumaratunga, was severely injured in another LTTE terrorist attack and has survived at least four attempted assassinations by the same group. They have murdered government ministers, local politicians and moderate Tamil leaders. They have attacked naval ships, oil tankers, the airport in the country's capital Colombo and Sri Lanka's most sacred Buddhist relic, the Temple of the Tooth. They have also attacked Colombo's World Trade Centre and the Central Bank, as well as the Joint Operations Command, the nerve centre of the Sri Lankan security forces. Unlike other suicide terrorists they do not deliberately target civilians, but they kill large numbers of them regardless. In the attack on the Central Bank in 1996, for example, ninety people were killed.

Until the escalation in the use of suicide terrorism among the insurgents in Iraq, the LTTE had carried out more suicide attacks than any other terrorist group. Different academics count incidents differently, so while there may not be agreement on the precise figures there is agreement on the scale. By one such account, Robert Pape calculates that between 1987 and 2001 a total of 143 Tamil Tigers carried out seventy-six suicide attacks killing 901 people.[7] Most other reliable accounts put the figure much higher. *Jane's Intelligence Review* says there were 168 LTTE suicide attacks in this period, while Ricolfi says 191.[8] The LTTE themselves claim to have carried out 147 suicide operations between 1987 and 1999, but they claim responsibility publicly only for military attacks, not for their attacks on civilians, politicians or economic targets.[9] More important than the precise number of attacks is the fact that until recently the most consistent and deadly deployer of suicide attacks was not a religious group but a nationalist one.[10] The LTTE's ideology is the entirely secular one of national liberation. Their commitment is fuelled by hatred of the enemy and a desire to take revenge for their attacks, not by God.

The Tamil Tigers have an elite unit called the Black Tigers that specializes in suicide missions. The Birds of Freedom, a special unit of female terrorists, contribute Black Tigresses. The LTTE deploy the Black Tigers strategically both to compensate for their military weakness relative to government forces and to carry out difficult operations, like the assassination of senior politicians without having to worry about an escape plan. The commitment of members of the movement to the cause of national liberation is evident in the fact that each member carries a cyanide capsule that she or he will take in the event of arrest. This demonstration of commitment also has a practical side as members of the group know that taking the capsule will spare them brutal treatment by the security forces. Over 600 Tamil Tigers are reported to have died in this way.[11] Very few are successfully arrested and then only after their stomachs have been pumped to remove the cyanide. Taking one's life to avoid torture and probable death is a defensive act of prudence, though it shows the power of the commitment to the cause. Willingly volunteering for offensive martyrdom operations is something else.

Just as Islamists reject the notion of suicide and prefer martyrdom, so too do the Tamils. The Tamil word for suicide is *thatkolai*. The Tamil Tigers prefer to use *thatkodai,* meaning to give yourself.[12] As with other terrorist movements, the LTTE has more volunteers for the role of martyrdom than they have need for. Those who wish to become a Black Tiger or Tigress write a letter of application to the organization's leader Vellupillai Prabakharan. He then goes through each application and selects only those he considers most suitable based on his sense of their emotional stability, motivation, experience and family circumstances. His preference is for young people, usually aged between fourteen and sixteen, and for girls, who form about two-thirds of the suicide squads.[13] This preference appears to be more tactical than philosophical. As Palestinian groups have found, women generally find it easier to conceal the explosives in their clothes and tend to be searched less rigorously when stopped.

The LTTE, just like other groups, have developed a cult of hero worship around those who deliberately die for the cause. Prabakharan apparently has said: 'The death of a liberation hero is not a normal event of death. This death is an event of history, a lofty ideal, a miraculous event which bestows life. The truth is that a liberation tiger does not die . . . Indeed, what is called "flame of his aim" which has shone for his life will not be extinguished. The aim is like a fire, like a force in history, and it takes hold of others. The national soul of the people has been touched and awakened.'[14] Those selected for suicide receive special training and are considered the elite corps. Prior to going out on an operation they are said to have a final meal with Prabakharan himself and to have their picture taken with him.[15] He has said of them: 'The Black Tigers are different and are also unique human beings. They possess an iron will, yet their hearts are so very soft. They have deep human characteristics of perceiving the advancement of the interest of the people through their annihilation.'[16]

The Tamil Tigers ensure that their martyrs are accorded renown among the Tamil community. The names of deceased Black Tigers are publicized along with their rank so that they can be honoured in Tamil newspapers and websites. Their garlanded photos adorn the walls of the Tigers' training camps. When they go on their mission many carry identity cards to ensure that their identity will be known. Sometimes they film their attacks. CDs with songs of tribute to the martyrs and videos of their attack on the airport can be bought in shops in Tamil-controlled areas. They have their very own 'heroes' day', July 5, which is the anniversary of the first LTTE suicide attack in 1987. This day of remembrance is separate from the movement's 'heroes' day' on November 27 each year. This pattern is exactly the same as the practice in Lebanon where 'Martyrs' Day' is celebrated each year on November 11 in com- memoration of Hezbollah's first suicide bomber who blew himself up at an Israeli military post on that date in 1982.

Local Tamil districts construct memorials to Black Tigers who came from their area. These memorials consist of a photograph that is garlanded with flowers on Black Tigers Day and a flame of sacrifice lit in front of each one. Those who have died for the cause are given the title *mahaveera*, meaning brave one, and their mother is called *veeravati* or brave mother.

The memory of those who have given their lives for the cause is kept alive in their communities. In Kantharuban Arivuchcholai orphanage in Tamil-controlled territory there is a shrine. It con- tains a picture of Kantharuban, who blew himself up in 1991, and a picture of the first and most famous of the Tamil Tigers' suicides, Captain Miller, who drove a truck full of explosives into an army camp and killed forty soldiers. There is also a photograph of twelve other Tigers who swallowed cyanide capsules after being captured by Indian troops in 1987. The children in the orphanage learn that Kantharuban, an orphan himself, requested at his meal with Prabakharan on the eve of his operation that a home be built for children like him.[17]

Along with the appeal of attaining renown, the desire for revenge is everywhere. Twenty-two-year-old Mahendran, whose three brothers were killed fighting for the Tigers, explained why he too was thinking of joining: 'The harassment that I and my parents have suffered at the hands of the army makes me want to take revenge.

It is a question of Tamil pride, especially after so much sacrifice.'[18] Another young man destined to be a suicide terrorist explained that he thought the action was necessary to get a reaction, to get a homeland: 'This is the most supreme sacrifice I can make. The only way we can get our *eelam* [homeland] is through arms. This is the only way anybody will listen to us.'[19]

Those who volunteer to be suicide terrorists in Sri Lanka do not do so with visions of virgins in paradise on their minds, nor with guarantees that Allah will look after those they have left behind. They volunteer to avenge the atrocities committed against their communities, to further the cause of national liberation and to bring glory to themselves. They do so because they have been personally affected by the conflict in which they live, because their community supports their action and because their movement's ideology legitimizes it. Religion has nothing to do with it. A man whose three sons died fighting for the Tamil Tigers, one of whom was a Black Tiger who blew himself up, described learning of his third son's death: 'It was heartbreaking but I also knew that they had done it for a cause, for the country, for the people. I bore the sadness, with the thought that they were doing a very desirable thing.'[20]

The PKK and the LTTE are not the only secular groups to have deployed suicide terrorists. Many of the martyrdom operations in the Middle East have been carried out by secular rather than religious groups. The current wave of suicide terrorist attacks began in December 1981 and the target, ironically in light of how the tactic has since developed, was the Iraqi government of Saddam Hussein. This attack took place in the context of the Iran–Iraq war. This is the war that witnessed the phenomenon known as human-wave attacks, in which thousands of very young Iranians, many completely unarmed, stormed Iraqi positions or deployed their bodies to de-mine vast tracts of land in massive suicidal assaults.[21] Not much is known about this Iranian wartime tactic, but its influence on the godfathers of modern suicide terrorism, the Lebanese Hezbollah, is unmistakable.

In the first reported attack a man drove a car laden with explosives into the Iraqi embassy in Beirut killing himself and sixty-one others and injuring many more. The Iraqi government blamed Iranian and Syrian intelligence officials. In this period there were estimated to be over a thousand Iranian revolutionary guards in Lebanon.[22] They sought to influence the outcome of the ongoing civil war by bankrolling and training the groups that were to emerge as Hezbollah. The systematic use of the tactic of suicide bombing began a little over a year later.

The year 1983 witnessed the full-scale emergence on the modern scene of suicide terrorism. On April 18, 1983 a truck containing a large amount of explosives was driven into the American embassy in Beirut and killed eighty people. On October 23 both the US Marine barracks and the headquarters of the French paratroopers were hit by car bombs driven by suicide terrorists: 241 people (220 Marines and twenty-one other US servicemen) were killed in one blast and 58 French paratroopers and two civilians in the other. A couple of weeks later, on November 4, a driver bent on suicide drove a car full of explosives into the Israeli government building in Tyre, southern Lebanon, killing eighty-eight people, almost exactly a year after a similar attack in the same place had killed ninety people, including fifteen civilians. The following month, the American embassy in Kuwait was hit by yet another suicide attack.

These early attacks were carried out by Islamist militants, but, as with every successful military tactic, its adoption soon spread. By 1986 several secular Lebanese groups like the Socialist National Party, the Communist Party, the Lebanese Ba'ath Party and the Syrian Ba'ath Party were all carrying out suicide attacks. These secular groups were backed by the Syrian government, whose agents recruited, trained and equipped the operatives.[23] Like the Tamil Tigers and the PKK their targets were primarily political and military, but they showed wanton disregard for civilian casualties.

Aiming specifically at civilians, however, is not the preserve of religious groups. Secular Palestinian groups also employed suicide attacks and they deliberately targeted Israeli civilians on the spurious grounds that there are no civilians in Israel. Two secular Palestinian groups have carried out suicide attacks, the Al-Aqsa Martyrs Brigades and the Popular Front for the Liberation of

Palestine (PFLP), though the two Islamist groups Hamas and Palestinian Islamic Jihad (PIJ) have carried out significantly more.

The inspiration for the idea of suicide terrorism appears to have come from Iran to Lebanon, but from Lebanon it spread a long way. A number of Tamil insurgents received training in Lebanon in the early and mid-1980s and brought the tactic back to Sri Lanka. Moreover the Israeli decision to deport 415 Palestinian militants to Lebanon in 1992 had disastrous unintended consequences, as the Palestinians learned the value of the tactic from Hezbollah. In this way the skill-set was transferred from Shiite (Iran and Hezbollah) to Sunni (Hamas and later al-Qaeda) Muslims, as well as to secular Palestinian and Tamil groups. The modern phenomenon of suicide terrorism, therefore, can be traced to the Lebanese civil war of 1973–86.[24] A tradition of martyrdom is helpful in securing the commitment of recruits, as was the case for Shiite Muslims in Hezbollah and for their Iranian backers, but it is by no means necessary, as demonstrated by the Sunni and secular examples.

Variations on Suicide Terrorism

There have been a number of variations on suicide terrorism. The human-wave attacks deployed by the Iranians in the Iran–Iraq war are one example. The Kamikaze attacks launched by Japan in the later stages of the Second World War are better known. Peter Hill has demonstrated that these attacks were not as effective as was claimed by the Japanese, but they were more effective than conventional attacks. Moreover, their most pronounced effect was on the morale of their potential victims. The fear they inspired was such that American commanders stopped warning their crews when mass attacks were coming.[25]

There was a marked diminution in the enthusiasm of the Kamikaze recruits as the war progressed and younger and more educated volunteers were solicited. The crucial motivational factors appear to have been less a commitment to an almost mythical emperor and more a commitment to family, country and colleagues. One wrote: 'I didn't see myself throwing my life away for him [the emperor] nor for the government either, nor for the nation. I saw myself dying to defend my parents, my brothers and sisters.' He went on to explain his commitment to his colleagues: 'I couldn't bear the idea of sacrificing someone else by quitting. I knew that if I did, I'd regret it for the rest of my life, even if I never knew his name. I hated the thought that I'd fail and they'd say "Those reservists are no good." I couldn't do that to the others.'[26]

Recent research on the Kamikazes reveals a number of other similarities to contemporary suicide terrorists that have not been widely acknowledged. Pilots were given an escort on their missions just as Palestinian handlers often accompany contemporary shaheeds on their missions into Israel. The escort helped guide and protect the Kamikaze and later would report on the mission, but they were undoubtedly also used as an element of control to make it more difficult for the pilot to change his mind. Moreover, the writings of those who participated suggest that they were not one uniform group of like-minded individuals, even though they each volunteered for this highly unusual suicide mission. Rather, as with any group of significant size, they reflect a variety of motivations.

Another significant similarity between the Kamikaze and contemporary suicide terrorists is the degree of glory that came with the role. Like other groups today they were rewarded with renown, with glory for themselves and their families. Families of Kamikaze were given the title *homare no ie*, meaning household of honour. They received more tangible benefits too – increased pension rights, better rations and places of honour at official ceremonies. The pilots were eulogized in the press and public statements and were referred to as god-heroes. In this they were elevated even higher than other soldiers killed in battle who already became national gods.[27]

Like contemporary shaheeds, the Kamikazes were deployed by the weaker side in the conflict. Like their contemporary counterparts they inflicted more damage on the enemy than conventional attacks, and, again like contemporary suicide terrorists, the fear they inspired outweighed the damage they inflicted, considerable as it was. They appear to have been motivated by a sense of commitment to their communities and their colleagues, as well as by a desire for glory. The two significant differences are that the Kamikazes' targets were exclusively military and their action was ordered by the military hierarchy, acting on behalf of the government, during a time of inter-state war. These two differences make their actions both easier to understand on a personal level and easier to exculpate on a moral one. They were motivated by desire for renown and reaction but not revenge and they were sustained by their commitment to their colleagues, the support of their community and the ideology of Japanese nationalism.

Another variation on the theme of suicide terrorism is the action of the imprisoned members of the IRA who starved themselves to death in an attempt to secure political-prisoner status. This action is also easier to understand in moral terms in that they did not kill anyone else in killing themselves, but given the protracted and painful manner of their death it is perhaps even harder to understand in personal terms. Just as the Shiite tradition of martyrdom facilitated the emergence of suicides in the Iran–Iraq war and their transfusion to the Lebanese Shiites in Hezbollah, the tradition of punishing oneself to shame one's enemy also has a long tradition in Celtic culture. It was not uncommon under the ancient Gaelic legal system known as Brehon Law for a man who was owed something by his neighbour to sit outside the other's house and refuse to eat until the embarrassed neighbour righted the wrong. While this tradition lay in the cultural background, it was probably not foremost in the minds of those who decided to go on hunger strike in the Maze prison in Belfast in 1981. A historical example that was, however, foremost in their minds was that of Terence Mac Sweeney, the lord mayor of Cork, who had died on hunger strike in Brixton prison in 1920 during Ireland's war of independence against Britain.

With his death, Mac Sweeney joined the pantheon of Irish martyrs alongside the fifteen men executed for their role in the 1916 Easter Rising and Thomas Ashe, who died in 1917 after being force-fed while on hunger strike to demand political-prisoner status. Mac Sweeney's famous words, spoken during his inauguration as lord mayor, were to become the mantra of the movement:

'It is not those who inflict the most but those who suffer the most who will conquer.'

This is not the place to recount the story of the republican hunger-strikers.[28] The crucial distinction between these terrorists who committed suicide and suicide terrorists is that the former did not kill others while killing themselves. Theirs was a powerful claim to moral superiority over their enemy. In the short term the effort failed, in that the government of Prime Minister Margaret Thatcher allowed the first ten hunger-strikers to die and the families of the remaining prisoners authorized the authorities to feed them. Over the longer term, however, the hunger strike was an enormous success.

Given the depth of the suffering that the republican prisoners were prepared to endure for the sake of a principle, that they be treated as political prisoners, the government could no longer reasonably claim that they were wanton criminals. Sympathy for the hunger-strikers and fury at the intransigence of the government proved to be a recruitment bonanza for the IRA at home, a fund-raising bonanza abroad, and a public-relations bonanza everywhere. The 1981 hunger strike had been undertaken by the prisoners without official sanction from the IRA, but the movement soon capitalized on the event. The leaders took advantage of the popular sympathy for Bobby Sands, the first of the prisoners to go on strike. (The prisoners decided to start their strikes at staggered intervals in order to space out their deaths and thereby prolong the pressure on the government.) The IRA's political wing, Sinn Fein, ran Bobby Sands in a by-election for a seat at Westminster and he won handsomely. When he died a month later it was as an elected member of the British parliament. This political success also had the long-term and quite unanticipated consequence of demonstrating to the membership of the IRA the advantages of political over military action and proved a spur to the pragmatists within the movement who sought to develop a political strategy.

The action of the hunger-strikers cannot be explained in religious terms. There was no religious component to their behaviour, though like almost all Irish republicans they were all Catholics. The Catholic church unequivocally forbids suicide, and the church hierarchy was fairly unsympathetic, though priests drawn from the local community were more sympathetic to the prisoners and their families. Nor can they be said to have been trying to exact revenge. On the contrary, their moral claim was based on their willingness to suffer. They did expect to elicit a reaction, though it took some time for them to realize that the government was not going to give in. The reaction they received in the streets of Northern Ireland was undoubtedly a great consolation to them and helped sustain the later strikers. These men were also sustained by loyalty to their colleagues. Once Sands had died, others felt compelled to go all the way too: to fail to do so would be to let down their colleagues. They did, of course, achieve renown. To this day Bobby Sands and his nine fellow hunger-strikers, who all died after him, are celebrated as heroic republican martyrs. Their portraits are painted on gable ends, songs recount their stories, and their deaths are annually commemorated.

Unlike contemporary suicide terrorists they were motivated by a desire not for revenge but for reaction and renown. They were sustained in their protracted self-inflicted torture by their commitment to the colleagues who had died before them and the support they received from their communities and the ideology of Irish nationalism.

The growing popularity of suicide terrorism has led to an increase in efforts to explain the phenomenon. Many of the arguments I made earlier about terrorism generally can also be applied to suicide terrorism. The most popular are that suicide terrorists are either crazy religious fanatics or desperate people responding to poverty and privation. Neither of these arguments that emanate from opposite ends of the ideological spectrum is convincing. I have already demonstrated that a great many suicide terrorists have not been religious at all, much less religious fanatics.

The claim that they are crazy, which is popularly made in the press and by politicians, is not consistent with any of the research on the subject. Moreover, as I have pointed out, suicide terrorists do not act alone; they are selected, trained, supervised and encouraged by a group. Moreover, those who do the selecting from among the many volunteers competing for the honour consistently

WHY DO TERRORISTS KILL THEMSELVES?

claim that they do their best to ensure that those who are chosen are psychologically sound. Hamas made a point of telling the Palestinian community in Gaza, which produced more volunteers than the organization was prepared to deploy, that they would only take 'normal' people. They were not interested in those who might be depressed or suicidal or crazy.[29] A PIJ representative spoke in similar terms: 'We do not take depressed people. If there were a one-in-a-thousand chance that a person was suicidal, we would not allow him to martyr himself. In order to be a martyr bomber you have to want to live.'[30] Fayez Jaber, speaking for the Al-Aqsa Martyrs Brigade, also insists that his organization accepts only fully mature, psychologically sound volunteers and not those who are trying to avoid personal or family problems.[31]

Nasra Hassan interviewed the families and trainers of a large number of suicide bombers in the Gaza Strip, as well as a number of volunteers who for one reason or another had not been able to carry out their task. She wrote of them: 'None of the suicide bombers – they ranged in age from eighteen to thirty-eight – conformed to the typical profile of the suicidal personality. None of them were uneducated, desperately poor, simple minded, or depressed. Many were middle class and, unless they were fugitives, held paying jobs. More than half of them were refugees from what is now Israel. Two were the sons of millionaires. They all seemed to be entirely normal members of their families.'[32] The simple, uncomfortable truth is that suicide terrorists are not crazy in any meaningful sense of the word.

The notion that poverty drives people to suicide terrorism is also exposed by the demographics of those who volunteer for the role, from the Egyptian Mohammad Atta with his PhD in urban planning to Briton Shehzad Tanweer, son of a prosperous small businessman. It is nevertheless the case that successful professionals have not volunteered to be suicide terrorists, and a great many of those who have done so came from economically deprived areas like the Gaza Strip. The act of martyrdom, however, is not an act of desperation, as can be seen in the evident exuberance of the young people in the Gaza Strip who flock to Hamas headquarters to volunteer. Explanations, therefore, must lie elsewhere. I believe that suicide terrorism, like terrorism generally, requires a lethal cocktail of a disaffected individual, a supportive community and a legitimizing ideology, and that in taking their own lives in this brutal way they are seeking revenge, renown and reaction.

The growth in popularity of the tactic has exceeded social scientists' capacity to keep up. All the carefully constructed data sets calculating the lethality of attacks or percentage of attacks carried out by different groups have been confounded by the extraordinary escalation in suicide attacks in Iraq since the American invasion of the country. There have been more suicide attacks in Iraq alone in the years since the fall of Saddam Hussein in April 2003 than in the rest of the world since the tactic was first adopted in 1981. In May and June 2005, there were more suicide attacks in Iraq than have been recorded by the Israelis since the tactic was first used in their country in 1993.[33]

We know very little about those who are carrying out these attacks in Iraq.[34] Many are local Iraqis, others are foreign, especially Saudi, Syrian and Algerian mujahideen. They are members of a number of different groups with none enjoying a monopoly. Many of the attacks have been carried out by al-Qaeda in Iraq, which is led by Abu Mus'ab al-Zarqawi and is part of the al-Qaeda consortium. Among other groups that have deployed suicide attackers are Ansar al-Islam and Ansar al-Sunna. Many of these groups are made up of Iraqis, while others consist largely of foreign fighters recruited to join battle against the US. There can be little doubt that the objective of these attacks is to expel the US from Iraq. In volunteering, the young men are seeking to avenge the occupation of Iraq and the American war on terror, which they perceive as a war on Islam. They are also seeking a reaction. They are clearly hoping that they can raise the cost of occupation to the point that the US government, either acting alone or under pressure from the American public, will decide to withdraw. It is unlikely that they expect to get renown. There are simply so many recruits and so many attacks that it is difficult to see how they are being managed.

Some light was shed on the situation by an interview that reporter Aparisim Ghosh managed to arrange with 'Marwan', a young Iraqi martyr-in-waiting. Like his colleagues in Gaza he described the day he learned that he had finally been put on the list of suicide candidates as 'the happiest day in my life'. He is hoping that with the rate of attacks he will not have to wait long. 'I can't wait. I am ready to die now,' he says. Marwan, who came from a successful middle-class family, explained that he had expected the US to bring down Saddam Hussein and then leave, but the US remained as an army of occupation. He described himself as radicalized by an incident in April 2003 in which US soldiers fired at a crowd of demonstrators at a school, killing twelve and wounding many others. He witnessed the incident and decided to join the fight against the US in earnest.[35]

Marwan claims to be fighting first for Islam, second to become a martyr and win acceptance into heaven, and third for his country. He concedes that he has given little thought to the nature of the Islamic state he would like to see established, declaring: 'The first step is to remove the Americans from Iraq. After we have achieved that, we can work out the other details.'[36]

As in other places, many of these volunteers make a videotaped testimony prior to their operation, and their names are glowingly recorded on jihadist websites, both to encourage others and to lionize the volunteers. Unlike in other cases, however, Iraqi insurgents are not guaranteed the same kind of glory that their Palestinian and Tamil counterparts get. This is largely due to the nature of the occupation and insurgency. There are no family celebrations on the death of a martyr, for example, for fear of reprisals against the family. But Marwan claims not to be worried about this. He says: 'It doesn't matter whether people know what I did. The only person who matters is Allah – and the only question he will ask me is "How many infidels did you kill?"'[37]

The godfathers of suicide terrorism in Iraq do manage to ensure group support for the volunteers, providing them with a mentor to support them through the final weeks and providing a ritual set of preparations to be followed prior to the operation. Nevertheless they appear to have sought to persuade their volunteers to do without the degree of renown that other martyrs are assured of, or rather to settle for renown in the afterlife instead of renown on the ground. The appeal of earthly glory, however, is not entirely absent, even here. Marwan said that he hoped that he would be chosen for a high-profile attack, the kind that will be posted on headlines everywhere, and that al-Zarqawi himself will direct it personally.

Another variation on the profile of suicide terrorists that has come to light in recent years is the significant number of women martyrs. The Kurdish and Tamil terrorist groups have been using women as suicide terrorists for many years, but this has gone largely unnoticed in the west. Generally speaking, women are under-represented in terrorist groups, but they are over-represented among PKK and LTTE suicide terrorists. In recent years too women have been very much in evidence among Chechen suicide terrorists, and their attacks have been deliberately targeted at civilians, as when two young Chechen women strapped themselves with explosives and blew themselves up at a crowded outdoor rock concert in Moscow in July 2003. It was only when Palestinian groups started to deploy women, however, that people in the west began to pay attention – and were horrified.

Islamic fundamentalists have a view of women as property to be protected that would appear to be incompatible with their playing the role of soldiers, much less martyrs. Al-Qaeda, for example, have not yet deployed a woman on a suicide mission, although in late 2005 al-Qaeda-affiliated organizations appeared to be willing to do so. The experience of other Islamist groups suggests that expediency can trump dogma on this issue. Therefore, if al-Qaeda find it to be in their interest to deploy women as suicide terrorists, they are likely to adjust their religious rulings on the subject accordingly. The use of women against Israel appears to be a consequence of the rivalry between religious and secular groups battling for the role of legitimate representative of the Palestinian people. The first women martyrs acted under the rubric of the secular Al-Aqsa Martyrs Brigade, the suicide-terrorist offshoot of Yasser Arafat's Fatah movement.

Women are not recent converts to the cause of Palestinian terrorism, as the redoubtable Leila Khaled, leader of many terrorist exploits in the 1970s, can attest. But on January 27, 2002 Wafa Idris, a twenty-six-year-old Red Crescent volunteer, became the forty-seventh Palestinian suicide bomber and the first woman to act in the name of the Palestinians. Just as in 1985, when Syrian President Hafez al-Assad decided to try to secularize suicide bombing in Lebanon and thereby win support away from the religious extremists, so too Yasser Arafat at the outbreak of the second intifada in September 2000 decided that he could not leave all the martyrdom operations to the Islamist members of Hamas and PIJ. Over a year later the ever-manipulative president of the Palestinian Authority decided to try another twist and exploit one of the advantages of the secular groups, their female supporters. In January 2002 Arafat addressed a crowd of over a thousand Palestinian women. He pronounced them to be the equal of men and declared: 'You are my army of roses that will crush Israeli tanks.' In this speech he coined the feminine form of the word 'shaheed', chanting 'Shahida, shahida until Jerusalem.'[38]

That afternoon Wafa Idris blew herself up in a Jerusalem shopping mall, killing an eighty-one-year-old Israeli man and injuring more than 130 people. Initially reluctant to admit their connection to her, once it was clear that the reaction on the street was overwhelmingly positive Fatah claimed her publicly as one of their own and instructed her family to rejoice in her death. A few weeks later the Al-Aqsa Martyrs Brigade officially opened a woman's unit, the Shawaq al-Aqsa, in Idris's honour.

The secular groups were not the only ones to respond to popular sentiment. Initially Sheikh Ahmed Yassin, the spiritual leader of Hamas, declared that any man who recruits a woman to be a martyr is breaking Islamic law: 'He is taking the girl or woman without the permission of her father, brother, or husband and therefore the family of the girl confronts an even greater problem since the man has the biggest power over her choosing the day that she will give her life back to Allah.'[39] Even Hamas soon changed its tune. Yassin later said that, as there were plenty of men 'demanding to participate', they didn't need women. He wrote in *Al-Sharq al-Awsat*, the London-based newspaper, that women would require male escorts and that it was preferable to use men.[40] Later still he completely reversed his earlier position and insisted that 'The Prophet always emphasized the woman's right to wage jihad.'[41]

Dr al-Rantisi, the Hamas spokesman until he was assassinated by the Israelis, explained to writer Barbara Victor that the fatwa had been adjusted and that women are welcome as shahidas, but they must first produce one son and one daughter. 'After she fulfils her demographic role then she can participate in armed struggle.'[42] The movement was not long in finding a candidate. On January 14, 2004 Fox News announced: 'Homicide Bomber-Mom Kills Four at Gaza Border'. A twenty-two-year-old mother of a three-year-old boy and one-year-old girl blew herself up at the main border crossing. Hamas and Al-Aqsa Martyrs Brigade issued a joint claim of responsibility. Hamas conceded that this was a first for them, but explained the move in purely tactical terms, as prompted by Israeli security impediments to their male bombers. Before her death Reem al-Reyashi made the now familiar videotape. Smiling into the camera she explained that she had dreamed since she was thirteen of becoming a martyr and dying for her people. She added, inexplicably: 'God gave me two children and I loved them so much. Only God knew how much I loved them.'[43]

Reem was not the first mother to volunteer to be a suicide bomber. Exactly a year earlier forty-year-old Suhad Gadallah was prevented from blowing herself up only by the swift action of a passing young Israeli. She left at home a handicapped husband and four children between the ages of five and fifteen. She explained her action in the familiar language of revenge: 'My eldest son, Abdullah, was twenty when he was shot and killed by the soldiers. My child is dead. I had no reason to live. I only wanted to avenge his death. I knew Allah would care for my other children and my husband.'[44]

Much has been made in the west of the motivating power of the promise of seventy-two virgins awaiting the martyr in paradise. This prospect undoubtedly holds less appeal for women. Several women who have been incarcerated by Israel for attempting to become martyrs told the writer Manuela Dviri that a woman martyr 'will be the chief of the seventy-two virgins, the fairest of the fair'.[45] Sheikh Yassin, having decided that he would permit female martyrs, interpreted the Koran as saying that women martyrs become 'even more beautiful than the seventy-two virgins'. They are not, however, guaranteed their own seventy-two virgins: 'If they are not married they are guaranteed a pure husband in paradise.' While not prepared to grant women equality on that front, Yassin does so on another. Like their male counterparts, 'They are entitled to bring seventy of their relatives to join them there without suffering the anguish of the grave.'[46]

Interviews with the family and friends of the first female Palestinian suicide bombers suggested that the motives of these women might be somewhat different from those of their male counterparts. Behind the usual rhetoric, these female trailblazers were also fighting powerful personal demons. Wafa Idris had been divorced by her husband because of her failure to produce a child, and she had been forced to return to her fatherless family who could ill afford to support her. Her one child was stillborn, bringing shame on herself and her family. A month later Darine Abu Aisha followed in her footsteps. This twenty-year-old university student was profoundly depressed and under intense pressure from her family to marry. She had been forced by Israeli guards to kiss a male cousin in public at a border crossing, which had deeply shamed her. The cousin then offered to marry her, but she wanted a professional career, not marriage.

Ayat al-Akhras's action appears to have been a mix of a desire to take revenge against the Israeli occupation and to save her family from the disgrace and the danger of deriving their livelihood from her father's work for an Israeli construction company. Hiba Daraghmeh had been raped at the age of fourteen. And so the litany continued. Among those who tried and failed to blow themselves up, familiar stories of being raped or bearing illegitimate children are reported.[47] An Israeli guard in the prison which houses jailed would-be female martyrs describes the inmates and their motivations:

There are 30 of them, between 17 and 30 years old, some of them are married and others aren't, some of them have children. Their stories come out of the *Thousand and One Nights*. Some of them did it to make amends for a relative who was a collaborator, others to escape becoming victims of honor killings, and for the psychologically frail or depressed it was a good way to commit suicide and at the same time become heroines.[48]

If this is the case it suggests that the movement's insistence on taking only psychologically sound volunteers does not extend to women.

With the increase in numbers of female martyrs, however, the profile appears to have been normalized. Since those first few attempts, female suicide bombers seem to reflect a cross-section of Palestinian society from the lawyer to the housewife. With Andalib Suleiman, the normalization seems complete. She appears to have been motivated not by a desire to exorcize any personal demons but rather by a desire to become a superstar. She was fascinated by the celebrity of martyrs and replaced the pop-star posters on her bedroom walls with those of martyrs. Her trainer explained that she wanted to be a shahida to avenge the killings of women and children by the Israelis, to prove that women were as brave as men and that her family were resolute fighters. 'She also wanted the assurance that after she died she would be famous all over the Arab world.'[49] Female suicide terrorists in the Palestinian territories, therefore, clearly share their male counterparts' desire for revenge and renown. They appear, however, to stress nationalism more and religion less than the men. This difference is probably attributable to the fact that nationalism is more compatible with gender equality than religion, and many of the women bombers wish to make a claim for their sex as well as for their communities. Even in death, however, they do not quite attain equality. The families of male suicide bombers receive a lifetime stipend of $400 per month from the sponsoring organization, while families of shahidas receive $200 per month.[50]

Organizations and Individuals

From the point of view of terrorist organizations or of the men who lead them there is nothing surprising about suicide terrorism. It is a very effective tactic for the weaker side in a conflict. The costs are low and the payoffs are high. Sheikh Yassin was quoted by the Beirut newspaper, the *Daily Star*, making a point often heard among Palestinians: 'Once we have warplanes and missiles, then we can think of changing our means of legitimate self-defence. But right how, we can only tackle the fire with our bare hands and sacrifice ourselves.'[51] Prabakharan, the leader of the Tamil Tigers, spells out another advantage of the tactic: 'With perseverance and sacrifice, Tamil Eelam can be achieved in a hundred years. But if we conduct Black Tiger operations, we can shorten the suffering of the people and achieve Tamil Eelam in a shorter period of time.'[52] For the weaker side in a conflict, suicide terrorism is adopted as a means of offsetting the imbalance with a more powerful enemy.

The trick for the organization is to ensure a steady stream of volunteers. In at least one case, a terrorist group decided to launch a suicide attack but was unable to find any volunteers. Inspired by the success of the 9/11 attacks, the leadership of the FARC (Fuerzas Armadas Revolucionarias de Colombia) tried to recruit a volunteer to fly an aircraft into the Presidential Palace during a ceremony installing the newly appointed president, Ãlvaro Uribe. In spite of offering two million dollars in compensation to the family of the pilot, they were unable to find one. The organization had to be content with setting off several bombs outside the palace.[53]

When leaders of terrorist groups speak of suicide attacks they are hard-nosed and tactical. When volunteers speak of suicide attacks they are emotional and excited. Bin Laden's right-hand man, Dr Ayman al-Zawahiri, speaks in a cost-benefit fashion of the advantages of inflicting the maximum number of casualties with the minimum number of losses among the mujahideen.[54] Sayyed Nasrallah, the secretary general of Hezbollah, was even more explicit:

> In Lebanon, in order to carry out an operation with an outcome of 8 or 9 dead soldiers, it would need training, equipping, observations, frontier groups, rockets, explosives . . . After all these preparations, the outcome would only be 3 or 4 deaths due to the strong fortifications of the enemy. On the other hand, one single [martyr] without any training or experience, driving a bus without any military back-ups, was able to kill 8 or 9, wound 21, and scare the entire 'Israeli' entity.[55]

A Palestinian security official explained to Nasra Hassan that, apart from a willing candidate, all that is needed are items like nails, gunpowder, a battery, a light switch and a short cable, mercury, acetone and the cost of tailoring a belt wide enough to hold the explosives. 'The most expensive item is transportation to a distant Israeli town. The total cost of a typical operation is about $150.'[56] The most expensive suicide operation in history was the 9/11 attacks, and they cost an estimated $500,000 while inflicting tens of billions of dollars in damage, quite aside from the enormous human cost. In marked contrast, those planning to volunteer, do not speak in terms of costs and calculus at all but rather of the glory of their death for the cause. One would-be Palestinian martyr who survived his operation said of the preparations: 'Those were the happiest days of my life.' He went on: 'We told each other that if the Israelis only knew how joyful we were they would whip us to death.'[57]

It has not gone unnoticed among the families of some martyrs that the leaders of the organizations have not offered their own children as shaheeds. When this suggestion was made to him Sheikh Yassin responded cleverly but implausibly: 'We do not choose martyrs to die. Allah chooses them.'[58] This is not to suggest that the leaders of these movements do not believe their own rhetoric. I expect they do. It does suggest, however, that they are altogether more pragmatic about martyrdom operations than are the many young people who volunteer for them. As one Hamas leader explained: 'Our biggest problem is the hordes of young men who beat on our doors clamouring to be sent. It is difficult to select only a few. Those whom we turn away return again and again, pestering us, pleading to be accepted.'[59] A senior al-Qassam leader agreed: 'The selection process is complicated by the fact that so many wish to embark on this journey of honour. When one is selected, countless others are disappointed.'[60]

The organizations that recruit them understand the motivations of their followers. Once they have selected a volunteer, the organization then engages in a well-honed training process that is geared to these motivations and that involves indoctrination in the ideology of the group, an emphasis on group solidarity and on commitment to the community, and a pledge as insurance against defection. During the period of indoctrination the volunteers, who are already converts to the cause to begin with, are subjected to a constant barrage of information and ideology designed to strengthen their commitment. The organization appeals to the desire for revenge by telling stories and showing movies of atrocities against Muslims or Israeli atrocities against Palestinians. The operation is explained in terms of the group's ideology – religious fundamentalism in the case of Islamist groups or nationalism in the case of secular groups. (Most Palestinian groups include both, with greater or lesser emphasis depending on the nature of the organization.) The action is legitimized and glorified in terms of the movement's ideology and the history of the community from which the volunteer comes. The organization appeals to the desire for renown by glorifying the actions of earlier martyrs and treating them in heroic terms. It is at this point too that an effort is made to strengthen the commitment of the volunteer still further by outlining the rewards that will come to him and his family.

The trainers also understand the power of group solidarity and play on this to their advantage. In Hamas and PIJ the preparation for suicide attacks is often done in cells, consisting of three to five volunteers. These cells are characterized as 'martyrdom cells' to differentiate them from the regular military cells.[61] In their account of the road to Martyrs Square, Oliver and Steinberg provide riveting accounts of tight social networks and intense small-group loyalty. At one point they write: 'What the rank and file [of Hamas] seemed to live and die for, in the end, was neither hospitals nor politics nor ideology nor religion nor the Apocalypse, but rather an ecstatic camaraderie in the face of death on the path to Allah.'[62] The powerful sway of group solidarity is further evidenced by the clustering of the places of origin of so many suicide bombers. Luca Ricolfi has observed that a significant majority of suicide bombers come from a small number of refugee camps around the West Bank towns of Hebron, Nablus and Jenin. He points out that on May 17–18, 2003 three students from Hebron Polytechnic University each carried out a martyrdom operation. Even more striking is the case of the 'Jihad Mosque', a soccer team from Hebron that provided eight volunteers out of its eleven-man team. Six of the eight were next-door neighbours and members of the same extended family.[63]

Some volunteers opt to make group videos on the eve of their operation, and these films clearly convey the depth of the cama-raderie among them. Eve-of-operation videos have become part of the ritual of suicide attacks. Young people pose before the camera against a range of backgrounds and explain what they are about to do and why. In many cases these videos are carefully scripted, with the volunteer reading a statement written by their sponsoring terrorist group. In others, however, they are more informal. In a video called 'The Giants', three soon-to-be martyrs take turns on centre-stage before coming together to make a col-lective vow to complete their operation. They had been told that 'In Islam it's a horrible thing to run away' and that there is a verse in the Koran that says that anyone who runs away in the middle of a battle goes straight to hell.[64] Through these videos the vol-unteers explicitly, or more often implicitly, pledge publicly that they will go through with their mission. The leaders of the ter-rorist organizations know that they have willing volunteers for martyrdom, but they take steps to ensure that they do not change their minds. Ariel Merari has argued convincingly that this is the main purpose of these videos. In the case of Hamas and PIJ, the candidate is formally referred to as 'the living martyr', *al-shahid al-hai*, from that point on.[65] It would be deeply shameful to oneself and one's family to change one's mind having gone this far. The videos serve other purposes too. They act as useful propaganda tools and help in the glorification of the martyr that in turn helps to attract new volunteers.

What appears to be a profoundly individual action, blowing oneself up in an effort to kill others, is actually a very social one. Individuals often volunteer with their friends and, even when they do not, they are drawn from a community which is supportive of their action. Their determination is fired by a sense of commitment to their group, and they expect to be rewarded with renown in their community. Public opinion polls suggest that support for suicide attacks among the Palestinian population has fluctuated and ranged from lows around 20 per cent in the early 1990s to highs around 75 per cent a decade later. A poll in March 2005 suggested that Palestinian support for bomb attacks inside Israel had dropped from 77 per cent in September 2004 to 29 per cent in March 2005, though only 40 per cent believe the perpetrators should be punished.[66] Other polls in May 2005 see the Palestinian population as evenly divided on the subject.[67] Individual attacks like the suicide bombing of Maxim's restaurant in Haifa, which killed twenty-one Israelis including four children and injured sixty others, have attracted the support of 75 per cent of Palestinians.[68] Among the tight social and family networks that produce volunteers the percentages are possibly even higher.

In attempting to ascertain what it is that drives an individual to volunteer to be a martyr in the first place the evidence is very strong that, as with terrorism generally, the key motivators are revenge, renown and reaction. From Chechens to Tamils to Palestinians to Saudis, among both women and men, young and old, the words of volunteers for suicide are replete with the language of revenge. A senior member of al-Qassam told Nasra Hassan: 'After every massacre, every massive violation of our rights and defilement of our holy places, it is easy for us to sweep the streets for boys who want to do a martyrdom operation. Fending off the crowds who demand revenge and retaliation and insist on a human bombing operation – that becomes our biggest problem.'[69] During the October 2002 theatre-hostage crisis in Moscow, Al-Jazeera aired a pre-recorded tape featuring five of the female Chechen hostage-takers in which they expressed their willingness to die and explained that they were acting in order to 'avenge their losses'. There is a special unit of Chechen terrorists called the Black Widows, made up of women who become terrorists once their husbands are killed. The final videotapes made by living martyrs repeatedly speak of the desire to avenge the atrocities committed against their communities. Posters and commemorative cards made to the martyrs declare: 'The Right of Revenge is Ours.' A popular-music genre emerged in Gaza in the mid-1990s known as 'revenge songs'. Sometimes the desire is to avenge a personal injury, the death or arrest of a relative, and sometimes it is to avenge the ill-treatment of people they do not know but with whom they identify. Often it is to avenge a sense of humiliation. The longer the conflict continues, the more atrocities there are to be avenged.

While the desire for revenge has proven to be a powerful motivator in the human condition generally, it has not sufficed to propel people to commit suicide in large numbers. There are other motivations at play too and these are the social motivations, the desire to be loyal to one's peers and to be revered in one's community. I get the sense from watching some of the eve-of-operation videos, especially the less carefully scripted ones, that the volunteers' desire to be the centre of attention is being briefly indulged by the movement's leaders before they are dispatched to war as cannon fodder.

PKK leader Abdullah Ocalan, speaking of the first female Kurdish suicide terrorists, said: 'These women were fully aware and fully desirous of being free women with an important message to pass on and capable of being examples to all women the world over.'[70] The leaders of the organizations understand the power of this appeal and hence have created a culture of hero worship around the shaheeds. Songs extol their virtues and their bravery. Their likenesses adorn walls in the streets of their communities and the homes of their would-be emulators. Their stories are told on the internet for all the world to see. Calendars depict a 'martyr of the month'. An underemployed youth has no way of realizing a dream to be a superstar like Diego Maradona or Britney Spears (especially if s/he is not good at soccer or singing). But s/he knows just how to become a Wafa Idris or a Captain Miller, and s/he doesn't need any special talents to do so.

In addition to the worldly renown that the volunteers expect to achieve, they are guaranteed a direct route to paradise, where everything they have wanted in this life will be provided. Volunteers are also promised places in paradise for seventy of their nearest and dearest friends and relatives. Many volunteers conclude that it is an offer they cannot refuse. They give up the life they enjoy now and in so doing take a strike at the hated enemy, and force the enemy to respond to them; in return they provide for their family in this world and the next while acquiring for themselves an honoured place in heaven. If you believe in the payout, it's not a bad deal. The fact that there are so many volunteers in secular groups that do not offer a place in paradise indicates that this is no more than an added inducement, not an explanation of the decision to become a martyr.

Once a martyr dies the family holds a celebration, not unlike a wedding. Hundreds of friends and neighbours flock to the home and parents distribute sweets to the neighbourhood children. Parents and siblings speak of their pride and are honoured in their communities. Interviews after the fact, however, suggest that at least in some cases the families are just playing a part, doing what is expected of them while privately grieving in an altogether understandable way. Mabrook Idris, mother of the first female Palestinian suicide bomber, initially declared: 'I am proud that my daughter died for Palestine, proud that she gave her life for us all. Thank God. Thank God.' As word of Wafa's death spread, the leaders of al-Aqsa arrived at her home in Ramallah with sweets and posters emblazoned with photographs of Wafa. The atmosphere was joyous – a neighbour described it as 'a wedding with eternity'. Not long afterwards, however, the mother confessed: 'If I had known what she was going to do, I would have stopped her. I grieve for my daughter.'[71] The father of Ayat al-Akhras used almost the same words: 'Had I known she was planning to do such a thing I would have locked the door and thrown away the key.'[72] Another mother told Nasra Hassan that had she learned of her son's plans, 'I would have taken a cleaver, cut open my heart, and stuffed him deep inside. Then I would have sewn it up tight to keep him safe.'[73]

While the family express public pride and private grief, the euphoria of the martyrs themselves seems genuine. In 1983 a young guard at the Marine barracks in Lebanon caught a glimpse of the man driving the truck full of explosives towards the building. He remembers no physical features, only that the man had an enormous smile on his face.[74] Israeli survivors of suicide attacks on buses similarly describe the bombers as wearing a big smile. This is what is known in the Shia tradition as the bassamat al-farah or 'smile of joy', prompted by one's impending martyrdom. Over twenty years after the Lebanese attack, the Iraqi martyr-in-waiting, Marwan, described how he was asked to mentor a friend in the final weeks before his suicide attack. 'My friend was happier than I had ever seen him. He felt he was close to the end of his journey to heaven.'[75] In their final video the three 'Giants', Abu-Surer, Uthman and al-Hindi, cannot contain their excitement. Smiling and laughing into the camera they are savouring every moment of being centre-stage. They are the very epitome of the 'happy death' constantly celebrated in the slogans of the intifada. Hamas slogans declare: 'I will die smiling in order that my religion live' and 'O Muslim, say Allahu Akbar with joy'. Nationalist groups simply replace religion with the homeland as in 'How sweet is death for the sake of the homeland' and 'Mother I am happy, happy to die for freedom'.[76] Far from performing lonely acts of desperation, these martyrs are going gleefully to their premature graves.

While individuals choose martyrdom in order to exact revenge and attain renown, they also want to advance their cause. They want to elicit a reaction from the enemy because, in reacting, the enemy is acknowledging their importance. Few volunteers believe that their individual action alone can cause Turkish, Russian, Sri Lankan or American withdrawal or Israeli destruction, but they certainly hope that their action in concert with others will bring about political change in the long term and that in the short term it will be at least acknowledged by the enemy. It some cases the suicide action is carefully designed to ensure the maximum number of casualties possible, as was the case on 9/11, but in many instances in which suicide bombing has become almost commonplace, one gets the sense that the volunteers are more enamoured of the dying than the killing. On their videotapes they speak at length about their deaths and far less about those they are going to kill. They seem so caught up in the euphoria of it all. Moreover, they very often detonate themselves in situations in which they do not cause nearly as many casualties as they might. In one fairly extreme example, in August 2001 the twenty-eight-year-old Muhammad Mahmoud Nassr approached a waitress in the Wall St Café in Haifa. He was carrying enough explosives in his belt to destroy the restaurant. He lifted his tee-shirt to show the belt to the waitress and asked if she knew what it was. The terrified customers fled the restaurant in a panic. When he was left alone he cried 'God is great' and blew himself up, and nobody else.

This difference speaks to the range of suicide attacks. Just as a range of different groups stage suicide attacks, there is also a range of different types of suicide attack. One of the specialities of al-Qaeda is the sophisticated operation that involves a significant group of terrorists working together on a number of co-ordinated attacks. In these cases there is indeed an emphasis on the killing. These latter are, of course, altogether more dangerous.

A large part of the appeal of suicide attacks, especially to the leaders of terrorist organizations, is that historically they have been effective in eliciting a reaction, even in getting results. In the case of Lebanon, the suicide attacks against American and French forces led directly to the withdrawal of the multilateral force. 'We couldn't stay there and run the risk of another suicide attack on the marines,' wrote President Ronald Reagan in his memoirs, explaining the American decision to withdraw.[77] Osama bin Laden has often invoked this example as evidence of American cowardice. The withdrawal had portentous ramifications for Lebanon and permitted the unimpeded growth of Syrian influence in the country. By 1985 these attacks arguably led to Israel's decision to concede most of the gains it had made during its 1982 invasion of Lebanon and to retreat to a narrow strip of land in southern Lebanon from which it subsequently withdrew in May 2001. Later suicide attacks by Hamas and PIJ in Israel were designed to derail the peace process launched by the Oslo agreement in 1993. They largely succeeded. Suicide attacks also influenced the outcome of the 1996 Israeli elections. Prior to the elections Shimon Peres, widely perceived as a dove, was twenty points ahead of his hawkish rival, Benjamin Netanyahu. Yet after suicide attacks in Jerusalem and Tel Aviv the majority of the Israeli electorate decided that the situation required a hawk and the election went the other way. There can be no doubt that the massive and quite unprecedented escalation in suicide attacks against the US and its allies in Iraq since the beginning of the American occupation is designed to force the US to withdraw.

On the face of it, neither Sidique Khan nor Shehzad Tanweer appear to fit into the type of situations just described. They were both

British born and lived in suburban England, where the biggest rivalries are over soccer and cricket teams, not national liberation or religious fundamentalism. They appear not to have left behind much that might help explain their action, and those who know them best seem to be among the most baffled. Less than two months after the attack, however, a brief videotape was aired on Al-Jazeera television depicting Sidique Khan wearing a red keffiyeh and speaking in a broad northern-English accent. Khan described himself as a soldier and said that he was acting to avenge the atrocities against his people (meaning other Muslims). Ayman al-Zawahiri was then shown praising the London bombings and describing them as 'a sip from the glass that the Muslims have been drinking from'.[78]

The four bombers carried identification with them on their mission, so they presumably wished to be identified. Even their families had no idea what they were up to. Indeed the first lead in the case was when the family of another of the terrorists, Hasib Hussain, called the police out of concern that he had not returned home.

The statement claiming the London action by al-Qaeda Europe declared it to have been designed 'to take revenge against the British Zionist Crusader government in retaliation for the massacres Britain is committing in Iraq and Afghanistan'. The statement then threatens other governments that 'they will be punished in the same way if they do not withdraw their troops from Iraq and Afghanistan'.[79] At this point we do not know whether the claim is legitimate, nor do we know whether it reflects the motivations of each of the bombers. It is reasonable to assume, however, that it does.

From what we know of other suicide terrorists it is reasonable to assume that these four were also motivated by a desire to take revenge for British and American action in Iraq and Afghanistan. We do not know whether they desired renown, but given the motives of others they probably did. They certainly achieved it. Pulling off the first suicide operation in the heart of Europe and at a time when the world's leaders were in the country was bound to ensure that their names would be circulated the world over. In his message Khan said: 'I'm sure by now the media's painted a suitable picture of me.' So he was evidently anticipating being recognized. We do not know whether the example of their Spanish counter- parts came to mind. (On March 11, 2004 a group of Moroccan immigrants detonated ten explosions on commuter trains in Madrid, killing 191 people. The bombing is widely credited with ensuring the unexpected defeat of the conservative party of Prime Minister Aznar and the surprise election of the Socialist Party dedi- cated to withdrawing Spanish forces from Iraq.) One could cer- tainly imagine the British team thinking that it would be far better to die gloriously than to be hunted down by the police and waste away in prison for the rest of their lives. It is also reasonable to assume that they thought they could expect a reaction. The reac- tion they were probably hoping to achieve was a British withdrawal from Iraq. The war is deeply unpopular in Britain and one could well imagine them thinking that they could bring about such a withdrawal, as the Spanish train bombers had done.

While revenge, renown and reaction were certainly available to them, they also had a legitimizing ideology in radical Islam and they were, almost by definition, disaffected individuals. The missing piece seems to be the supportive community. These men were born and grew up in suburban Britain, not in the Gaza Strip.[80] Everything we know about suicide terrorists suggests that there must have been a collective component to this. The supportive community was evidently not their family, neighbours and friends. They were probably deeply committed to one another. The most likely explanation for the fact that one of the four bombs exploded an hour after the others and on a bus rather than a train is that the perpetrator, Hasib Hussain, was prevented from taking the intended Underground train and took a bus instead. Knowing his colleagues had exploded their bombs he could have defected from the group but instead decided to improvise within the terms of the original plan. His commitment to his colleagues was presumably such that he acted as they had out of loyalty to the group and their project.

The question then becomes, where did this small group get the social support they needed to sustain them? Khan and Tanweer had travelled to Pakistan together and presumably made contact there with radical fundamentalists. They may have had support from a small number of local extremists affiliated with nearby mosques, but there is no evidence so far to support this. It is also possible that they managed to attain the support of a virtual ulema or Muslim community, through the internet. Thanks to the powers of the internet one can gain access to Islamist websites, or read and watch endless propaganda against the west, or communicate with radical imams in any part of the world, all from one's bedroom in Leeds. The internet has truly provided the means of globalizing terrorism, and even globalizing the tactic of suicide terrorism.

One of the striking novelties of the London bombings is that they reverse the usual pattern of terrorist violence. Usually grievances emerge locally and if there is an external or international component it builds on the local resentments. In this instance the grievances were external and the action was local. Terrorist violence usually starts locally and then goes global. In this instance it started globally and then went local. It is not an auspicious development.

What is so shocking about Khan and Tanweer, aside from the inhuman horror they inflicted on hundreds of people, is that they did not come from a community that overtly supported their action, nor did they suffer discrimination or privation themselves, nor were they acquainted with people whose grievances they sought to avenge, nor were they known to be members of a radical group, nor were they even understood to be interested in politics. As a friend said of Tanweer: 'It's not in his nature to do something like this; he is the type of guy who would condemn things like that.'[81] They did not appear to fit any established profile of a suicide bomber and they were acting in a country and a region that had not previously experienced a suicide attack. The London attacks, therefore, represent a sinister escalation in the terrorist threat.

Having examined the emergence of terrorism and the causes and motives of terrorists it is now time to turn our attention to the situation facing western countries today to see how this knowledge can help us confront the threat we face. It has often been said that the world changed on September 11, 2001, but did it? It is worth examining what exactly changed and what did not that day, and why that question matters. It is also worth inquiring how our knowledge of other terrorist groups and government actions against them can help us fashion an effective response to the threat from al-Qaeda and its offshoots today. In the second part of this book I will turn to the war on terror and the prospects for its success. I will argue that they are slim. I will suggest, however, that there are lessons to be derived from the experience of other countries in countering terrorism. I will argue that there is a direct correlation between a democratic government's ability to understand the nature of the terrorists they face, their ideology, their organization and their appeal, and the ability of the government to counteract that threat. I will suggest, in short, that our current policies are not the right ones if we wish to contain the threat of terrorism.

PART II

The Counter-Terrorists

Americans are asking, why do they hate us? They hate what we see right here in this chamber – a democratically elected government. Their leaders are self-appointed. They hate our freedoms – our freedom of religion, our freedom of speech, our freedom to vote and assemble and disagree with each other.

George W. Bush, September 2001[1]

Later [after the attack on the USS *Cole*] the Mujahideen saw that the gang of black-hearted criminals in the White House was misrepresenting the event, and that their leader, who is a fool whom all obey, was claiming that we were jealous of their way of life, while the truth – which the Pharaoh of our generation conceals – is that *we strike at them because of the way they oppress us in the Muslim world, especially in Palestine and Iraq, and because of their occupation of the Land of the Two Holy Places.* When the Mujahideen saw this they decided to act in secret and to move the battle right into his [the US president's] country and his own territory.

Osama bin Laden, March 2003[2]

6

What Changed and What Did Not on 9/11

Night fell on a different world – a world where freedom itself is
under attack.

George W. Bush, September 20, 2001[1]

At the time of the Clerkenwell explosion terror took possession
of society.   Lord Campbell, 1868[2]

Before boarding the plane on that bright, clear September
morning the young man telephoned his wife to tell her, three
times, that he loved her.[3] She was not able to accompany him as
she was studying in dentistry school in Germany. Only the night
before he had written her a love letter. It began: 'Hello my dear
Aysel. My love, my life. My beloved lady, my heart. You are my
life . . . I love you and will always love you.' The letter ended by
declaring: 'I am your prince and I will pick you up. See you again!!
Your man always.'[4]

The couple had been separated for fourteen months while each
attended school in different countries. He went to Germany five
times to visit her during this time and she came to visit him in the
States once. Six months earlier he had travelled home to visit his
father who was undergoing heart surgery. Before returning to school
he spoke to Aysel, who found him to have been deeply moved by
his father's illness. He said that he wanted to have children soon so
that his father could see them before he died. His father had been
generously supporting his studies, sending him $2,000 a month and
making sure that his young wife was well supported. The family had
been pleased to see the handsome happy-go-lucky playboy get

married. In the elite private schools in which he had been educated, he seemed, or so his family had complained, more interested in girls than geometry. While not spectacularly wealthy, his family were very comfortably off. They owned two homes, drove fashionable Mercedes cars and liked good whisky. Their only son and middle child enjoyed spending their money. When visiting his wife the young man would take her to Paris to eat, drink and see the sights, and when she came to visit him they went to the Florida Keys. Rather than staying with those he knew, he was quick to make friends with his classmates at his new school and took a fun trip with them to the Bahamas. He often stayed in their apartments, cooking dinner for them in the evening and making everyone an early-morning cup of tea. 'He was a friend to all of us,' said the head of his school.[5]

Unlike the other passengers who said goodbye to their family members that morning, however, the twenty-six-year-old Lebanese student Ziad Jarrah knew that he would not be seeing them again. He boarded United Airlines flight 93 on the morning of September 11 with no intention of ever stepping off the plane.

By exploring the degree to which the terrorism we encountered on 9/11 in the United States differs from the terrorism that preceded it, this chapter challenges the view that we inhabit an entirely new world in which the experience of other countries has no relevance, America's national security doctrine is inadequate and protection of its civil liberties unaffordable. The most profound change effected on 9/11 was less the act itself than the reaction it elicited in the US. The scale of the attack was unprecedented, the expressive nature of the violence was rare, the profile and the organization of the suicide bombers were novel and the exposure of US vulnerability was dramatic.

Nevertheless, there was a great deal that did not change. The terrorist preference for conventional technology, symbolic targets, spectacular actions and even suicide bombing was far from new. Religiously motivated violence appeared new but was not, and the prominence of the political motives mixed in with the religious ones was under-appreciated. Despite previous attacks on American citizens abroad, the attacks on American soil aroused a sense of inse-curity that was entirely new, and counter-terrorist policy changed accordingly. The biggest change that occurred on 9/11, therefore, was not in the forces arrayed against it but in America's reaction to those forces.

The horror of the attack and the fear it inspired led Americans to believe that the world had changed. They believed that it was no longer safe to fly. They believed that they were vulnerable to attack by weapons of mass destruction in ways previously unknown. But the real change came from within the US, not outside. It came from the newfound sense of insecurity. With it came a loss of perspective and, ultimately, a willingness to support a response that was destined to make the situation worse.

The scale of the atrocity committed on 9/11 was, simply, unprece-dented in the lengthy annals of terrorism. The final casualty figure of 2,976 was much less than the early reports had suggested. Nevertheless, almost ten times as many people were murdered that day as in any other terrorist action. Earlier mass-casualty attacks had killed about 300 people. Previously the point of terrorism had been for the psychological impact to be greater than the actual physical act. This is how terrorists have leveraged their relative weakness, but in this instance the physical act itself was unprecedented in its destructiveness outside of wartime. Of course, from the terrorist's point of view, they were at war. Bin Laden had declared war on the US in 1996. The destruction in New York, Washington and Pennsylvania made this war a reality, and America countered with its own declaration of war.

One of the most striking things that changed on that day, there-fore, was that for the first time terrorists had succeeded in killing very large numbers of people, the kind of casualties that had previ-ously only occurred in inter-state or civil warfare. Historically ter-rorists have not taken the opportunities available to them to murder on a grand scale. They have not needed to. They could further their objectives and provoke widespread terror without inflicting wide-spread casualties. The most frequently cited aphorism on this point was made by the RAND analyst Brian Jenkins in 1974: 'Terrorists want lots of people watching, not lots of people dead.' When the IRA called in a warning to evacuate a building in London because they had placed a bomb inside, they could successfully terrorize all of London without killing anybody. They could quite easily have left a bomb and not run the risk of detection by calling in a warning. They did not need to kill large numbers of people to make their point. It was enough to demonstrate that they could. Moreover, they knew that to have committed a large-scale atrocity would have alienated their supporters at home. The perpetrators of the 9/11 attacks, on the other hand, clearly wanted to kill as many people as possible.

Most terrorist groups rely for support on members of their ethnic group or adherents of their ideology, so operatives have been careful to ensure that their actions do not alienate this support base. When the audience is God, however, you do not need to be so constrained. God is unlikely to announce his reaction, so terrorists are free to interpret his reaction as they choose. Like most other terrorist groups with religious motives, however, al-Qaeda also has an audience on the ground. For al-Qaeda this audience is vast and geographically dispersed: it is the entire Muslim world, amounting to 1.2 billion people, as well as the population of the United States whose policies they seek to change. In order to make an impression on such a vast group, the action had to be quite spectacular, as indeed the 9/11 attack was.

This was not the first time terrorists had tried to kill the maximum possible number of people. The group of New Jersey Islamists who drove a yellow Ford Econoline rental van filled with 1,500 pounds of urea-nitrate into the basement of the World Trade Center in February 1993 had clearly intended to kill as many people as possible. They succeeded in killing six and injuring more than a thousand. Philippines authorities had similarly discovered plans for inflicting mass casualties when in 1995 they found a laptop used by Khalid Sheikh Mohammad, the mastermind of the 9/11 attack. This computer contained plans for simultaneously blowing up eleven aircraft over the Pacific. The plan required that a bomb be left under a seat and that the bomber leave the plane during a stopover. The same laptop contained a number of other plans too, including flying a light aircraft into CIA headquarters in Langley, Virginia, and an alternative plan to fly aircraft into major US buildings, including the World Trade Center.[6]

This was the first time, however, that terrorists had succeeded in inflicting such massive casualties. The previous year nineteen Americans had died as a result of international terrorism, and 405 people had died worldwide.[7] The year before that, five Americans and 233 people of all nationalities had died at the hands of international terrorists.[8] A leap from 200 to 400 to 3,000 is dramatic by any standard. Another way of getting a sense of the enormity of the escalation is to look at the UK. Britain had been fighting a campaign against the IRA, a thoroughly professional and ruthless terrorist organization, for several decades in Northern Ireland. Yet Britain lost sixty-seven of its citizens in the September 11 attacks, more than in any single terrorist attack by the IRA in over thirty years.

So while the scale of the attack was unprecedented, the nature of the violence was also quite different from what had previously been experienced. That nineteen men were willing to kill themselves in order to hurt American civilians seemed unfathomable. Suicide terrorism has fascinated Americans since the 1990s, when it began to be used on a significant scale by the Palestinians. None of those earlier attacks matched this large, synchronized attack. No longer did one or two operatives hit an American military target like the Marine barracks in Beirut or the USS *Cole* off Yemen, or even a symbol of American power like the US embassies in Nairobi and Dar-es-Salaam, which were bombed in 1998. These attacks, though horrific, could somehow be seen as the action of individual extremists attacking military or government targets, deranged fanatics acting on behalf of their organization. But for a group the size of an American football team willingly to blow themselves up in unison in order to kill American office workers seemed completely beyond the bounds of comprehension.

Americans have tended to see themselves as being on the side of those who sought to overthrow the yoke of colonialism. They have never seen themselves as colonial oppressors and were spared the political traumas experienced by many of their allies in accommodating themselves to the demand for independence that swept the former colonies after the Second World War. Americans are not very familiar with the writings of Franz Fanon, who was born in the French colony of Martinique in 1925 and wrote of the Algerian struggle for independence. His writings have not resonated in the US. In his seminal work, *The Wretched of the Earth*, Fanon wrote of violence as liberating, as behaviour that is necessary to the perpetrator as a means of freeing himself from oppression. This is not the instrumental violence of the robber or the mafia member. It is expressive violence to cleanse the soul.[9] And this was the kind of violence that confronted the American public on September 11 and for which they were quite unprepared.

The first thing that changed, therefore, was the scale and the nature of the violence that confronted the US. The second essential innovation of 9/11 was that this attack hit America at home. American vulnerability was exposed. In the words of the president: 'Our nation has been put on notice: we are not immune from attack.'[10] Previous attacks had occurred overseas. The United States, unlike most of its allies, has been relatively untouched by domestic terrorism. The Days of Rage of the Weathermen, the violent offshoot of the Students for a Democratic Society (SDS) in the 1960s, were a distant memory. Aside from the earlier attack on the World Trade Center, the one notable exception was the bombing of the Alfred P. Murrah Federal Building in Oklahoma City on April 19, 1994 which left 168 people dead, including nineteen children. That bombing was carried out by a twenty-six-year-old American survivalist, Timothy McVeigh, who was in police custody ninety minutes after the attack.[11] While deeply shocking, McVeigh's action, for which he was executed on June 11, 2001, appeared to be a one-off attack by a deranged extremist. He did not pose an ongoing threat to the US.

Not only has the US been spared domestic terrorism but it has also been extraordinarily lucky in managing to conduct its wars largely beyond its own shores. Other than the Japanese attack on the Pacific Fleet in Pearl Harbor on December 7, 1941, which resulted in the deaths of 2,403 American servicemen and sixty-eight civilians, one has to return to the Civil War to find domestic casualties on the scale of 9/11. On 9/11, however, the victims, with the exception of some of the 125 people killed in the Pentagon, were all civilians.

The ability of al–Qaeda to carry out a sophisticated attack within the United States was deeply shocking. It exposed the fact that for the first time in its history America's oceans and geographic location no longer sufficed to keep its enemies at a distance. In the words of Vice President Dick Cheney: '9/11 changed everything. It changed the way we think about threats to the United States. It changed our recognition of our vulnerabilities. It changed in terms of the kind of national security strategy we need to pursue, in terms of guaranteeing the safety and security of the American people.'[12] The American public were confronted with the reality of globalization. The world was a smaller place and they no longer felt safe. In a poll conducted by CBS News a month after the attack, 88 per cent of the respondents said that they considered it likely that there would be another terrorist attack in the US within a few months.[13]

The American public were also confronted with the fact that the United States, both its government and its people, was deeply reviled by a group of radical Islamists half a world away, of whom they had never heard. Some reacted by asking: How do we get them? Applications to join the military and intelligence services soared. Others reacted by asking: why do they hate us? These people sought to learn more. Most were simply baffled, saddened and frightened. For the US public this was a dastardly attack out of the blue by crazy, evil people. It was an unconscionable, unprovoked assault on innocent civilians. For the perpetrators of the violence, however, this was a glorious blow by the weak against the strong. It was giving Americans a taste of their own medicine. It was in effect the story of David and Goliath. In bin Laden's own words:

> They carried out the raid by means of enemy planes in a courageous and splendid operation the like of which mankind had never before witnessed. They smashed the American idols and damaged its very heart, the Pentagon. They struck the very heart of the American economy, rubbed America's nose in the dirt and dragged its pride through the mud. The towers of New York collapsed and their collapse

precipitated an even greater debacle: the collapse of the myth of
America the great power and the collapse of the myth of democracy;
people began to understand that American values could sink no lower.
The myth of the land of freedom was destroyed, the myth of American
national security was smashed and the myth of the CIA collapsed, all
praise and thanks to Allah.[14]

Americans would have been stunned to learn that al-Qaeda
believed that they had warned the US time and time again to
change its policies in the Middle East and that the US had arro-
gantly ignored all warnings. While the American public focused on
the individual tragic stories of fathers, mothers and children whose
lives had been torn apart by the attack, the perpetrators saw the
victims as depersonalized agents of their message. The rancour they
felt was for America, the most powerful country in the world, not
for the individual people they murdered. They held individual
Americans collectively accountable for the actions of their government in that they financed it through their taxes and voted them
into office. The perpetrators' hearts had been hardened to the individual tragedies they inflicted as they believed that their side had
experienced many more. For their part, most Americans had never
heard of al-Qaeda or of Osama bin Laden.

For the US the world appeared to have changed on 9/11, but it's
not so clear that it did. Certainly the scale and the nature of the
violence visited on the US were unprecedented, but this change
was a long time in the making. The exhaustive work of the 9/11
Commission and the work of many academics before 2001 attested
to the growth in radical Islamic movements, their antipathy towards
the US, the impact of the successful outcome of the mujahideen
campaign against the Soviet Union, and the activities in terrorist
training camps in Afghanistan and elsewhere. Investigations into
earlier attacks outside the US had also revealed to the security services the extent of the transnational networks that were operating
and the degree of financial backing they enjoyed. There was no
shortage of evidence for the fact that the stability of America's most
powerful allies in the Middle East was often purchased by repression of domestic opponents, as in Egypt, or by exportation of the
radical message, as in Saudi Arabia.

None of this, however, had penetrated the popular consciousness in the US, so that 9/11 was seen as something coming completely out of the blue, a bizarre, brutal and unprovoked act of
religious fanaticism. Americans have long been renowned as a relatively insular people with comparatively low rates of foreign travel
and passport ownership. This fact is no doubt attributable in large
part to the size and geographic isolation of the US and the ease of
domestic travel, but it meant that there has not been a significant
interest in foreign developments, especially when they did not
directly impinge on the daily lives of Americans. This tendency to
look inward was reflected in Washington, where foreign policy
appeared to be conducted with an eye to American interests somewhat narrowly defined and an even keener eye to domestic politics
and not at all with an eye to the impact of these policies on the
ground in other countries.

A case in point is the deployment of American troops in Saudi
Arabia at the end of the first Gulf War. Few Americans were aware
of the commitment that was made, ostensibly to serve as a trip-wire
in the event of aggression against the friendly Saudi regime. This
deployment was enormously unpopular on the ground and was
used as a rallying cry for Islamic extremists, most notably bin
Laden. He argued repeatedly that the deployment of American
troops was humiliating and was evidence of nefarious American
designs on Saudi oil reserves and independence. Most Americans
were quite oblivious to the deployment and, insofar as they were
aware of it, considered it an act of altruism.

Before September 11 I heard Michael Sheehan, the co-ordinator
for counter-terrorism in the State Department between 1998 and
2001, respond to a question posed by a student: why do they hate
us? He replied with the government's line that they hate us because
we love freedom, because we love democracy. I countered with
another question: 'What if we learned that, in fact, what they hated
was our policies? If we learned that the deployment of our troops
in Saudi Arabia was what caused the enmity against us, would this
cause you or the administration to re-evaluate the wisdom of our
policies?' He responded emphatically: 'No. We will never let terrorists determine our policies.' He won the debating point. He was

a smart and dedicated public servant and he was voicing the official line. But I was stunned then, and remain so now, by how short-sighted a policy this was. Americans did not know and did not care whether their troops were on the ground in Saudi Arabia. There were many alternatives to this deployment that would have provided ample reassurance to Saudi Arabia – an additional American aircraft carrier in the Gulf, for example. But the US insisted on its right to implement a policy that was hugely unpopular and it appeared to be completely oblivious to the way it could be used against Americans. This was the hubris of great power.

The American government did not see the events of September 11 as an attack on American policies. They saw them as an attack on the American way. President Bush was speaking for many of his fellow countrymen when he said in his address to the nation on the night of September 11: 'America was targeted for attack because we're the brightest beacon for freedom and opportunity in the world. And no one will keep that light from shining. Today our nation saw evil, the very worst of human nature.'[15] Four years later his position remained unchanged: 'Our enemies murder because they despise our freedom and our way of life.'[16] The American public, however, appear to have had a more nuanced view. In a Harris poll conducted just over a week after the attacks Americans were asked: 'Which ONE of the following do you think is the main reason why those who attacked us and their supporters hate the United States?' Twenty-six per cent answered, 'Our democracy and freedom', 20 per cent answered, 'Our values and our way of life.' Both of these responses were consistent with the administration's interpretation. However, others thought differently: 22% responded, 'Our support for Israel'; 17 per cent thought it was 'Our influence on the economy and lives of Middle Eastern countries' and 11 per cent answered that they hated us because of 'Our economic and military power.'[17]

Vice President Cheney was quite right when he said that September 11 changed everything. On the evening of that day most Americans thought the same. An Ipsos-Reid poll taken at that time found that 74 per cent of Americans agreed with the statement that 'the events are a turning point that will fundamentally change things forever'.[18] Americans thought the change was external. However, the real change effected on September 11 2001 was not an external one. It was internal. Terrorism and even religious terrorism had been around for centuries. Al-Qaeda and other extremist Islamist groups had been operating and trying to hit the US for years. They succeeded this time, but the disproportion between the harm they inflicted and the impact that they had was quite considerable.

Terrorism is above all a game of psychological warfare. As pointed out earlier, terrorists are invariably weaker than their opponents, so they try to compensate for this weakness by achieving dramatic effects. They were extraordinarily successful in inflicting almost 3,000 casualties on the US in a single day, but in fashioning a reaction to this atrocity we should perhaps put those deaths within the context of other casualties, especially other preventable casualties, the US suffered that year.

Slightly fewer than 3,000 people were killed in the attacks on September 11, 2001. Over 900,000 Americans died that year. Of these 131,117 died of acute causes. The 3,000 casualties inflicted by al-Qaeda, while enormous, pale in comparison to the 30,000 suicides and 16,000 homicides in the US in the same year, or even the 15,000 Americans who died in falls in 2001. Over 42,000 Americans died in car crashes in 2001 and over 40 per cent of these, 17,500, died in alcohol-related traffic fatalities. In other words, six times as many Americans were killed by drunk drivers in 2001 as were killed by the terrorists on 9/11.[19] What's more, equivalent numbers of Americans are killed by drunk drivers every single year. But we seem only to remember those killed by terrorists. This is not for a moment to belittle the terrible human tragedy that accompanied every single one of those 2,976 deaths, but it is to marvel at the attention they have received and the response that has been elicited compared to the far greater number of deaths due to other preventable causes, like drunk drivers. As the findings of the 9/11 Commission make abundantly clear, the attacks on September 11 were preventable too.

One can only imagine what the reaction might be to calls requiring Americans to submit to sobriety tests in order to use the highways or for posting policemen with breath-analyser kits outside popular watering holes. While the individuals who lost their lives in New York, Washington and Pennsylvania have rightly been memorialized nationally and the country has vowed to punish those responsible, other people who were killed that day have been forgotten by everyone except their families and friends. Take the case of Barbara Cordova, who was on her way to bring her granddaughter home to dinner when she was killed by a speeding drunk driver. The driver, despite a long record of other driving offences, was punished with one year's probation, twenty-four hours of community service, $400 in court fines and a requirement to participate in an alcohol-treatment programme.[20]

It is part of the genius of terrorism that it causes us to emphasize the harm it inflicts as compared to other tragedies. The spectacular effect of terrorist atrocities is magnified by the way they play into the hands of the media, providing extraordinary pictures and video footage as well as compelling stories of heroism, chance and tragedy. As will be argued later, an essential element of any successful counter-terrorism strategy must be the development of public resilience so that we cannot be so easily manipulated by terrorists. As long as we react so strongly, those seeking a reaction will find the tactic an appealing one.

The real change, therefore, was in American's diminished sense of security and the government's response to this. Americans no longer felt safe in their homes. On the face of it American citizens were a great deal safer in the autumn of 2001 than they were throughout the Cold War, when the armed might of the Soviet Union, including over 10,000 strategic and close to 30,000 non-strategic nuclear warheads were trained on the US and its allies. During the Cold War, America's enemy was a global superpower in possession of vast arsenals rivalling its own and an army considerably larger than that of the US. It was ruled by authoritarian leaders espousing a hostile and expansionist ideology utterly at variance with America's belief in democracy. America's enemy in 2001 appeared to be a band of fighters living in caves who received refuge from one of the poorest and most isolated countries in the world.

It seems to have been a combination of the novelty and the unexpectedness of the attack, along with the visual spectacle of seeing two of the largest and most famous buildings in the country collapse, that contributed to the impact of the 9/11 attacks. After all, the Soviet nuclear weapons had been trained on the US for decades and they never hurt it. Casualties on the roads occur every year, but not all at the same time, nor are they visible. Moreover, the numbers of deaths in alcohol-related accidents, while still enormous, are less than the annual carnage of 25,000 of twenty years ago (due largely to the more widespread use of seatbelts). So Americans had become used to the Soviet menace and other threats to their security.

It is perhaps worth remembering that when the threat from communism was first felt after the Second World War there was an intense popular reaction, with 'Reds' being sought under beds, in Hollywood, in academia and, most of all, in the government. Alliances were struck with unsavoury dictators who shared none of America's commitment to civil and human rights and democratic principles but who shared its loathing of communism. Then the US embarked on costly foreign wars when it mistook nationalism for communism and failed to understand the profound distinction between the two. By 2001, over a decade after the end of the Cold War, even the threat from communism had become a distant memory. But its place in the American psyche was more than supplanted by the threat of terrorism.

American 'exceptionalism', the sense that America is different from (and implicitly superior to) the rest of the world, has been a powerful aspect of US political culture. America's size, wealth and geographic location enabled it to develop apart from and without intense involvement in the affairs of other countries. Those occasions when the US has been drawn, reluctantly, into conflicts overseas in order to protect its interests, as in the two world wars, have tended to be followed by periods of retreat or isolation. The disregard for multilateral institutions and preference for unilateralism exhibited by the Bush administration represented an approach to 'entangling alliances' that had a long lineage in American history and a strong resonance with the American public.

With the shock of the 9/11 attacks and the unprecedented out-pouring of support from around the world, the American reaction was to see this attack as *sui generis*, an act of unparalleled evil to which the US had to respond. As the president said: 'This is a new kind of evil.'[21] There was little sense that there was much to be learned from the experience of others. This was a uniquely American event. Yet citizens of over eighty countries died in the attacks. The rest of the world rushed to condemn the atrocity and to make common cause with the US, insisting that they were all Americans and that this was an attack on all humanity. Nevertheless, the prevailing sense among Americans was that this was different. This was about them.

As subsequent official inquiries have indicated, the attacks revealed startling inadequacies in domestic preparedness and conse-quence management. They revealed glaring weaknesses in intelli-gence-gathering capacities and astonishing failures of co-ordination and information sharing among different security agencies. The president responded with the creation of an entirely new federal agency with cabinet-level representation, the Department of Homeland Security, in order to confront the new threat.

The threat was not as new as people thought, though its newness added to the fear it inspired. There were two aspects in particular of al-Qaeda violence that left Americans thinking that indeed the world had changed. First was the belief that if al-Qaeda could destroy the World Trade Center, it would not hesitate to use weapons of mass destruction against the US. Second was the sense that the organization was driven by irrational religious fanat-ics whose behaviour was likely to be both unpredictable and unconstrained.

As pointed out in earlier chapters, the mixture of religious and political motives is far from new. Indeed al-Qaeda, having been founded in 1988 and having declared war on the US in 1996, was not new either. What was new was that this time they were lucky. This time their plan worked and they successfully hit their target, to devastating effect. Americans had previously experienced the power of the fusion of radical Islam and politics in the person and the actions of the Ayatollah Khomeini of Iran. He, however, had confined his direct attacks to Americans abroad.

Unlike many countries in Europe, the US does not have a large Muslim community. Estimates vary widely, but the most accurate suggest that there were 2.8 million Muslims in the US in 2001. This represents less than 1 per cent of the population and is significantly less than the Muslim populations in allied countries like Britain, France, Germany and Spain. Not having much exposure to Islam, many Americans seemed frightened and prepared to confound the extremist perversion of Islam represented by bin Laden and his relatively small group of followers with the vast global religion. Only a religion seemed capable of legitimizing such action. President Bush sought to make clear in his public pronouncements that al-Qaeda did not speak for Islam; he added that Islam's 'teachings are good and peaceful and those who commit evil in the name of Allah blaspheme the name of Allah'.[22] Nevertheless, the view that there was indeed a clash of civilizations in the making received growing currency. Asked in October 2001 whether they thought the attacks were the start of a major conflict between the people of America and Europe and the people of Islam or only a conflict with a small radical group, 28 per cent of Americans thought that the west was in conflict with Islam. A year later that figure had grown to 35 per cent.[23]

For all the religious rhetoric of bin Laden, however, he has persistently articulated a set of political demands linked to American policy in the Middle East. In the wake of the attack, public discourse focused not on these political demands but on the grandiose religious rhetoric. In the president's words: 'Al-Qaeda is to terror what the mafia is to crime. But its goal is not making money; its goal is remaking the world – and imposing its radical beliefs on people everywhere . . . These terrorists kill not merely to end lives, but to disrupt and end a way of life.'[24] Later he was to refer to their ideology as 'Islamo-fascism'.[25] There can be no doubt that terrorist groups that have enjoyed a mix of religious and political motives have been both more transnational and less constrained than other terrorist groups. Religion, however, is rarely a cause of terrorism; rather religion serves to 'absolutize' conflicts, in the word of sociologist Mark Juergensmeyer, making compromise more difficult.[26]

Terrorist leaders have found religion to be enormously useful in legitimizing their actions and in winning recruits for the cause. Religion enables terrorist leaders to cast the conflict in terms of cosmic warfare and their followers to see themselves as soldiers in the divinely inspired army. Religion facilitates recruitment both by providing legitimacy and by providing rewards in the afterlife to people prepared to pay considerable costs in this one. The organizational networks available through religions have long been a powerful resource for the weak in their efforts to mobilize against the strong. In the case of apartheid South Africa, for example, which banned most forms of political organization among the black majority, churches remained one of the few places in which those seeking change could congregate. Churches, especially among diaspora communities, have also always served to draw in those seeking comfort in an alien culture. So both on a practical and an ideological level, at the level of personal rewards for the followers as well as tools for the leaders, religion and terrorism have often been linked.

In responding to the attacks on 9/11, Americans opted to accept al-Qaeda's language of cosmic warfare at face value and respond accordingly, rather than formulate a response to al-Qaeda based on an objective assessment of its resources and capabilities relative to their own. There is no doubt that the sheer spectacle of the crumbling towers appeared consistent with a view of cosmic warfare. But 3,000 casualties in a country long accustomed to more than five times that many homicides a year might have elicited a more moderate reaction. Part of the reason it did not was the sense that if, in the name of their God, they would fly planes into American buildings, what else would they do? The biggest fear is that they might try to use weapons of mass destruction.

Weapons of Mass Destruction

It is in some ways ironic that an attack using primitive box cutters and relying on no technological innovation since the jet engine managed to propel the fear of terrorist use of weapons of mass destruction to the top of the national agenda. But it did. In the words of the president: 'In the Cold War, weapons of mass destruction were considered weapons of last resort as they risked the destruction of those who used them. Today, our enemies see weapons of mass destruction as weapons of choice.'[27]

One month after 9/11, some 80 per cent of Americans, according to an ABC News poll, were worried about terrorist use of chemical or biological weapons (known by the shorthand CBW) in the US.[28] In October 2001 a total of 63 per cent of respondents told pollsters that they thought that the use of chemical or biological weapons was the biggest threat from terrorists 'right now', 9 per cent said they thought the biggest threat right now was from nuclear weapons or dirty bombs, and only 5 per cent said they thought the biggest threat came from planes being hijacked and crashed.[29]

Ever since the Japanese cult Aum Shinrikyo led by Shoko Asahara had released sarin gas on the Tokyo subway in 1995, American officials have been deeply troubled by the prospect that terrorists might use weapons of mass destruction against the US. On that day, March 20, at the height of the morning rush hour, five teams of two members of the Japanese sect smuggled small gas dispensers on to several subway trains in Tokyo. The trains were all due to arrive at the Kasumigaseki station, at the heart of the capital's government district, shortly after 8 a.m. The cult members were smartly dressed in business suits and carried umbrellas, as well as plastic bags of sarin concealed in the morning newspaper. As the trains pulled into the station they left the bags on parcel racks, punctured them with the tips of their umbrellas, quickly alighted from the trains and promptly swallowed an antidote. The dispensers released the nerve gas, causing pandemonium. Many thousands of commuters were overcome, twelve people died and 5,500 were injured. The attack was the first successful use of chemical weapons by a terrorist group, and it demonstrated just how easy it could be for terrorists to deploy chemical or biological weapons in an open society. The casualties in this instance would have been considerably higher if the chemists had made the concoction more concentrated. Moreover, it became clear once the group's headquarters were raided that they had the facilities to produce several other nerve agents as well.

The term weapons of mass destruction or, more often, WMD is used to describe broadly three types of weapons: chemical, biological and nuclear. Distinctions are not often drawn between the different types of weapon but it is actually very important to understand that they differ significantly from one another in their lethality, in their novelty, in the ease of their deployment and in their usefulness to terrorists. It is worth taking a moment to disaggregate this concept of weapons of mass destruction and to explore the nature of the different types of weapon that fall under this rubric.

Chemical Weapons

There are four major categories under which chemical agents can be classified according to their effects: blister agents, choking agents, blood agents and nerve agents. Blister agents are designed to cause injury rather than death. So if a murderous group wanted to cause chaos and overload a region's medical facilities without actually killing many people, they might opt for a blister agent like mustard gas. It is hard to imagine, however, how this approach would appeal to any known terrorist group. Choking agents were widely used in the First World War. They are designed to kill their victims, and their biggest attraction from a terrorist point of view is that they are so easy to obtain. Cyanide-based compounds are the main components of blood agents. These work best for individual assassinations rather than mass attacks because of the rapid rate of evaporation. The newest trend in chemical weapons has been nerve agents. These weapons, like sarin, tabun and soman, have been the main weapons stockpiled as chemical weapons. These were the type of weapons deployed by Saddam Hussein against the Kurdish city of Halabja in March 1988. In general they are hundreds of times more lethal than blister, choking and blood agents. They are particularly attractive to those seeking to do harm because of the small amount needed to do a lot of damage.

Among the advantages of chemical weapons for terrorists are that they are cheap and easy to obtain, little training is required in their use, and production of the crude agents is fairly straightforward. The most difficult part is dispersing the weapon correctly. Chemical weapons can also be quite dangerous to handle and difficult to control, so their appeal to terrorists has been limited. Over the years a number of terrorist groups have been linked to chemical weapons, but these episodes remain uncommon. Lacking the dramatic effect of a bombing or hijacking and entailing considerable risk to the handlers, they have not been an attractive option for terrorists.

Prior to 9/11 there was little to indicate that terrorists had acquired a capacity to develop chemical weapons, although there were a number of reported attempts to do so. Aum Shinrikyo was a highly unusual case, as the testimony presented at the trials of those accused in the Tokyo attack attested. In spite of indications of their illegal activities, their status as a religious organization protected them from police investigation. The organization had global assets estimated at $1 billion and a membership estimated at about 50,000. They had twenty scientists with graduate degrees among their membership and had extensive, elaborate and modern technical facilities. Indeed, Masami Tsuchiya, Aum's top scientist, who held a master's degree in organic chemistry from Tsukuba University and who confessed to having created the sarin, explained that he had joined the cult because it had far better laboratory facilities than his university.[30] They recruited the top science graduates from Tokyo's best universities. They practised for five years and made nine attempts before successfully pulling off the sarin gas attack. Two further failed attempts followed the March attack. In all, they launched twelve attacks and only the Tokyo attack made an impact, though far less than intended by the group. The experience of Aum suggests that developing these weapons is not as easy as it is often presented and requires scientific expertise, significant funding and secure laboratories. These means are not readily available to a terrorist group, though they could, of course, be provided to one by a sponsoring state. Aum itself was dismantled after the Tokyo attack and has re-emerged as a peaceful group.

There were many reports, prior to 9/11, of al-Qaeda's interest in securing chemical weapons, though these reports rarely had much effect on the public. In one instance they did. On August 20, 1998, charging that al-Qaeda was producing chemical weapons at the al-Shifa pharmaceutical factory in Khartoum, Sudan, the US bombed the factory, killing one worker and injuring twelve others. This action was partly in retaliation for the bombing of the American embassies in Nairobi and Dar-es-Salaam. Subsequent reports suggested that the information on which the attack was based was inaccurate and the factory's owner, Salah Idris, filed suit against the US government claiming compensation. In response the US Treasury unfroze Idris's American bank accounts, thereby implicitly acknowledging that the administration lacked the evidence to justify their action against him.[31]

There were a variety of other reports in the 1990s of plans by al-Qaeda to develop and deploy chemical weapons, in particular cyanide. There were reports of crude laboratories in Khost, Jalabad and Charassiab, Afghanistan.[32] There were also reports that bin Laden had bought chemical and biological weapons from former Soviet states.[33] More fanciful reports declared that bin Laden had bought no fewer than three CBW factories in the former Yugoslavia and had hired a number of Ukrainian biologists and chemists to train his members.[34] Ahmad Rassam, who pleaded guilty to plotting to bomb Los Angeles International Airport, claimed in court that he had witnessed a dog being gassed with cyanide. These claims were consistent with an al-Qaeda video broadcast on CNN showing dogs being killed by toxic chemicals, probably a crude nerve agent or hydrogen cyanide gas.[35] The Italian government claims that by arresting nine Moroccans in February 2000 they foiled a plan to poison the water supply of the US embassy in Rome using a cyanide compound.[36] When US forces toppled the Taliban, however, they found evidence only of very primitive laboratory facilities.

Most of the reports since 9/11 have been about al-Qaeda's interest in these weapons while in Afghanistan. An al-Qaeda computer that fell into the hands of *Wall Street Journal* reporter Alan Cullison in Kabul, for example, contained details of a project, code-named

'Curdled Milk', that was under the direction of Ayman al-Zawahiri and included plans to launch a chemical and biological weapons programme.[37] With the capture of Khalid Sheikh Mohammad in 2003, more detailed information of the progress of this programme appears to have been acquired. According to reports, captured documents indicated that al-Qaeda had the requisite material to manufacture cyanide and two biological toxins and were close to producing anthrax bacteria.[38] Other post 9/11 reports claimed that al-Qaeda members were being trained in secret camps near Baghdad in how to use chemical and biological weapons by instructors from a secret Iraqi military intelligence unit.[39] The US found no evidence to verify these reports once it had occupied Iraq.

While there can be little doubt that some members of al-Qaeda displayed a keen interest in acquiring chemical weapons, there is very little evidence that they succeeded in doing so to any significant degree. The ability of the organization to pursue this interest, moreover, was far greater prior to the fall of the Taliban when they could operate openly in Afghanistan. It appears, therefore, that the fear of their using chemical weapons increased just as their capacity to do so declined.

Biological Weapons

Far from being new, biological weapons have been around as long as warfare itself. The term essentially means the intentional use of biologically derived agents or disease to undermine the adversary's strength, whether in terms of military force, population or resources. There are two categories of biological warfare agents, micro-organisms, which are living organic germs such as anthrax, and toxins, which are the byproducts of living organisms or essentially natural poisons such as botulism or ricin. There are also a great many natural and man-made variants. Biological warfare includes such well-honed ancient practices as catapulting carcasses of dead animals into a besieged city to spread disease or placing dead horses in the enemy's water supply (a common practice in the American Civil War).

One of the most famous cases of biological warfare in American history occurred during the French and Indian war (1754–67). The English believed that the Indians holding Fort Carillon were loyal to the French. In 1763 in an apparently altruistic gesture they offered blankets to the Indians but before handing them over they exposed the blankets to the smallpox virus. The Indians got sick, the epidemic spread, and the British attacked and defeated them easily.

There have been a variety of very minor incidents of the use of biological weapons by terrorists. In the 1980s a number of Red Army Faction (RAF) safe houses in Germany and France were found to have baths full of biological agents. More serious were a number of assassination attempts made with ricin-tipped umbrellas. One of the more famous of these incidents was the murder of Georgi Markov, a BBC World Service journalist and active critic of the communist Bulgarian regime. He was killed by being poked with a ricin-tipped umbrella while waiting at a bus stop in London in 1978. Although labelled terrorism at the time, these assassination attempts were actually the covert action of governments trying to eliminate difficult dissidents overseas.

Generally, biological agents are many times deadlier than chemical agents pound for pound. Ten grammes of anthrax spores, for example, would kill as many people as a ton of the nerve gas sarin. Indeed, if the Aum Shinrikyo group had used anthrax instead of sarin, they would have killed many more people in Tokyo. One of the big advantages of biological weapons from the point of view of the terrorist is how difficult they are to detect while they are being produced or transported. If one were carrying a biological agent in a briefcase on to an aircraft, for example, there are no mechanisms that would identify it. Alternatively the agent could easily be concealed in an aerosol can. Readers of Tom Clancy novels will have come across many other ideas.

The fact that members of al-Qaeda were willing to kill as many people as possible led to the fear that they would not hesitate to use weapons of mass destruction. These fears were greatly exacerbated by a series of anthrax attacks that occurred shortly after the demolition of the World Trade Center. Exactly a week after 9/11 five letters containing anthrax were mailed to media outlets in the United States. Three weeks later two further letters were mailed, this time to two Democratic senators and this time containing a more potent and highly refined form of anthrax. In all, seven letters were mailed, five people died and nobody has yet been charged with the crime. The consensus among the investigators is that these letters were mailed not by a member of al-Qaeda but rather by an American with a grudge and probably one who had worked in one of the country's most sophisticated bio-labs like the Level 4 Lab at Fort Detrick, Maryland. The appearance of anthrax greatly contributed to the sense of fear and insecurity as local officials were deluged with calls from a frightened public fearing that any white powder they encountered might be anthrax.

Al-Qaeda's continued interest in biological weapons and particularly in ricin is evidenced by a number of arrests in Europe associated with the discovery of traces of the toxin and equipment for its production. These include the December 2002 arrest of Menad Benchellai, known as 'the chemist' because of his chemical-weapons training in Chechnya or Afghanistan and later in Georgia. He had a makeshift laboratory in the spare bedroom of his parents' home in Lyon, France, where he developed ricin and stored it in Nivea face cream jars before giving them to a chemist for safe keeping. Two years after his arrest several members of his family were charged with involvement too. Authorities believe that there are interconnected cells of North Africans attempting to develop ricin operating in France, Britain and Spain, but the case has yet to be proven.[40]

In January 2003 nine Algerians were also arrested in London after a makeshift ricin lab appeared to have been found in their flat above a chemist's shop. This incident was deeply troubling to the British public and was invoked by the British prime minister Tony Blair, as well as by the American secretary of state Colin Powell, in an effort to gain support for the American-led invasion of Iraq. It transpired, however, that no traces of ricin were found in the flat.[41] In April 2005 four of those charged were acquitted and charges against four others were dropped. Only one man was convicted and that was for murdering a policeman in the course of the raid. While the alleged discovery of ricin received worldwide attention, the revelation that no traces of ricin were found, just a number of recipes downloaded from the internet, went largely unnoticed.[42] This case shows how much the media can help to exaggerate our reactions. Finding a ricin factory in London was big news, all the more so when the members of two governments constantly referred to it. The fact that there was no factory after all does not make such a good story and so it gets lost.

One of al-Qaeda's manuals, known as *The Encyclopaedia of Jihad*, actually commends ricin as relatively easy to produce and harmless to the developer, and provides instruction on its production from readily available castor beans.[43] While undoubtedly deadly, ricin is more appropriate for assassination than for mass attacks. Given the relative ease with which it can be produced, one can understand its appeal to terrorists, though far more readily available ingredients like fertilizer could inflict much greater harm. Remember that Timothy McVeigh had managed to take down the Murrah Federal building with an easily obtainable agricultural fertilizer called ammonium nitrate and some motor-racing fuel called nitromethane.

Earlier claims about al-Qaeda's cache of bio-weapons also appear to have been exaggerated. A number of defendants on trial in Egypt claimed that al-Qaeda had obtained biological-weapons substances including the Ebola virus and salmonella bacterium through the mail from countries of the former Soviet Union, as well as anthrax-causing bacteria from east Asia and botulinum toxin from the Czech Republic.[44] Shortly after 9/11 there were also reports that Mohammad Atta, the leader of the suicide team, had a meeting in Prague with an Iraqi intelligence agent who allegedly gave him a vial of anthrax. The Czech government have vehemently challenged the veracity of this claim.[45] There were reports from US forces in Afghanistan in late 2001 that the homes of al-Qaeda leaders in Kabul tested positive for anthrax, but these claims too have been challenged. John Walker Lindh, the so-called 'American Taliban', allegedly told his interrogators that battlefield rumours were rife that there was going to be a second wave of attacks from al-Qaeda in the US and that they would be biological.[46] It appears that most rumours about biological weapons were just that, rumours, and many may have been elicited in response to the evident American interest in the subject.

American forces did appear to find a biological-weapons plant under construction in Afghanistan. It was apparently being built to produce anthrax, though no traces of any biological agents were found there.[47] The French interior minister and subsequently prime minister, Dominique de Villepin, told a conference on bio-terrorism in Lyon in January 2005 that al-Qaeda affiliates moved to the Pankisi Gorge region of Georgia after the fall of the Taliban in order to continue their efforts to produce anthrax bacteria, ricin and botulinum toxin.[48] Still other reports have said that two groups closely allied to al-Qaeda, Ansar al-Islam and Jemaah Islamiyah, have both sought to develop biological weapons.[49]

Many of these reports were of questionable reliability. Most appear to have been ignored prior to 9/11 and to have been taken at face value afterwards. The truth probably lies in between. As with chemical weapons, al-Qaeda have clearly had an interest in developing biological weapons, not least because of their scare value. There is not much evidence to suggest, however, that they have succeeded in acquiring these weapons in any meaningful numbers. Having lost the sanctuary of Afghanistan, it has become extremely difficult for them to acquire the capacity to produce them in significant quantities.

It is worth remembering the experience of Aum Shinrikyo in this respect. In spite of their excellent facilities, their trained scientists and their immunity from police oversight, Aum did not succeed in deploying biological weapons. Initially they opted for biological weapons over chemical weapons because of their greater lethality. In their first several attempts Aum actually tried and failed to use biological toxins. They developed an anthrax bomb which they twice tried to deploy, once from a truck and once from a sky-scraper, to no effect. After four failed attempts with biological weapons they turned to chemical weapons and produced sarin. The first time they used it they killed one of their own scientists, so they diluted the gas. It was this diluted concoction that was deployed in the fatal attack in Tokyo. This attack was in turn followed by two further failed attempts, one involving cyanide.[50] None of this is to suggest that we should ignore the possibility that terrorists might use chemical or biological weapons. Followers of bin Laden have a demonstrated interest in acquiring them. It is to suggest, however, that the fears of their use that were prompted by 9/11 are probably overblown, that chemical and biological weapons are more difficult to develop and to deploy effectively than is widely believed and that, thanks to the destruction of their sanctuary in Afghanistan, al-Qaeda are likely to find it more difficult to acquire them now than before 9/11. The constant allegations of weapons finds, however, greatly fed into the fear generated by the 9/11 attacks.

Including biological and chemical weapons under the broader rubric of weapons of mass destruction is itself questionable, though it predates 9/11. In fact chemical and biological weapons have in the past inflicted far fewer casualties than more conventional forms of weaponry. Biological weapons, though relatively easy to acquire, are extremely difficult to deploy effectively, while chemical weapons have to be used in vast quantities in order to be effective. It is probably for these reasons that biological and chemical weapons have seen so little use by states in wartime. On the relatively rare occasions when they have been used, they have not been responsible for a significant percentage of the overall casualties. The First World War saw the heaviest use of chemical weapons, which caused 5 per cent of the overall casualties. Chemical weapons caused less than 1 per cent of the Iranian casualties when used by Iraq in the Iran–Iraq war.[51] Reporting every purported incident in which a terrorist might have acquired these weapons and thereby feeding the public fear that mass casualties are just around the corner is, of course, exactly the kind of reaction terrorism attempts to elicit.

Nuclear

The biggest fear of all, of course, is that terrorists might use nuclear weapons. In the 2004 presidential debate both President George Bush and the Democrats' contender Senator John Kerry ranked nuclear proliferation and in particular weapons falling into the hands of terrorists as the biggest security threat facing the United States. The risk of 'loose nukes' had been a constant concern to American administrations since the end of the Cold War. The fear was that the collapse of the Soviet Union would facilitate trafficking in nuclear weapons. There was considerable concern about the quality of security in Russian nuclear facilities. There were also concerns that underpaid Russian scientists might attempt to sell their knowledge or some of the contents of their labs or that the Russian mafia might attempt to raise significant amounts of cash by acquiring nuclear materials. Any of these groups, it was thought, could take advantage of the permeability of Russia's southern borders. These concerns were heightened when Aum Shinrikyo broke the taboo on terrorist use of WMD. The imperviousness to any constraints on civilian casualties exhibited on 9/11 led to widespread concerns that al-Qaeda would not hesitate to use nuclear weapons.

Official pronouncements from the government tended not to distinguish between different types of weapons of mass destruction. But evidently the public did. Specifically the public consistently found that a nuclear attack posed less of an immediate threat than a chemical or biological attack, by 13 per cent to 75.[52] Even so, fully 16 per cent said they expected terrorists to detonate a nuclear device in the US within a year and a further 23 per cent said they expected it within the next five years.[53]

Notwithstanding the availability of nuclear materials, technologies and expertise there was nothing to suggest that al-Qaeda had the ability or even the motive to use nuclear weapons against the US. The consequence of such an action would be so catastrophic, however, that the possibility was widely discussed. Developing nuclear weapons is far from being as easy as popular discussions imply. Nevertheless, the task would be rendered a lot easier with a sponsoring state to provide protected facilities in which to work or even the fissile material itself. It was precisely the fear that Saddam Hussein was developing weapons of mass destruction and that he might put them into the hands of terrorists that led the American public to support the invasion of Iraq.

Bin Laden himself did not help matters. On the contrary he appears to have been happy to exploit American fears. He simply insisted that he had the same right to possess nuclear or any other weapons that the west had. In an interview with Al-Jazeera television in 2001 he was asked how true were the reports that he sought to acquire nuclear, chemical and biological weapons. He replied:

> We are seeking to drive them [the US] out of our Islamic nations and prevent them from dominating us. We believe that this right to defend oneself is the right of all human beings. At a time when Israel stocks hundreds of nuclear warheads and when the western crusaders control a large percentage of this weapon, we do not consider this an accusation but a right.[54]

As with chemical and biological weapons, prior to 9/11 there were a great many reports that bin Laden had acquired nuclear weapons, but these reports did not penetrate the popular consciousness in the United States. In the case that the US brought against bin Laden for the embassy bombings, prosecution witness Jamal Ahmad al-Fadl testified that as early as 1993–4 he had been charged by al-Qaeda with acquiring uranium in Khartoum. In August 1998, a leaked Israeli intelligence report stated that bin Laden had paid over 2 million sterling for a 'suitcase' bomb to a middleman in Kazakhstan. A few months later Russian intelligence services informed their American counterparts that bin Laden had given a group of Chechens $30 million in cash and two tons of opium in exchange for twenty nuclear warheads.[55] In September 1998, a full three years before 9/11, an alleged aide to bin Laden, Mamduh Mahmud Salim, was arrested in Germany for trying to obtain highly enriched uranium for al-Qaeda.[56] There were other reports of expensive failed efforts by bin Laden to acquire enriched uranium in eastern Europe.[57] In December 2000 Arab security sources alleged that a shipment of about twenty nuclear warheads originating in Kazakhstan, Turkmenistan, Russia and the Ukraine had been intercepted en route to bin Laden.[58]

Reports after 9/11 were even more alarming. One report, this time in November 2001, claimed that al-Qaeda had acquired a Russian-made suitcase nuclear bomb from central Asian sources. The device is reported to weigh 8kg and to possess 2kg of fissionable uranium and plutonium. The report said the device, serial number

9999, was manufactured in October 1998 and could be set off by a mobile phone.[59] On February 8, 2004 the Egyptian newspaper *Al-Hayat* reported that al-Qaeda had bought tactical nuclear weapons from the Ukraine in 1998 and was holding them in storage. The Ukrainian government denies the claim and insists that they transferred all nuclear weapons to Russia by 1996.[60] No evidence was discovered in Afghanistan to suggest that al-Qaeda had nuclear weapons but evidence of their interest in such weapons was found. A London *Times* reporter discovered a blueprint for a 'Nagasaki bomb' in files in an abandoned al-Qaeda house in Kabul. The 'superbomb' manual, as it was called, discusses the advanced physics of nuclear weapons and dirty bombs. There can be little doubt, therefore, that al-Qaeda has contemplated the acquisition of nuclear weapons.[61]

Asked in September 2001 and again two months later whether they thought bin Laden currently had access to nuclear weapons, 63 per cent of Americans replied yes.[62]

A Dirty Bomb

A far more likely scenario than a nuclear attack is a dirty bomb. Often confused with nuclear weapons, a dirty bomb uses conventional explosives to disperse radioactive materials. Even a small amount of radioactive material, if properly milled into fine particles and dispersed by a conventional explosive, could spread radioactive particles over an area of several blocks. The most devastating aspect of a dirty bomb is the panic it would in all likelihood cause. The lethality of a dirty bomb, however, is quite limited when compared to the impact of even a crude nuclear bomb in which there is a nuclear chain reaction that could kill tens of thousands of people within a three-mile radius of the blast while thousands more would suffer radiation poisoning from such an attack.

A month after 9/11 the London *Sunday Times* reported on meetings at which bin Laden sought to purchase nuclear and radiological materials.[63] In November 2001, the Italian organized-crime office alleged that bin Laden had obtained seven enriched uranium rods from mafia connections. The rods had apparently been made in the US.[64] In early 2003 British intelligence sources indicated that they had found documents suggesting that al-Qaeda members had built a dirty bomb in Afghanistan with the assistance of medical isotopes provided by the Taliban.[65] Other reports claim that bin Laden bought radiological materials through contacts in Chechnya.[66] There have also been many reports of intercepted efforts to purchase radioactive materials by al-Qaeda operatives.

The case that generated most concern in the US was that of Jose Padilla, a former gang member and a US citizen who was arrested in Chicago in May 2002 on the grounds that he was planning to organize a dirty-bomb attack on the US for al-Qaeda. Padilla has been held as an enemy combatant, the only American citizen arrested in this country to be so classified. Two years after his arrest the Justice Department revealed that in fact he had been planning not to deploy a dirty bomb but instead to blow up some apartment buildings. The plan apparently was a far more modest one that involved Padilla and an accomplice renting two apartments. They then planned to turn on the natural gas and set off conventional explosive devices simultaneously in each building.[67] As an enemy combatant Padilla has not yet been brought to trial. In the minds of most Americans, however, he has been incarcerated for planning a dirty-bomb attack on the US. In December 2005 the Bush administration decided to change course and sought to have Padilla released from military custody and tried in a civilian court. In the case both of Padilla's dirty bomb and of the Algerian ricin ring in London, the conviction that al-Qaeda were pursuing WMD appears to have outweighed the actual evidence that they have done so. Reports of these cases helped to instil fear and exacerbate the sense of insecurity occasioned by 9/11. From the terrorists' point of view the mere suggestion that they have or plan to use WMD serves their purpose by exaggerating their capabilities and frightening their adversary.

Bin Laden has long understood the essential role of terrorism as communication. His regular video and audio appearances, as well as those of his senior associates, have sought to intimidate the enemy and hearten his followers. As a regular follower of the western media, he is well aware of the fear that weapons of mass destruction evoke in the American public. He has deliberately fuelled concerns about his possible use of WMD by declaring it to be a religious duty to acquire them and that al-Qaeda have a right to use them. He has been very successful and I expect deliberately so in exploiting these fears.

On a number of occasions bin Laden and al-Zawahiri have claimed to have nuclear weapons. In an interview in early 1999 with *Time* magazine bin Laden asserted that acquiring any kind of weapon, including chemical, biological and nuclear ones, was a 'religious duty'. This assertion has been invoked regularly since to demonstrate his determination to obtain these weapons. He said: 'Acquiring weapons for the defence of Muslims is a religious duty. If I have indeed acquired these weapons, then I thank God for enabling me to do so. And if I seek to acquire these weapons, I am carrying out a duty. It would be a sin for Muslims not to try to possess the weapons that would prevent the infidels from inflicting harm on Muslims.'[68] A Pakistani reporter, Hamid Mir, claims to have interviewed bin Laden in November 2001 and to have heard him assert: 'We have chemical and nuclear weapons as a deterrent and if America used them against us we reserve the right to use them.'[69] Five months later, the al-Qaeda leader Abu Zubaydah claimed that al-Qaeda has the interest and the know-how to produce radiological weapons and knew how to smuggle them into the US.[70] In March 2004 Ayman al-Zawahiri went considerably further. He told Hamid Mir that al-Qaeda possessed nuclear weapons purchased in central Asia. Al-Qaeda's second in command stated that operatives had been sent to central Asia to purchase portable nuclear material. He is quoted as having said: 'If you have $30 million then there is no problem going into the central Asian black market, getting in contact with some penniless Soviet scientists and purchasing lots of compact nuclear weapons.'[71]

In making these claims al-Qaeda is undoubtedly attempting to advance the essential psychological aspect of their terrorist campaign. Aware of American fears of WMD, al-Qaeda will further their efforts to acquire them and by announcing that they have them will try to acquire the benefits of possession even if they lack the reality. One gets the clear impression that bin Laden is skilfully engaged in a game of manipulation, trying to stoke the fears that he has generated. In fact the risk of WMD was actually greater before 9/11 than afterwards because of the sanctuary provided in Afghanistan and access to opium to trade for weapons. Most Americans became aware of the risk only after 9/11 and it then became a preoccupation. The American government likewise became obsessed with the fear that an enemy state might provide terrorists with weapons of mass destruction.

In all the discussions of America's vulnerability to WMD there was almost no public discussion of the nature of the threat, no distinctions drawn between chemical, biological, nuclear and radiological weapons nor any public discussion of the limitations of these weapons. Rather, government statements have tended to group all forms of weapons of mass destruction together as an apocalyptic means of destroying the country. In fact, as I have pointed out above, there are very real differences between the few types of weapons which are linked under the rubric of WMD. Moreover, the lethality of any biological and chemical weapons or dirty bombs likely to be acquired by terrorist groups will pale in destructiveness compared to natural disasters like Hurricane Katrina, or indeed the San Francisco earthquake of 1906 and the Galveston Hurricane of 1900, in which 3,000 and 9,000 died respectively and hundreds of thousands were left homeless.

Accurate estimates are hard to come by, but even if one were to include nuclear weapons, the numbers killed by all forms of WMD throughout history come to about 400,000.[72] This is a high figure, but it is tiny when compared to the tens of millions killed by conventional weapons. Nuclear technology has unquestionably come a long way since the atom bombs were dropped on Hiroshima and Nagasaki, killing over 100,000 people. The detonation of a nuclear bomb would undoubtedly be devastating and would indeed constitute a turning point in history. But the conflation of this risk with that posed by a hapless Frenchman concocting ricin in his parents' spare bedroom serves only to undermine our ability to formulate coherent and effective counter-terrorist policies. While the probability of any terrorist group obtaining access to nuclear weapons is very low, the consequences would be so enormous that the risk has to be taken very seriously and focused policies developed to address it.

The fear inspired by the 9/11 attacks and the US government's response to those attacks led Americans to conflate the threats instead of analysing them, gauging the risks and responding appropriately. Just as distinctions were not drawn between the types of weapons that could be used against the US, distinctions were also not drawn between the enemies it faced. The fear that terrorists might acquire WMD from an enemy state was such that Americans did not stop to analyse the relations between the terrorists and those states. The US developed a plan to prevent Saddam Hussein giving weapons to Osama bin Laden without any consideration of the likelihood that he would do so or of the relations between the two men. Middle East experts in the State Department and terrorist experts around the country were quick to point out that Saddam Hussein was exactly the kind of secular and corrupt Islamic leader that bin Laden was dedicated to overthrowing. They sought to remind the country that when Saddam had invaded Kuwait in 1990 bin Laden had approached the Saudi authorities and offered to mobilize the mujahideen who had fought successfully in Afghanistan to fight the Iraqi leader and expel him from Kuwait. Knowing only that both Saddam and bin Laden were their enemies, and ignoring the fact that they were each other's enemy too, Americans conflated the threat and eventually created a self-fulfilling prophecy.

Saddam Hussein, of course, was notorious for having deployed chemical weapons against Iran and against the Iraqi Kurds in the course of the Iran–Iraq war. Of the 600,000 Iranians who died in that war, about 5,000 were killed by chemical weapons deployed by Iraq.[73] Estimates of the number of Kurds killed by Iraqi chemicals weapons in Halabja range from several hundred to 5,000. The fact that Saddam was prepared to use chemical weapons was considered enough to justify the conviction that he would hand some of these weapons over to terrorists to use against the US. The heightened sense of insecurity caused by the 9/11 attacks appears to have prevented public discussion of the logic of this assumption. The US felt that it could not afford to take the chance.

Part of the impact of 9/11, therefore, was the heightened fear that terrorists might use chemical, biological or, worse, nuclear weapons. In fact, however, terrorists were no more likely to use these weapons after 9/11 than before. Indeed, given the loss of their sanctuary in Afghanistan, they were even less likely to do so. What changed on 9/11 was that terrorists demonstrated that they could land a powerful blow on the US. They did not demonstrate that they had the wherewithal to repeat the act or to wage a military campaign against the US, Americans just assumed that they could. The public attitude towards weapons of mass destruction changed dramatically. In a poll conduced by the Pew Research Center in April 1996, as many as 72 per cent of Americans indicated that they believed there was a chance that terrorists could use a weapon of mass destruction to attack a US city but only 13 per cent said they were worried a great deal about this and 27 per cent said that they were 'somewhat worried.' By contrast 59 per cent said they were not worried about these dangers. These findings confirm the experience of Republican Senator Richard Lugar, who made this issue a central plank in his unsuccessful presidential campaign. One year after the Oklahoma City bombing 66 per cent of Americans said that they were not worried about terrorism in public places in the US.[74] September 11 changed all that.

Through a combination of failures on America's part and a long series of lucky breaks on theirs, al-Qaeda managed to hit the US and hit it hard. But they could not follow up. They did threaten the lives of American civilians, but they posed no real threat to the security of the state itself. It would be extraordinarily difficult for them to repeat their attack on the US. It would of course not be at all difficult for them to hit the US in the way that the bombs in Bali, Madrid and London hit those cities, but to launch another such sophisticated attack would be very hard indeed and would require all the lucky breaks to fall their way again. The tactic of commandeering an airline and flying it into a building had a life span of a couple of hours. As soon as the heroic passengers on United Airlines flight 93 knew what was intended, they thwarted the plan. Added to the sense that they were willing and anxious to kill the largest possible number of Americans and therefore would not hesitate to use WMD was the fear that their next act would have to surpass the 9/11 attack in ferocity in order to keep up their momentum: hence the attraction to them of WMD.

Before 9/11 Americans ignored reports that al-Qaeda was interested in WMD. After 9/11 their interest became a *casus belli*, even though the evidence suggests that the ability to acquire these weapons was weaker after 9/11 with the overthrow of the Taliban. What changed was that the American public was now prepared to believe that terrorists wanted WMD and would use them. When this conviction was added to the widespread belief that al-Qaeda was linked to Saddam Hussein and the fear that he would give these weapons to al-Qaeda, the combination became a crucial factor in mobilizing support for the war on Iraq which was to have such portentous ramifications for the campaign against terrorism.

It is not quite true therefore that, in the words of President Bush, 'September 11 changed our world.' Rather it was America's reaction to September 11 that changed the world. The US suffered a terrorist attack unprecedented in its scale and destructiveness and in so doing lost its sense of security. The US also lost its sense of perspective. At home Americans became convinced that it was unsafe to fly, even though the facts clearly indicated otherwise. For the ten years from 1992 through 2001, including the deaths on 9/11, the risk of death while flying in the US was one in ten million or one in every 15 billion kilometres travelled.[75] Instead Americans took to their cars, an altogether more dangerous form of transport. Economists have calculated that among the uncounted casualties of 9/11 are the extra 1,200 fatalities on the road occasioned by the diversion from air to road transport after 9/11.[76] Abroad the American government conflated the threats it faced and based its policies on the vulnerabilities it felt, rather than on those threats. The heinousness of the atrocity, moreover, blinded the US to some of the legitimate objections to its policies overseas. One thing that did not change was Americans' confidence in the rectitude of their actions or the unassailability of their moral position.

Domestically, a weak and unpopular president, recently elected with a highly questionable mandate, was transformed into a war leader by a population seeking security. The enormous scale of the atrocity seemed to merit a powerful response and the US replied with the most potent weapon in its armoury, a declaration of war. But the war was declared not on those who had committed the atrocity, but rather on the tactic they had used to hurt it. It was a war America could not win.

7

Why the War on Terror Can Never Be Won

The security forces set about their work in a manner which might have been deliberately designed to drive the population into our arms. On the pretext of searching they burst into people's homes by day and night, made them stand for hours with their hands up, abused and insulted them . . . These attempts to frighten the people away from EOKA always had exactly the opposite effect to that intended: the population were merely bound more closely to the Organization and the young scorned the threat of the gallows.

General George Grivas, leader of EOKA[1]

The story had already started with the Shah's visit of '67, when Ohnesorg was shot – a completely harmless man. After that, things were different.

Two days earlier he had been in the Extrablatt office making an order, and I had happened to be helping out at the sales desk where I saw him briefly. Then three or four days later I was standing by his casket, and that gave me a really crazy flash. It's hard to describe it: something terrible got started in me. I couldn't get over it, that some idiot comes along and guns down an unarmed man.

I had been in a lot of barroom fights, and even though they were often really tough, you always kept some semblance of fairness . . . But a thing like this was just straight out murder to me.

Benno Ohnesorg. It did a crazy thing to me. When his casket went by, it just went ding, something got started there.

Bommi Baumann, member of June 2nd Movement[2]

The statements just quoted by two former terrorists, one a hardened Cypriot military commander, the other a young German radical, both attest to the difficulty of using the military to defeat terrorism. In the pages that follow I will argue that the experience of other countries suggests that the military alone cannot success-fully be deployed by democracies to defeat terrorism. I will argue that when the history of the immediate post-9/11 years comes to be written it will be seen as a period marked by two major mistakes and two major missed opportunities. The mistakes were a declaration of war against terrorism and the conflation of the threat from al-Qaeda with the threat from Saddam Hussein. The missed opportunities were the failure to educate the American public to the realities of terrorism and to the costs of America's sole superpower status and the failure to mobilize the international community behind the US in a transnational campaign against transnational terrorists.

As soon as the enormity of the atrocity became clear on September 11 the government reacted with a declaration of war. In an address to the nation on the night of the attack the president announced: 'Immediately following the first attack, I implemented our government's emergency-response plans. Our military is pow-erful, and it's prepared . . . America and our friends and allies join with all those who want peace and security in the world, and we stand together to win the war against terrorism.'[3] Nine days later, when the president addressed a joint session of Congress and the American people on September 20, 2001, the declaration of war on the tactic of terrorism was cast as a declaration of war on the emotion of terror: 'Our war on terror begins with al-Qaeda, but it does not end there. It will not end until every terrorist group of global reach has been found, stopped and defeated.'[4]

The scale of the attack was so enormous that this seemed a jus-tifiable response. On September 18 the US Congress authorized the president to 'use all necessary and appropriate force against those nations, organizations, or persons he determines planned, authorized, committed or aided the terrorist attacks that occurred on September 11, 2001, or harbored such organizations or persons, in order to prevent any future acts of international terrorism against the United States by such nations, organizations or persons'.[5]

Only hours after the attack on Pearl Harbor the US Congress voted a declaration of war against Japan and President Roosevelt signed the declaration the following day, December 8, 1941. In 2001 the memory of Pearl Harbor was often invoked. Also invoked were the 1996 fatwa of Osama bin Laden entitled 'Declaration of War against the Americans Occupying the Land of the Two Holy Places [Saudi Arabia]' and his second fatwa two years later: 'The ruling to kill the Americans and their allies – civilians and military – is an individual duty for every Muslim who can do it in any country in which it is possible to do it, in order to liberate the al-Aqsa Mosque and the holy mosque from their grip, and in order for their armies to move out of the lands of Islam, defeated and unable to threaten any Muslim.'[6] As bin Laden had declared war against the US, and in bombing American cities had committed an act of war against it, there was little doubt that war was the appropriate response. Nor was there much doubt about the outcome of this war: 'people have declared war on America and they have made a terrible mistake,' said the president.[7] Polls indicated that more than 90 per cent of the American public were confident of victory.[8]

Bin Laden's al-Qaeda was not the first violent group to declare war on America. On July 31, 1970, in Berkeley, California Bernadine Dohrn, an attractive young woman in her signature outfit of short skirt and high boots issued communiqué no. 1 from the Weather Underground, a militant offshoot of the SDS. It was entitled 'A Declaration of a State of War'. The statement read in part:

> All over the world, people fighting Amerikan imperialism look to Amerikan youth to use our strategic position behind enemy lines to join forces in the destruction of the empire . . . Tens of thousands have learned that protest and marches don't do it. Revolutionary violence is the only way . . . We will never live peaceably under this system . . . Within the next fourteen days we will attack a symbol or institution of American injustice.[9]

The words of the Weather Underground proved to be more violent than their deeds. Although they did bomb more than two dozen buildings, they sought to avoid human casualties, and they generally succeeded in that aim. But on the evening of August 24,

1970 members of the group drove a van filled with ammonium nitrate and fuel oil and detonated it outside the Sterling Hall building of the University of Wisconsin in Madison. A post-doctoral student in chemistry, Robert Fassnacht, who was working late, was killed in the explosion. The Weathermen had been trying to destroy the Army Mathematics Research Center. They believed that their violence was morally justified because their goal was to end greater violence and gross injustice by the US in Vietnam.

Nor was this the first time an American president had spoken of a war on terrorism. In his 1986 speech to the United Nations General Assembly President Ronald Reagan said: 'the United States believes that the understandings reached by the seven industrial democracies at the Tokyo summit last May make a good start towards an international accord in the war on terrorism.'[10] The phrase 'war on terrorism' had also been fairly widely used much earlier by the press to describe the efforts by Russian, European and eventually American governments to stop assassination attempts by international anarchists in the late nineteenth century.[11]

Of much more recent memory were other, metaphorical wars. In his State of the Union Address on January 8, 1964, President Lyndon Johnson declared a 'War on Poverty' which was designed to address the plight of 35 million Americans living in poverty that year. In 1971, President Richard Nixon declared a 'War on Drugs'. He called for an 'all-out offensive' on the problem of drug abuse in America and created the Office of National Drug Control Policy to respond to the problem.

This war was, of course, different. On September 12, 2001, NATO declared the action against the US to be an attack against all nineteen members of the alliance. This was the first time in the history of the western alliance that NATO invoked Article 5 of the Washington Treaty, which stipulates that an armed attack against one member of NATO will be considered an attack against every member. At the same time NATO and its erstwhile enemy, Russia, intensified their co-operation. It was clear that we were no longer in the realm of a metaphorical war.

The depth of support from around the world was unprecedented. In London the band outside Buckingham Palace movingly played

'The Star-Spangled Banner'. The headline of France's main daily newspaper, *Le Monde*, famously declared 'Nous sommes tous Américains'[12] (We are all Americans). German Chancellor Gerhard Schröder, who later won re-election largely on the strength of his opposition to the American-led invasion of Iraq, promised the US 'uneingeschränkte Solidarität' (unlimited solidarity).[13]

When the history of this period in American foreign policy comes to be written I believe this moment will be seen as a lost opportunity of major proportions. Here was a chance to recast international relations. Countries that had been allies and those that had been rivals throughout the Cold War could have been united against the threat of transnational terrorism. They were anxious to be used in this way. The US accepted their condolences but not their offers of support. It did not use the mechanism of NATO or any other international institution to fashion or implement a response. It felt strong enough to react on its own and so it did. An under secretary of defense later explained that the US 'was so busy developing its war plans that it did not have time to focus on co-ordinating Europe's military role'.[14]

A year after the attack NATO held a summit meeting in Prague. Lord Robertson, the secretary general of NATO and former British defence secretary, had very high hopes for the meeting. The plans for the summit envisioned the adoption of a comprehensive package of measures to combat terrorism and even the creation of a NATO Response Force, a technologically advanced, flexible and inter-operable force that would be available for immediate deployment following a decision by the NATO Council. Robertson hoped that NATO would become the focal point of the international fight against terrorism and demonstrate that NATO had changed to adapt to the new security environment. The meeting was intended both to discuss the expansion to former members of the Warsaw Pact and to demonstrate the strength of the traditional Atlantic alliance. As it turned out, the summit was dominated by the contentious issue of a possible war with Iraq. Secretary Rumsfeld's remark that 'the mission determines the coalition not the coalition the mission' was seen as a deliberate attempt to undermine NATO, the very embodiment of the Atlantic alliance. That remark was eclipsed in unpopularity only by Rumsfeld's subsequent dismissal of France and Germany (who opposed war in Iraq) as 'old Europe' in favour of the 'new Europe' of the east, countries that were more supportive of the US administration's plans to invade Iraq. When asked later why he did not use NATO to go into Iraq, Rumsfeld said: 'It hasn't crossed my mind.'[15]

It was soon widely believed in other countries that the US ignored the interests of everyone but itself. While all governments are expected to think of their own interests first, alliance leaders and superpowers are also expected to take into account the interests of others. By offering immediate and unconditional support to the US, western leaders were expressing genuine sentiments, but they were also expecting that in return they would be consulted by the US. They were soon disappointed.[16] These feelings were not limited to the elites. A Pew Research Center poll in May 2003 found that over 70 per cent of citizens in such generally friendly countries as Canada, Spain, the Netherlands and Russia believed that the US does not take the interests of others into account. Eighty-five per cent of the French, 66 per cent of the Germans and 55 per cent of the British felt the same way.[17]

The shared interest in combating terrorism and the declared willingness of NATO to dedicate itself to that end could have been used to transform international institutions into an effective means of pooling diverse and complementary resources for a common purpose. In so doing the security community that had emerged since the Second World War and that had effectively eliminated the legitimacy of the use of force to resolve conflicts between its members could have been extended to other countries anxious to join. To have invested in remaking the international order in this way, however, would have required a willingness to consult others and ultimately to constrain the exercise of American power. Unlike the Truman administration at the end of the Second World War, which took a long-range view of American interests, and used the opportunity afforded by the end of the war to remake international institutions, the Bush administration focused on the short-term response, and led a 'coalition of the willing' into Afghanistan and later Iraq.

There are any number of reasons why an American president of any ideological hue might have responded to the 9/11 attacks with a declaration of war. The enormity of the attacks seemed to call for it. Moreover, there is no more effective means of mobilizing a country domestically than by declaring war. Rivals come together, differences are forgotten and the country rallies first behind the leader and later behind the boys who fight in its name. There is another, more pragmatic reason. The accretion of power to the executive that inevitably occurs in time of war has always been an attractive by-product for national leaders.

The public was also overwhelmingly in favour of a declaration of war, though it is perhaps reasonable to point out that no other options were made available to them. Had they been proffered a list of options they might have responded differently. Two days after the attack 68 per cent of Americans polled by the *Los Angeles Times* said that they considered the country to be in a state of war.[18] There was overwhelming popular support for a resort to military force in response to the attacks. Opinion polls showed 85–92 per cent support for military action.[19] The public was also overwhelmingly confident that the US would find and punish the people responsible for the attacks. In a series of polls by different polling agencies in the weeks after 9/11 more than 90 per cent of the respondents expressed confidence in America's ability to catch the people responsible for the September 11 attacks.[20]

In spite of the popularity of the declaration of war, to declare war on what is, after all, a tactic does not appear to make a great deal of sense. One would never hear of war being declared on, say, precision guided bombing. It's not so much the tactic that ought to be the focus of our attentions as those who deploy the tactic. Later, the war on terrorism became the global war on terror (GWOT), which is an even more nebulous notion. Terror, like fear, is an emotion, so declaring war on an emotion is hardly a strategy conducive to success. When the president was not declaring war on terrorism or terror he was declaring war on evil. At a meeting with King Abdullah of Jordan, President Bush said: 'I have assured His Majesty that our war is against evil, not against Islam.'[21] Two months later he gave the same message to the Warsaw Conference: 'We do not fight Islam, we fight against evil.'[22] In January 2002 the president told a town meeting in California: 'Our war is a war against evil.'[23] On another occasion the president assured Americans that 'We will rid the world of evildoers.'[24]

There were, of course, alternatives available to declaring war on terrorism, terror and evil. The administration might, for example, have declared war on al-Qaeda or on Afghanistan, the state that harboured them. Had they done so there would have been some clear matrices of success or failure by which progress could have been measured. One might even be able to know, for example, when the war was over. But the scale of the atrocity and the desire to respond in sufficiently epic terms suggested that a war against a state or an organization wasn't enough. America wanted to wage war not just on al-Qaeda but on 'every terrorist group of global reach'.[25]

The problem with a declaration of war is that warfare conjures notions of victory and defeat. Yet as was obvious at the time and as we have begun to realize since, it is very difficult ever to declare victory in a war on terrorism or terror, much less evil. The US succeeded in defeating the Taliban in Afghanistan but that has not brought it victory in the war on terrorism. Indeed, according to polls, 87 per cent of the American public believed that, if the Taliban government of Afghanistan were toppled but Osama bin Laden and his top aides were not captured or killed, they would not have been successful in achieving their objectives in the war on terrorism.[26] The US has succeeded in severely curtailing the freedom of operation of the al-Qaeda leadership. It has captured many, but by no means all, of their leaders and destroyed their command, communication and training systems, yet this has not brought it victory in the war on terrorism.

If victory means making the US invulnerable to terrorist attack then it is never, ever, going to be victorious. So casting a conflict in terms of a war one cannot win is a big mistake. It is conceding far too much to one's adversary to allow them to demonstrate that you have not won the war. By dispatching any operative into any Starbucks or subway station or shopping mall in the country and blowing it up, a terrorist group could demonstrate that the most powerful country in the history of the world has not been able to beat them. This is making it much too easy for the terrorists.

Terrorists want to be considered soldiers at war with an enemy. Most aspire to gain enough support for their cause that they can, one day, field a real army. The concept of jihad as invoked by Islamic extremists, for example, is all about war. Terrorists constantly refer to themselves as soldiers. Sidique Khan, the teacher's aide from Leeds who blew up a London Underground train, declared: 'We are at war and I am a soldier. Now you too will feel the reality of this situation.'[27] Dermot Finucane remembers how proud he was that his brother John, a member of the IRA, was getting a military funeral. Terrorists constantly use military forms of address to one another and military forms of organization and discipline. In 1981 the ten republican prisoners jailed in Northern Ireland did not starve themselves to death to force the British out of Ireland. They did not starve themselves to death to unite the island of Ireland. They starved themselves to death in order to win political-prisoner status for themselves. It is enormously important for terrorists' sense of themselves that they be considered and treated as soldiers. The ultimate goal of any war must be to deny the adversary what it is that he wants. Terrorists want to be considered at war with the US, so for America to concede this to them is to grant them what they want, instead of doing its utmost to deny them what they want.

Terrorists like to be considered soldiers at war both because of the legitimacy they believe it brings their cause and also for the status they believe it confers on them. For the US to declare war on a bunch of radical extremists living under the protection of an impoverished Afghanistan is to elevate their stature in a way that they could not possibly hope to do themselves. Terrorists wish to be on the 'wanted' poster. (When Dermot Finucane finally made it on to the 'wanted' poster he was disappointed to have had to share the honour with thirty-five others.) To be elevated to the status of public enemy number one is just what a terrorist group want. It gives them stature among their potential recruits, which in turn wins them more followers. Declaring war on terrorists, in effect, hands them the renown they seek.

The language of warfare also induces what Michael Howard has called a 'war psychosis'. People expect immediate action. Certainly the Bush administration felt compelled to take immediate action in response to the attacks of 9/11 rather than wait for the Pentagon to produce carefully calibrated war plans. But the experience of other countries in combating terrorism makes abundantly clear that successful counter-terrorist campaigns require, above all, patience and a long-time horizon. The Provisional IRA emerged in the early months of 1970. They finally declared an end to their terrorist campaign and destroyed their arsenal thirty-five years later in 2005. It took an enormous amount of patience and careful planning by the British government to achieve that.

The other point, of course, is that a declaration of war has standing in international and domestic law. Such a declaration prompts the expectation in the international community that one will abide by the international conventions on the conduct of warfare. The most famous of these are known as the Geneva Conventions. They have a long lineage in international relations. Efforts to regulate the conduct of warfare have been around as long as warfare itself, but historically agreements bound the participants only in the conduct of a particular war. The first attempt to establish international standards for all wars was launched by the Swiss businessman Henri Dunant, who founded the International Red Cross in 1863. Dunant was appalled by the carnage caused by the Battle of Solferino in northern Italy. He visited Emperor Napoleon III and persuaded him to order the unconditional release of all captured doctors. In 1864 Dunant invited thirteen countries to attend a conference on the humane conduct of war. The outcome of the conference was the first Geneva Convention, which provided for the neutrality of military hospitals and medical transports; the treatment of wounded soldiers and medical staff as non-belligerents; the return of prisoners to their home country if they are unable to fight; and the adoption of the white flag with a red cross as a symbol of neutrality.

In 1899, the first Geneva Convention was supplemented by treaties on the use of asphyxiating gases and expanding bullets. In 1906, the second Geneva Convention, which extended the principles to war at sea, was signed. In 1929, after the trauma of the First

World War, two more Geneva Conventions were brought into being. They dealt with the treatment of the wounded and of prisoners of war. The atrocities of the Second World War, both on the battlefield and in prisoner-of-war camps, provided a further impetus to efforts to regulate the conduct of war. The result was the 1949 Geneva Convention, which modernized the earlier conventions and added another, pertaining to the treatment of civilians in time of war. In 1977 two further protocols were agreed, extending the protections to other forms of warfare like civil wars and wars of self-determination. Terrorism is not specifically mentioned. The Geneva Conventions are not the only agreements governing the conduct of war – there are also a number of international laws and agreements – but the attempt to contain the atrocities of war represented by the Geneva Conventions has widespread international legitimacy and overwhelming support among democratic states.

When the US declared a war on terrorism the international community expected that the US would be bound by the rules of warfare and in particular by the international conventions on treatments of civilians, the wounded and prisoners. The White House counsel and subsequently the attorney general, Alberto Gonzales, however, argued that the war on terrorism was a 'new paradigm [that] renders obsolete Geneva's strict limitations on questioning of enemy prisoners and renders quaint some of its provisions'.[28] The White House adopted the term 'enemy combatant' and used it as a blanket category to cover Afghan fighters and foreign mujahideen fighting in Afghanistan, as well as foreigners arrested in the US. The rubric was also extended to Americans captured both in the field and, most controversially, in the US. At the time many in the State Department argued vehemently against discarding international conventions and later believed that the abuses of prisoners carried out in Iraq and Afghanistan were a direct consequence of the decision to abandon the accepted norms of behaviour. The Abu Ghraib prisoner-abuse scandal in turn did an incalculable amount of damage to America's moral standing in the world and to the effort to win support for its campaign against terrorism.

By declaring war yet refusing to be bound by the agreed constraints on warfare and refusing to conduct its war through existing international institutions, the US alienated its allies and confirmed the worst views of neutrals and adversaries. In 2001, for example, according to a poll conducted by the Pew Research Center, three out of four Indonesians had a positive view of the US. Two years later, four out of five had a negative view.[29] A BBC poll in summer 2003 revealed that the vast majority of Jordanians and Indonesians considered the US to be more dangerous than al-Qaeda. A majority in India, Russia, South Korea and Brazil saw the US as more dangerous than Iran.[30] The US government believed that the atrocity committed against America was so great that it could not afford to have any constraints on the exercise of its power in response. Ironically, it was precisely the unbridled deployment of that unrivalled power that alienated America's allies, turned neutrals against it, swelled the ranks of its adversaries and destroyed its chances of achieving its objectives.

Warfare, of course, also implies the deployment of the military. Again, the experience of other countries in countering terrorism makes very clear that the military is too blunt an instrument to be relied upon exclusively to counter terrorism.

The war in Afghanistan was the first step in the war on terrorism. It had massive domestic popular support and overwhelming international support as well. Public support among Americans for military action in Afghanistan was a heady 94 per cent.[31] When the Taliban refused to turn over bin Laden and the leadership of al-Qaeda, the US dismissed all responses short of complete compliance as prevarication and immediately inserted American and British special forces into the country to make contact with local opponents of the Taliban regime.

On October 7, less than a month after the attacks on New York and Washington, US and British forces began an aerial bombing campaign targeting al-Qaeda and Taliban forces. The campaign was initially entitled 'Operation Infinite Justice' but was quickly renamed 'Operation Enduring Freedom' when it was pointed out that only God could dispense 'infinite justice'. The paltry Taliban air defences were soon destroyed (the US did not lose a single aircraft to enemy fire). Within a few days most al-Qaeda training sites had been badly damaged. The capital Kabul fell on November 12 and the al-Qaeda fighters retreated to the Tora Bora cave complex. Kunduz fell on November 25 and on December 7 Mullah Mohammad Omar, the leader of the Taliban, slipped out of the former stronghold of Kandahar, the last Taliban-controlled city. Meanwhile, by the time tribal forces backed by US special operations troops and air support took over the last defence post of the cave complex at Tora Bora on December 17 it became apparent that the al-Qaeda leadership had also slipped away. The war in Afghanistan succeeded in toppling the brutal Taliban regime but did not capture either the Taliban or al-Qaeda leadership, nor has it brought peace to the country.

The war in Afghanistan taught the lesson that had already been taught many times previously, that winning battles does not necessarily equate with winning wars, especially when it comes to fighting terrorists. The Russians had not been able to translate overwhelming military force into victory in Chechnya. The Israelis had not been able to translate their overwhelming military force into success in Lebanon or the occupied territories. The Peruvian government had also failed to achieve success against the Shining Path through the use of military force. As pointed out earlier, a seventy-man intelligence unit within the Peruvian police force was able to achieve what wave after wave of military deployment had failed to accomplish, the destruction of the Shining Path. These cases suggest that military force alone cannot win against terrorism, no matter how glaring the asymmetry in power. On the other hand, there are a few Latin American cases in which the military were successfully deployed against terrorism domestically, but never in a democracy.

In Chechnya, despite fighting two all-out wars in 1994–6 and 1999–2002 the formidable armed might of the Russian army was unable to defeat terrorism. The Russian army, moreover, was able to operate without many of the constraints on the use of force imposed on armies in more mature democracies. Casualty figures range from 40,000 to 70,000 on all sides, and yet Chechen terrorism continues.[32] Ominous too is the fact that the conduct of the war has radicalized the terrorist movement in Chechnya. While initially Chechen terrorists were nationalists seeking independence from the Russian Federation, now Chechen terrorist groups have been infiltrated by radical Islamists and consequently are becoming more absolutist, less willing to constrain their violence and less likely to accept a negotiated settlement. Some of their actions, like the Beslan school massacre that killed 331 people including 186 children, rank among the most heinous acts of terrorism ever.

No country has as much depth of experience in fighting terrorism as Israel. Yet, in spite of having a superbly trained, equipped and motivated army, Israel was unable to defeat Hezbollah in Lebanon. Israel initially invaded Lebanon in 1982 to displace the Palestinian presence there, but by 1985 Hezbollah had succeeded in driving Israel back to a 'security zone' along the southern border. For fifteen more years Israeli forces clashed with Hezbollah before finally withdrawing from Lebanon altogether in May 2000. In the course of this fighting 21,000 civilians, 2,100 Lebanese fighters and over 900 Israeli soldiers are estimated to have been killed.[33] During the conflict the Israeli army won many of the battles, often suffering one casualty for every ten inflicted, but Israel was unable to translate these military victories into political success. Furthermore, the Israeli government discovered that the country was willing to accept far fewer casualties than the adversary. Hezbollah were well aware of this difference and exploited it skilfully. In one prisoner exchange in January 2004, for example, 700 Lebanese and Palestinian prisoners were exchanged for one Israeli businessman and the bodies of three Israeli soldiers. In spite of all their experience and all their military prowess and in spite of having a willing proxy on the ground in the form of the Southern Lebanese Army (SLA), the Israelis were not able to defeat Hezbollah. Indeed, when Israel finally withdrew from Lebanon in 2000 in spite, or more likely because, of its policies of armed invasion, targeted assassinations and collective punishment, Hezbollah was a stronger organization than when Israel first crossed the border in 1982.

There are a number of reasons why it was difficult for Israel to prevail in Lebanon. Hezbollah proved to be a resilient and skilful organization. It had powerful state sponsors in Iran and Syria. The Lebanese state was so weak as to be ineffectual and hence unable to serve as a useful ally of Israel even if it had wanted to. Moreover, the fact that Israel did not control the territory of Lebanon means that it was unable to develop an effective intelligence network. The actions of the Israeli army and Hezbollah's success against it served to generate more support for Hezbollah among the population at large. Added to this, Israel was constrained by domestic opinion at home. Israelis were both uncomfortable with the role of their democratic state as an army of occupation and unwilling to bear significant casualties among their citizen soldiers. Israel was also constrained by international opinion abroad that was deeply critical of many of its more forceful actions. These same factors are likely to constrain any other democracy in its effort to use military force against terrorists.

There are, however, some success stories. In a number of countries, especially in Latin America, the military have been successfully deployed to defeat terrorist groups. In these instances, the military operated in a fashion that is entirely inconsistent with the principles of liberal democracy. Argentina provides one of the more notorious examples. After the death of Juan Perón, a state of emergency was declared and the military acted with impunity. A military junta assumed power in a coup in March 1976. Later that year the junta launched what was known as the 'Process of National Reconstruction', better known as 'The Process', in an effort to stamp out left-wing terrorism (of which Perón was believed to have been fairly tolerant). The two main terrorist groups operating at the time, the Montañeros and the People's Revolutionary Army (ERP), exploited the vacuum left by Perón's death. As so often happens with the use of violence, the goal was soon broadened from defeating terrorism to exterminating all political opposition. The scale of human rights violations and 'disappearances' that ensued was staggering. People suspected of being terrorists, or related to or sympathetic to terrorists, were taken prisoner and never heard from again. The various units of the security forces competed with one another in their zeal to exterminate the terrorists. As one army commander, General Luciano Menendez, famously said: 'We are going to have to kill 50,000 people: 25,000 subversives, 20,000 sympathizers, and we will make 5,000 mistakes.'[34] The final death toll is unclear but it is believed that between 10,000 and 30,000 people were killed in the name of *el Proceso*.[35] More than a thousand people had direct involvement in the interrogation, torture and murder of suspects between 1976 and 1979. Terrorist attacks stopped.

Argentina is not the only example. In Chile the Movement of the Revolutionary Left (MIR) waged a terrorist campaign against the state between 1965 and 1989. Their base was in the countryside where they forcibly seized land for the peasantry, and from there they moved to the cities to launch campaigns of urban guerrilla warfare. There, as in Argentina, the military were deployed domestically against terrorism, and again gross violations of human rights resulted. The Chilean military believed the state to be threatened by terrorism, especially after the leftist Salvador Allende was elected president. He was ousted, with American assistance, in a military coup in 1973. The new regime immediately set about brutally quelling all opposition. The junta promptly established the National Directorate of Intelligence (DINA) to eradicate terrorist subversion. Much of the initial repression was driven by a mysterious 'Plan Z', thought to be a plot hatched by communists to take over the army. Troops were ordered to uncover the plot and eliminate those involved. Officers showing insufficient zeal were peremptorily dismissed. It now transpires that the plan was probably fabricated as an excuse for repression. Most of the terrorist leadership was killed or captured by the end of 1974, but MIR emerged again briefly in 1980 and again was soon suppressed. The Chilean government succeeded in eliminating the resort to terrorism but at a price – the gross violation of human and civil rights. The cost in human lives is difficult to calculate precisely. A public monument located in the General Cemetery of Santiago has the names of 4,000 victims who were executed or 'disappeared' for political reasons. A February 1995 report by the Corporation for Reparation and Reconciliation listed 2,095 extra-judicial executions and deaths under torture, and an additional 1,102 disappearances.[36]

In Brazil, too, the military successfully defeated a number of terrorist groups. As in several other Latin American countries, Brazilian terrorist groups started out in the countryside trying to establish a mass base and then moved into the cities to wage urban guerrilla warfare. Indeed, the manual of the urban guerrilla widely read by terrorist groups throughout the world, *The Mini-manual of the Urban Guerrilla*, was written by Carlos Marighella, the leader of the Action for National Liberation (ALN), one of the largest of Brazil's terrorist groups. The threat from terrorism in the mid-1960s caused the Brazilian government to evolve from a moderate military regime engaged in fostering economic stability into an ever more repressive military dictatorship determined to restore order. Brazilian terrorists proved particularly adept at kidnapping high-profile individuals, and in these instances the government negotiated concessions to win the release of the prisoners. Simultaneously the military intelligence service engaged in a brutal counter-terrorist campaign that included the use of death squads, torture of prisoners and widespread arrests. One of the government's most significant successes occurred in November 1969, when Marighella and a band of his followers were located and killed in a shoot-out. By the end of 1971 the tactic of urban guerrilla warfare had been abandoned in Brazil.

The lessons of Latin American counter-terrorism appear to suggest that if the military are deployed domestically and freed from constraints they can indeed defeat terrorism. They are free to operate in ways not open to democracies. Indeed the democratic government of Uruguay were replaced by military rule in 1973 precisely because of their failure to respond effectively to the terrorism of the Tupamaros. In this instance the Uruguayan military were encouraged to pull off a coup by the neighbouring military regime in Brazil, which felt that the Tupamaros posed a threat to their security. With the unbridled use of force the military did defeat the Tupamaros.

In Venezuela, however, the government of Rómulo Betancourt, the country's first democratically elected president and himself a former communist, demonstrated that even under the most difficult of circumstances a Latin American government could successfully counter terrorist movements without becoming a military dictatorship. In the early 1960s Betancourt withstood terrorism from several left-wing terrorist groups as well as threats from right-wing elements in the military. The Peruvian example also suggests that all-out war is not necessarily the most effective means of defeating terrorism. The tactics of the Argentinian,

Brazilian and Chilean military governments, moreover, are simply not available to democratic governments. They eradicated insurgent terrorism but in so doing replaced it with what was in effect state terrorism, the wanton abuse of force. No government could practise these tactics and remain a democracy because they entail the replacement of the rule of law, the essence of democracy, by the rule of force.

In declaring a war on terrorism, therefore, the US government did not have in mind the kind of war on terrorism practised by Latin American generals. They had in mind the legitimate conduct of war as employed on the western front against the Nazis in the Second World War. But the problem was that the US was not facing an enemy like the Nazis. President Bush has frequently compared al-Qaeda's ideology to that of fascism, Stalinism and Nazism, but he has done so to equate the fanaticism and immorality of their ideology not their military battalions. Using military armies against the Nazis could work because they were deploying military forces against their enemies, but al-Qaeda was deploying a handful of individual suicide bombers against the US. Its massed armies are not the best way to deal with them.

As the Cypriot nationalist George Grivas, head of the terrorist group EOKA, said of the British field marshal who was waging a campaign against him: 'Harding persisted in his error: he underrated his enemy on the one hand and overrated his forces on the other. But one does not use a tank to catch field-mice – a cat will do the job better.'[37] Declaring a war on terrorism is very much a case of using a tank to catch a field-mouse.

Some might reasonably argue that the experiences of Latin American countries or countries like Russia and Israel have little relevance for the US as its polity and its culture are so different. But the same argument could hardly be made of its closest ally, the United Kingdom, its partner in what Winston Churchill first called the 'special relationship'. Few countries have had the depth of experience in counter-terrorism and counter-insurgency of the United Kingdom. Many of the colonial movements seeking independence from Britain resorted to terrorist tactics at one point or another. Initially Britain relied simply on superior military force, but, for example in India, this strategy was ultimately unsuccessful. After the Second World War Britain was faced with a range of insurgencies in opposition to colonial rule. In Malaya and Kenya it was deemed to have been successful. The Cyprus conflict ended with compromise, and in Aden the British withdrew and Marxist insurgents took power.

On the basis of their extensive experience the British military devised what were known as the Thompson Principles, six principles of counter-insurgency warfare. These are:

1) the primacy of the political
2) co-ordination of government machinery
3) obtaining intelligence
4) separating the insurgent from his base of support
5) neutralizing the insurgent
6) post-insurgency planning

Armed with these principles, with years of experience and with a professional, highly trained and widely respected military, Britain faced the emergence of the Provisional IRA in Northern Ireland in 1970. There are a number of lessons to be derived from the British experience of using the military to counter a terrorist group. There is no doubt that the IRA was a very different type of terrorist group than al-Qaeda, but Britain enjoyed a great many advantages that the US does not have. The internal security forces of the state, the Northern Ireland police force and the locally recruited regiments of the British army were all entirely on the side of the British. Further, the British troops spoke the same language as the terrorists and the community from which they derived their support, which greatly facilitated intelligence gathering. What's more, the army was operating close to home in a geographically limited area without difficult logistical support issues to contend with. Despite all these advantages, and a $5 billion annual subvention from the British Treasury, and despite the fact that they were prepared to deploy up to 30,000 British troops on top of the local security forces, the British discovered that they could not defeat the IRA, which had only a few hundred members.

James Callaghan, Home Secretary in Harold Wilson's Labour government, ordered the deployment of British troops on August 14, 1969, in response to a request from the prime minister of Northern Ireland, James Chichester-Clark. The British government soon learned that it is altogether easier to deploy troops than to remove them. The deployment was intended to be a temporary measure but the troops were still there thirty-five years later. After the initial deployment it was feared that any withdrawal of troops might appear to constitute a victory for the terrorists, so the troops remained. They were sent in to restore order in the wake of disturbances caused by the civil rights movement, but also to protect the minority Catholic population from Protestant mobs and the actions of the undisciplined and highly partisan police force. Their arrival was initially welcomed by the Catholic community. The IRA was nowhere to be found.

Irrespective of the good intentions of the military, the arrival of the heavily armed soldiers and military vehicles on to civilian streets soon transformed the situation. The Provisional IRA was created in early 1970 to defend the Catholic community. The military soon found themselves on the side of law and order but in a divided society that made them partisan. The presence of the military on the streets enabled the IRA to portray the situation as one of British imperialism and provided target practice for novice terrorists. Early in the conflict three events involving the military served to alienate the Catholic population, win recruits for the IRA and win admiration for them even from people who were not prepared to support their methods.

Faced with marauding mobs and a complicit police force, Catholics barricaded themselves into 'no-go' areas. Realizing the danger of permitting the IRA to recruit and train with impunity, the British army launched 'Operation Motorman', the biggest military operation in Ireland in the twentieth century. Thirty-one thousand troops were deployed to pull down the barricades. The operation succeeded in breaking up the no-go areas and turning their inhabitants into enemies of the army. This operation was soon followed by the biggest political miscalculation of the entire conflict, the introduction of internment without trail. Again, it was the military that implemented the policy, carrying out night-time raids throughout Catholic areas and terrorizing whole neighbourhoods, not to mention the families of those arrested. That the policy was enforced almost entirely against Catholics, who by no means enjoyed a monopoly on the use of illegal violence, and that a great many of those interned were innocent of any connection to the IRA again infuriated the local population, turning them against the British government and into the arms of the IRA.

The third military action that proved to be both a tragedy in itself and a recruitment bonanza for the IRA was the incident known as 'Bloody Sunday'. On January 30, 1972, British soldiers of the Parachute Regiment, apparently believing themselves to be under attack, opened fire on civil rights marchers, killing thirteen on the spot. TV images of terrified youngsters ducking for cover and priests waving white handkerchiefs as they carried the wounded to safety completed the alienation of the population the military had recently arrived to protect. The heavy-handed tactics in which soldiers are trained can have an enormously powerful and negative effect when deployed in a civilian context, as the British military soon discovered. Their very physical presence, complete with weaponry and armoured cars, cannot help but instil fear, incite resentment and intimidate.

As often happens in such conflicts, the military themselves were among the first to appreciate the realities of the situation. The British army did not enjoy the deployment in Northern Ireland, seeing it as a distraction from the more important task for which they were trained, defending Europe from the Soviet Union. In 1978 the commander of the land forces in Northern Ireland, General J. M. Glover, wrote a secret intelligence estimate of the IRA. The report was bitterly criticized because it concluded that, Britain's overwhelming military strength notwithstanding, the IRA could not be defeated militarily. The report also rejected the government's view that the members of the IRA were thugs and criminals: 'Our evidence of the calibre of rank and file terrorists does not support the view that they are merely mindless hooligans drawn from the unemployed and unemployable.'[38] Glover concluded:

The Provisionals' campaign of violence is likely to continue while the British remain in Northern Ireland . . . PIRA will probably continue to recruit the men it needs. They will still be able to attract enough people with leadership talent, good education and manual skills to continue to enhance their all-round professionalism. The movement will retain popular support sufficient to maintain secure bases in the traditional Republican areas.[39]

Events were to bear out Glover's analysis.

The British government had not declared a war on terrorism in Northern Ireland but their deployment of the military in the province permitted the IRA to cast the situation as a war and themselves as the legitimate adversary of the British army. The presence of the army in a civilian setting and the heavy-handed tactics that necessarily go along with this attracted popular support for the IRA in their role as adversary of the British army. The presence of the military on the ground did help to curtail IRA violence, and after the first few years the military and the terrorists arrived at a stalemate punctuated by atrocities carried out by the IRA and successful security operations undertaken by the army. The resolution of the problem and the end of the terrorist campaign of the IRA, however, was brought about only by years of painstaking negotiation and engagement with the grievances that fuelled the support for the terrorists. The fact that 30,000 British soldiers supported by thousands more local security forces could not defeat a few hundred members of the IRA would certainly suggest that the American military operating thousands of miles from home, in an alien culture and often without the support of reliable local security forces, are unlikely to defeat every terrorist group of global reach.

The second major mistake of the post-9/11 period was the conflation of two very distinct security issues: the threat from al-Qaeda and the threat from Saddam Hussein. Reasonable people have disagreed on the wisdom of the war in Iraq, but from a counter-terrorist point of view there can be little doubt that it was a terrible mistake. There were three sets of arguments presented in support of the war. The first was that Saddam Hussein had weapons of mass destruction that he might himself use or give to terrorists to use against the US and its allies. This argument had widespread support in the US, especially among conservatives who regretted not finishing Saddam off the last time, in the first Gulf War of 1991. The second set of arguments was that Hussein was a genocidal maniac who had brutalized his countrymen and that as a humanitarian gesture he should be stopped. This argument appealed to liberals, especially those who felt that the west had unconscionably stood by and done nothing to stop genocide in Rwanda. Then there was the argument that Saddam was linked to al-Qaeda. In his famous speech at the United Nations in February 2003, Secretary of State Colin Powell laid out the American case for invasion. The bulk of his case rested on evidence of Iraqi development of weapons of mass destruction. He also argued that the fact that the Jordanian-born terrorist Abu Mus'ab al-Zarqawi had operated in the north-east corner of Iraq and had spent two months in Baghdad, where he received medical treatment, was evidence of collusion between Saddam and bin Laden.[40]

Reports from members of the administration, such as counter-terrorism co-ordinator Richard Clarke and Treasury Secretary Paul O' Neil, as well as from those who interacted with them such as Chancellor Schröder, all attest to the fact that immediately after the 9/11 attacks senior members of the administration believed that there must be a link between Saddam and al-Qaeda and started to anticipate action against Iraq. Deputy Defense Secretary Paul Wolfowitz, in particular, pushed hard for attacking Iraq right away. In a memo dated September 17, he argued that if there was even a 10 per cent chance that Saddam Hussein was behind the 9/11 attacks maximum priority should be placed on eliminating that threat. He also argued that the odds in fact were far more than one in ten.[41]

The American public continued to believe that Iraq was implicated in the September 11 attacks long after the evaporation of any evidence suggesting a link. A *Washington Post* poll in August 2003 found that 69 per cent of Americans believed that Saddam Hussein 'was personally involved in the September 11 terrorist attacks' – down from 78 per cent in the days following the attack.

A whopping 82 per cent believed that Saddam 'has provided assist-ance to Osama bin Laden and his terrorist network'.[42] This remark-able public misperception continued. A Harris poll conducted in February 2005 found that 64 per cent believed that Saddam Hussein had strong links to al-Qaeda, 47 per cent believed Saddam helped to plan and support the 9/11 attacks, and 44 per cent believed that several of the 9/11 attackers were Iraqis, when in fact none were.[43]

The public misperception was in large part attributable to state-ments from the president and senior members of the administration which indicated a connection. Those within the government and those outside who studied al-Qaeda knew of bin Laden's deep-seated animosity towards the secular and corrupt regime of Saddam Hussein. They knew that, as mentioned earlier, bin Laden had offered to fight Saddam to eject him from Kuwait. They also knew, as the 9/11 Commission reported, that bin Laden was sponsoring anti-Saddam Islamists in Iraqi Kurdistan and trying to attract them to join forces with him.[44] Nevertheless, in the absence of hard evidence of any link between Iraq and al-Qaeda, senior members of the administration repeatedly implied that there was evidence of a link. Vice President Dick Cheney, for example, several times referred to allegations of a meeting in Prague between 9/11 hijacker Mohammad Atta and a senior Iraqi intelligence officer. He told reporters in December 2001, March 2002 and September 2003 that reports of this meeting were credible.[45] They were not. In September 2002 Defense Secretary Rumsfeld asserted that American intelligence had 'bulletproof' evidence of links between al-Qaeda and Saddam Hussein.[46] As late as September 2003, Vice President Cheney described Iraq as 'the geographic base of the terrorists who have had us under assault for many years, but most especially on 9/11'.[47] The president was obliged to disavow these comments and said clearly on September 17, 2003: 'No, we've had no evidence that Saddam Hussein was involved with September 11.'[48]

Once the occupation of Iraq occurred and the troops failed to discover the existence of any weapons of mass destruction, the administration were obliged to retreat to the other rationales for the war, the link with terrorism and the humanitarian removal of a brutal dictator. Given the political predilections of this particular administration, the first argument had more resonance. The war in Iraq was then recast as the central front in the war on terror. In the words of the president: 'The terrorists regard Iraq as the central front in their war against humanity. And we must recognize Iraq as the central front in our war on terror.'[49] Speeches by members of the administration on the Iraq war are littered with references to the 9/11 attacks. In his famous speech on board the USS *Abraham Lincoln*, under the 'Mission Accomplished' banner, in which he declared the 'end of major combat' in Iraq, President Bush stated: 'The liberation of Iraq is a crucial advance in the campaign against terror . . . We have not forgotten the victims of September 11 – the last phone calls, the cold murder of children, the searches in the rubble. With those attacks the terrorists and their supporters declared war on the United States. And war is what they got.'[50] Two years later he told the troops assembled in Fort Bragg: 'The troops here and across the world are fighting a global war on terror. The war reached our shores on September 11, 2001 . . . Iraq is the latest battlefield in this war.'[51]

The 9/11 Commission investigated the allegations of connections between al-Qaeda and Saddam Hussein's regime and declared that they had found no evidence that any 'contacts ever developed into a collaborative operational relationship . . . Nor have we seen evidence indicating that Iraq cooperated with al-Qaeda in developing or carrying out any attacks against the United States.'[52]

By waging war in Iraq and conflating America's enmity with al-Qaeda and its enmity with Saddam Hussein, the US government have created a self-fulfilling prophecy. In October 2004 an erstwhile rival of bin Laden and one of the leaders of the Iraqi insurgency, al-Zarqawi, pledged his allegiance and that of the terrorist group Tawhid wal-Jihad to bin Laden in a statement posted on the internet and entitled 'Oath of loyalty of leader Abu Mus'ab al-Zarqawi towards the Sheikh of the Mujahideen, Osama bin Laden'.[53] Ironically, in autumn 2005, in a communication between al-Qaeda's second in command, Ayman al-Zawahiri, and Zarqawi, we appear to have uncovered a case of an attempt by the al-Qaeda leadership to moderate al-Zarqawi's violence.[54]

The insurgency in Iraq is driven by opposition to the US occupation of the country. The insurgents are made up of local nationalists determined to oust America from Iraq and foreign fighters who see the US army and want to eject it from the region. The little information we have on these insurgents all suggests that, far from being hardened members of terrorist groups, they have been recruited and radicalized by the US presence. They find America's claims that it is occupying Iraq to defend New York and deploying an army to import democracy so implausible that they do not believe it. Instead, they believe the claims of those who say the US is a self-interested army of occupation interested only in dominating the region and exploiting its oil wealth. Far from eliminating the terrorists, America's war in Iraq has spawned a whole new generation of terrorists. Iraq is proving to be the training ground for the next generation of terrorists, just as the Soviet invasion of Afghanistan was for the earlier generation of terrorists and just as those of us who studied terrorism for years before 9/11 said would happen if the US and its allies were to confound the threat from Iraq and the threat from terrorism.

While the American public was strongly supportive of the government's action, the international community was appalled. In the face of widespread scepticism within the international community and downright opposition from many other quarters, the US insisted that Iraq was indeed the central front of the war on terrorism and proceeded to invade, without the sanction of the United Nations. The war on Iraq deflected the attention of the military away from Afghanistan and the search for the perpetrators of the September 11 attacks, as well as diverting it from the vital task of rebuilding a country devastated first by war and then by the Taliban. Moreover, America's invasion seemed to confirm the view of its adversaries that it was in fact at war with Islam. In the court of public opinion its actions appeared to be altogether more in keeping with the motives attributed to it by its enemies and much harder to reconcile with its own professed principles. By injecting its army into the Middle East, America presented itself as an army of occupation against which its enemy has rallied, in essence repeating the folly of the Soviet Union's invasion of Afghanistan in

1979. Just as the Soviet war in Afghanistan proved to be a powerful mobilizing force for the mujahideen, so the US invasion of Iraq has proved to be a beacon for a new generation of Islamic radicals. In other words, America played right into the hands of its enemies.

The complete collapse in international support for the US in the face of the invasion of Iraq is simply extraordinary. The trend held in countries normally friendly, in those normally cautious or neutral and in those normally hostile. In France the number viewing the US unfavourably soared from 34 per cent in the summer of 2002 to 67 per cent in March 2003. In Germany the figure went from 35 to 71 per cent in the same period. In Russia the number rose from 33 to 68 per cent, in Indonesia from 56 to 83 per cent, in Turkey from 55 to 84 per cent, in Pakistan from 69 to 81 per cent, in Lebanon from 59 to 71 per cent and in Jordan from 75 to 99 per cent.[55]

The widespread unpopularity of the war in Iraq has undermined international support for America's war on terrorism and American credibility generally. A significant percentage of people in France (57 per cent) and Germany (49 per cent) have come to agree with the view that is common in the Muslim world, namely that the US is exaggerating the threat from terrorism. By contrast, only 13 per cent of Americans think so. In a March 2004 survey solid majorities in France and Germany and 44 per cent in Britain maintained that the war on terror was not a sincere effort to reduce terrorism. Believing in US competence and unwilling to accept US sincerity, citizens of other countries have come to conclude that there must be other motives behind the US war on terror. Majorities of those who doubt American sincerity in seven of the nine countries surveyed in 2004 believe that America's real motive is to control Middle Eastern oil. Almost as many believe that America's motivation is world domination.[56] In effect, they find al-Qaeda's propaganda more credible than that of the United States.

If the two mistakes of this period were declaring war on terrorism and painting Saddam Hussein and Osama bin Laden with the same brush, and the first missed opportunity was the unwillingness to mobilize a willing international community behind a campaign against al-Qaeda, the second significant missed opportunity was the chance to educate the American public in the realities of terrorism and in the implications of US global pre-eminence. Far from trying to educate the public, America's leaders played to their fears. While asserting that Muslims in general were in no way responsible, the US authorities summarily picked up about 1,200 Arab Americans and detained them for months without access to counsel or other protections. Rather than attempting to put the terrible atrocity of 9/11 into perspective, they fanned the outrage. Rather than countenancing the possibility that certain of America's actions might have reinforced resentment towards it, US leaders divided the world into good and evil and announced that those who were not with America were with the terrorists.

The US might have used the opportunity to think carefully about the question so many Americans were asking: why do they hate us? Instead of asserting, in essence, that it was because they are evil and we are good, it might have helped the American public to understand the perspective of the powerless. It might have helped Americans to understand that the purity of their motives, unquestioned in their own minds, is not self-evident to others. It might have had a national conversation about the price of being a global superpower, of being the most powerful country in history. Other great powers before have bred resentment, and not because they were more self-interested, or less competent, than the US. Other empires, however, have been run by a whole segment of the population in the imperial bureaucracies made up of the younger sons of the wealthy, or the adventurous in search of opportunity, who lived among their colonies overseas. The US has sought to run its empire by exporting only its movies and television shows, not its younger sons.

America has believed that the superiority of its values and its system of government is so self-evident that only the ignorant or the evil could reject it. Rather than use the shock of the 9/11 attacks, and the thirst for explanation so evident among the American public, to explore the complexities of its global position, its vulnerability to terrorism and the best means of countering it, the US declared that those who were not with it were against it. Rather than discuss how America as a society could develop resilience to terrorism and devise a policy to contain it, it simply resolved to smash it. Rather than use the opportunity to examine itself, it resorted to simplistic formulas of good and evil.

In responding to the attacks of 9/11 with a declaration of war on terror the US mirrored the behaviour of its adversary. Bin Laden has ignored the rich complexity and nuanced teachings of Islam and superimposed a highly simplified Manichaean view of good and evil. He represents the good servant of Allah. The US represents the infidel. In their response, Americans adopted the same black and white view of the world, only in their view they represent goodness and he represents evil. Nowhere was this similarity more in evidence than in the unfortunate use of the term 'crusade' in describing the war on terror. A few days after the attack President Bush told reporters that 'this crusade, this war on terrorism, is going to take a while'.[57] The word might have been dismissed as an unfortunate slip of the tongue had it not been repeated in a set speech to the troops in Alaska some months later. In that instance the president said of the Canadians: 'They stand with us in this incredibly important crusade to defend freedom.'[58]

While westerners may see the crusades as a romantic military episode in ancient history, in the Middle East today the crusades are well remembered. The charter of Hamas, for example, deals at length with the fate of the crusaders who held Jerusalem for 200 years before being expelled by the Muslim warrior Saladin. Hamas regards the Israeli occupation of Jerusalem today along the same lines. By their own account the crusaders slaughtered 70,000 Muslims when they conquered Jerusalem in 1099, and while they probably exaggerated the number the memory runs very deep. By using the term 'crusade' President Bush appeared to many in the Middle East to demonstrate that the US war on terrorism was actually a war of Christianity against Islam, just as bin Laden has sought to cast it.

One of the striking features of bin Laden's many statements is the endless litany of grievances against the west. He never takes into account the suffering he has inflicted on others, even of the hundreds of innocent Africans killed and injured in the attacks on the American embassy in Nairobi in 1998. In the US response to bin

Laden it appears that for Americans, too, only their suffering, only their grievances, matter. In fighting back at al-Qaeda they inadvertently killed a large number of civilians. By August 2002 the estimated number of Afghan civilian deaths from US bombing was 3,125 to 3,620 – that is, significantly more than the number of civilians killed by al-Qaeda on 9/11.[59] These numbers never became a topic of discussion, much less a cause of concern in the United States. Americans were so taken with the extent of their own suffering that they didn't consider the suffering they inflicted on others. It goes without saying that a significant difference between the civilian casualties in both cases is that the ones America suffered were intended while the ones it inflicted were accidental. The suffering of the victims, however, was undoubtedly the same.

In all his statements bin Laden has purported to be the defender of Muslims against American aggression. He claims his actions are in reaction to those of the US and that he seeks only to stop Americans from inflicting suffering on others. In just the same way, Americans claim that they are the defenders and he is the aggressor, that his attack on them was completely unprovoked, and that they wish only to stop those who inflict terror on others. On the day of the attack the president said: 'A great people has been moved to defend a great nation.'[60] A few days later he said: 'We did not seek this conflict but we will win it.'[61] For his part, bin Laden repeatedly claims to be the defender against the American aggressor. He argued: 'Our acts are a reaction to your own acts, which are represented by the destruction and killing of our kinfolk in Afghanistan, Iraq and Palestine . . . the one who starts injustice bears greater blame.'[62]

One of the most frequently used words in President Bush's speeches on the war on terrorism is 'freedom'. 'America was targeted for attack because we're the brightest beacon for freedom and opportunity in the world.'[63] 'Our enemies murder because they despise our freedom and our way of life.'[64] 'Either you stand for freedom or you stand with tyranny.'[65] 'We're responding to a global campaign of fear with a global campaign of freedom. And once again we will see freedom's victory.'[66] Bin Laden, however, also claims to be fighting for freedom and dismisses US claims to the contrary. In his address to the American people shortly before the presidential election in 2004, he said: 'I say to you that security is an indispensable pillar of human life and that men do not forfeit their security, contrary to Bush's claim that we hate freedom. If so, then let him explain to us why we don't strike, for example, Sweden? And we know that freedom-haters don't possess defiant spirits like those of the nineteen — may Allah have mercy on them. No, we fight because we are free men who don't sleep under oppression. We want to restore freedom to our nation; just as you lay waste to our nation, so shall we lay waste to yours.'[67]

Just as bin Laden seems to be supremely confident that Allah is on his side, US leaders have expressed equal conviction that God is on theirs. In the words of the president: 'Embedded in every soul is the deep desire to live in freedom. I understand freedom is not America's gift to the world; freedom is Almighty God's gift to each man and woman in this world . . . May God bless the people of this great state. May God bless our troops. And may God continue to bless the United States of America.'[68] By invoking God on its side in the war on terrorism the US facilitates a view of the conflict in the cosmic terms in which its enemies see it. This encourages Americans too to 'absolutize' the conflict, to demonize the enemy and to dismiss all responses short of all-out victory. It helps them, in other words, to see the conflict in the terms bin Laden sees it.

The president put it this way: 'In fact, we're not facing a set of grievances that can be soothed and addressed. We're facing a radical ideology with unalterable objectives: to enslave whole nations and intimidate the world. No act of ours invited the rage of the killers — and no concession, bribe or act of appeasement would change or limit their plans for murder.'[69] In so saying the president delegit-imizes any effort to engage with the grievances that might have intensified support for bin Laden. By invoking God on their side, America is inclined to see itself as representing all that is good in the world and the enemy representing all that is evil: 'We believe in human rights, and the human dignity of every man, woman, and child on this earth. The terrorists believe that all human life is expendable. They share a hateful ideology that rejects tolerance and crushes all dissent. They envision a world where women are

beaten, children are indoctrinated, and all who reject their ideology of violence and extremism are murdered.'[70] Hearing this just
confirms the terrorists in their view that God is on their side and
that this perversion of their perspective must be deliberate. In bin
Laden's words: 'Had he been truthful about his claim for peace . . .
he also would not have lied to people and said that we hate freedom
and kill for the sake of killing. Reality proves our truthfulness and
his lie.'[71] By invoking God in its response, therefore, the US is again
playing into the hands of the terrorists and sharing the view of
cosmic conflict propounded by its opponents.

By using the extreme language of conviction that bin Laden
uses, by declaring war, even a crusade, against him in response to
his war against the US, Americans are mirroring his actions. They
are elevating his stature, they are permitting him to set the terms of
their interactions. Given that he has a very weak hand and they
have a very strong hand, they should not be letting him set the para-
meters of the game.

The goal of any combatant in warfare is to deny the adversary
the objectives he seeks. As argued earlier, terrorists have both
primary and secondary objectives; al-Qaeda's rhetoric combines
both practical policy objectives and grand religious visions. But, as
I have argued, like other terrorists al-Qaeda seeks three objectives:
revenge, renown and reaction. The first they get for themselves, the
other two they must get from others. By declaring a war on terror
we are, in effect, giving al-Qaeda what they want. We are giving
them opportunities to seek revenge and we are handing them
renown and reaction. By declaring a war on terror, far from
denying them their objectives, we are conceding their objectives,
and this is why the war on terror can never be won.

Bin Laden has made it very clear in all his statements that he
wants revenge on the US for its actions in the Muslim world and
its support of Israel. By bringing its army to him America is making
it easy for him and those who follow him or are inspired by him to
exact this revenge. Moreover, by placing its troops in Afghanistan
and Iraq the US is ensuring that there will be many other actions
to be avenged, whether it is the killing of civilians in air strikes, the
abuse of prisoners or the desecration of corpses in Afghanistan, or

military operations and prisoner abuse in Iraq: those hurt by these actions are likely to swell the ranks of those seeking vengeance. Thanks to the role of the media, evidence of these abuses is presented for all the world to see so that those hungry for revenge are not just those who have suffered, but also others who identify with those who have suffered and are radicalized by the experience.

There is no surer route to renown than to be declared the greatest enemy of the most powerful country in the world. By offering millions of dollars for his head and declaring that it wanted him 'dead or alive' the US has elevated the stature of Osama bin Laden in a way he could only have dreamed of. The US has permitted him to play David to its Goliath. It is, of course, the case that his success in pulling off the 9/11 attacks guaranteed considerable glory for bin Laden in many circles. By reacting to the attack in the way it did, however, America greatly expanded those circles. If it succeeds in killing him it will turn him into a martyr and his renown will be consolidated for generations to come. If the US dosen't capture him he can continue to defy it and demonstrate its weakness. At this point it would be very hard for bin Laden to lose the war on terror.

A wiser response would have been for America to do everything in its power to capture him. Instead of relying on unreliable local forces whose interests it little understood, it should have focused its own efforts on the caves of Tora Bora. Had the US captured him alive it would have had an extraordinary opportunity to demonstrate to the world the strength of the American commitment to the rule of law. Had it captured bin Laden alive and then resisted the very human urge to exact revenge and instead handed him over to an international court of impeccable rectitude and reputation to be tried for crimes against humanity, America would have deprived him of glory, and have demonstrated, even to the sceptical, the vast difference between his values and its own.

There is no greater affront to terrorists than to be ignored. They deliberately attempt spectacular attacks in an effort to gain attention. The risk of ignoring a terrorist action, of course, is that it might incite its perpetrators to even more devastating attacks in order to get attention. So ignoring terrorists is not a feasible option, especially in a democracy in which the public demands action in the face of atrocity. By pursuing terrorists like the criminals they are, however, outside of the limelight and with painstaking and necessarily covert action, one can undermine their effectiveness without raising their profiles.

Terrorists have repeatedly and quite explicitly told us that they want to provoke a reaction and the more extreme the reaction the better for them. It will get them attention, and it will alienate the uncommitted and win recruits to their cause. On September 25, 1968, a leading Brazilian newspaper, *Jornal do Brasil*, published a manifesto spelling out the aims of the Brazilian terrorist group ALN. This is the group that was led by Carlos Marighella, author of *The Mini-manual of the Urban Guerrilla*. The manifesto declared the terrorist group's aim as to create a crisis in the country that would cause the government to adopt a military response. This in turn would lead to a mass uprising against the regime in which power would pass to the armed people. By responding to the 9/11 attacks with a declaration of war the US conceded the very objectives – revenge, renown and reaction – that al-Qaeda were seeking and it ensured that it could not win.

The urge to declare war in response to an atrocity on the scale of September 11 is very powerful and the decision to do so is very understandable. I have argued, however, that it is also very unwise. In the chapter that follows I will spell out an alternative strategy, a strategy that replaces the very ambitious goals to 'rid the world of the evildoers' and to 'root terrorism out of the world'[72] with the more modest and more achievable goal of containing the threat from terrorism. This strategy is based on the lessons that can be derived from the experience of other countries and especially other democracies in countering terrorism.

8

What Is to Be Done?

Happy is he who learns from others' mistakes.

Osama bin Laden, October 2004[1]

Ireland forces upon us these great social and great religious questions – God grant that we may have the courage to look them in the face and to work through them.

William Ewart Gladstone, 1844[2]

The bombing at Clerkenwell prison in December 1867, the details of which were recounted in Chapter Two, was followed by numerous arrests (including that of a police informant hired to spy on the terrorists), and rumours of impending atrocities were rampant. Fenians were alleged to be planning to dynamite the gasworks and the railway lines, to blow up the Crystal Palace and even to attack the British fleet. Protection for the royal family was increased dramatically while the police and the public became preoccupied by society's vulnerability to attack from the sewers. The newspapers fanned the public hysteria. *The Banner of Ulster* declared: 'Of all the fiendish ferocities ever perpetrated in any country, none exceeds that recently committed in the heart of London.'[3] The *Impartial Reporter* said it was 'the most frightful crime of modern times'.[4] The government was compelled to respond and put out a call for volunteers to act as special constables. More men came forward than volunteered during either of the subsequent world wars.

Five men and a woman were soon charged with the crime and brought to trial. The weakness of the crown's case was quickly evident as the case against two of the six collapsed and three others were acquitted for lack of evidence. One man, Michael Barrett, who presented several witnesses to support his alibi that he was in Glasgow at the time of the explosion, was convicted and sentenced to death. Queen Victoria was furious that the government were not taking a stronger line. In a letter to the home secretary the queen wrote that she was grieved 'to see the failure of the evidence against all but one of the Clerkenwell criminals . . . it seems dreadful for these people to escape . . . one begins to wish that these Fenians should be lynch-lawed and on the spot'.[5]

At his trial Michael Barrett did not fit the profile of the mindless murderer. He gave a thoughtful and eloquent forty-five-minute speech from the dock, delivered without hesitation and without notes. The *Daily Telegraph* reported that he 'was evidently a man of high intelligence'.[6] *The Times* remarked favourably on his 'look of determination and frank courage'.[7] One of the lawyers for the other defendants said, 'a less murderous countenance than Barrett's, indeed, I do not remember to have seen. Good humour was latent in every feature.'[8] Even the lord chief justice was unconvinced of the correctness of the result. Some members of the House of Commons like John Bright and John Stuart Mill requested clemency, but the prevailing sentiment was that even if Barrett had not committed the crime, he was clearly a Fenian and deserved to be hung. When Barrett's mother approached her local member of parliament for help in seeking a reprieve, he told her that her son and all other Fenians should be hanged, and the sooner the better.[9] On May 26, 1868, five months after the explosion, Michael Barrett was hanged before a crowd of about 2,000 onlookers in the last public execution in England.

A few days after the Clerkenwell explosion, at the height of the public and media hysteria, William Ewart Gladstone, then MP for South Lancashire and shortly to become leader of the Liberal Party, gave a speech in which he tried to press upon his listeners his belief that Irish violence was the product of Irish grievance and that it was the duty of the British people to address these grievances. He also reminded his audience that if the public were excited, the excitement would influence a jury and even a judge.[10] Gladstone's was a lone voice in trying to look behind the violence. While others cried for blood, he wanted to find out why Irishmen felt driven to violence against England.

Gladstone became prime minister for the first time a year after the Clerkenwell explosion with a mission to pacify Ireland. He had no illusions that it would be easy, but through the Irish Church Act of 1869 and the Irish Land Act of 1870 he sought to address the underlying religious and social issues that prompted support for Irish nationalist violence. He soon concluded that political change was also necessary and in 1886 he introduced his first unsuccessful Home Rule Bill for Ireland. In 1893, the year before he retired, he tried again and introduced the second, likewise unsuccessful, Home Rule Bill for Ireland. He did not succeed in his mission of pacifying Ireland. Too many others preferred a straightforward coercive response to Irish violence.

Nevertheless, Gladstone's endeavour to look behind the violence and to understand the factors that fuel it and his effort to introduce social, political and religious reforms to alleviate the conditions that breed support for violence represent a model of what can be done in the face of terrorism. Gladstone failed to pacify Ireland but had he succeeded the history of Britain and Ireland over the past hundred years would have been very different.

Nearly fifty years after Michael Barrett's death, on August 1, 1915, at the funeral for another Fenian, Jeremiah O'Donovan Rossa, a young Padraig Pearse, who was soon to lead the next Irish insurrection, gave one of the most famous speeches in the annals of Irish nationalism: 'Life springs from death; and from the graves of patriot men and women spring living nations . . . the fools, the fools, the fools! They have left us our Fenian dead, and while Ireland holds these graves, Ireland unfree shall never be at peace.'[11] Almost sixty years later, in 1973, the next generation of Fenians, this time called the IRA, planted a bomb outside the Old Bailey in London, right at the spot on which Michael Barrett had been executed over a century earlier.

Governments are invariably placed under enormous pressure to react forcibly and quickly in the wake of a terrorist attack. As I have argued, however, this response is not likely to be most conducive to long-term success against terrorists. Nor is there a simple solution to terrorism. Terrorism is a complicated and multifaceted phenomenon, but as I have tried to show here it is also one that can be rationally understood. An efficacious response is likely to be just as complicated as the problem. In the well-known words of H. L. Mencken: 'For every complex problem, there is a solution that is simple, neat, and wrong.' Gladstone's government recognized this long ago and introduced political, social and religious reforms as well as coercive policies in an effort to redress the problem of Irish terrorism. One does not need to go back as far as Gladstone to find examples of countries, even fully fledged democracies, which have had to contend with a threat from terrorism. Indeed, some of America's allies, which were anxious to help, were somewhat perturbed by the impression they gained from Americans that terrorism was unknown before 9/11. They argued that they had acquired a good deal of experience that might just be useful to the US.

In looking at the counter-terrorism experience of other democracies one point becomes clear. Whether it was Britain in dealing with the IRA, the Peruvian government in dealing with the Shining Path, the Italian government responding to the Red Brigades or India responding to Sikh terrorism in the Punjab, each of these governments learned from their early mistakes and significantly improved the effectiveness of their counter-terrorism policies over time. The US is in the fortunate position of being able to learn from the mistakes of others, but it appears instead to prefer to learn from its own. In this chapter, therefore, I will spell out some of the lessons that I think can be derived from the experience of others to enable the US successfully to contain the threat from terrorists.

Rule Number 1: Have a Defensible and Achievable Goal

The first point about which one must be clear is the purpose of the strategy. If the goal is to defeat terrorism or eliminate terror, not to mention evil, it simply cannot be attained. On the other hand, had the US government declared its goal on the evening of

September 11 simply to be to capture those responsible for the attacks, it might very well have been successful. This goal would have required a different political and military strategy in Afghanistan and it would have kept the US out of Iraq. Due to the impact of its response to 9/11 on al-Qaeda, and in particular the fact that the movement now has many of the characteristics of a diffuse and inspirational ideology rather than a military organization, even if America were to capture the remainder of those responsible it would not have defeated terrorism.

As a result, its task today is in many ways more difficult than it was in autumn 2001. Rather than having the objective of the defeat of terrorism, today its goal should be to contain the threat from terrorists. Terrorism is a tactic and it will continue to be deployed by those seeking change as long as it proves to be effective. Unlike the goal of eliminating terrorism, the goal of containing the terrorist threat is achievable. The particular brand of terrorism that currently poses a threat to the west is terrorism used by Islamic militants; therefore America's goal today should be to stop the spread of Islamic militancy. In order to contain the spread of Islamic militancy it must isolate the terrorists and inoculate their potential recruits against them.

If the US were to keep this more modest and more concrete goal firmly in sight and plan accordingly it would be able to ensure that its short-term tactics do not undermine the effort to realize its long-term objectives. If the goal were to prevent the spread of Islamic militancy America would take pains to ensure, for example, that its coercive policies against the presumed perpetrators of violence do not harm or alienate the broader populations in which its actions take place. The prevention of the spread of Islamic militancy is ultimately a political rather than a military goal, and as Thucydides said long ago, and British counter-insurgency strategy reiterated more recently, it is imperative to keep the political goal firmly in mind. The US needs to ensure that military actions do not make political goals harder to accomplish.

The nature of this goal, moreover, is such that it does not lend itself to unrealistic expectations that, like taking a beachhead or bombing a training site, it can be accomplished overnight. The nature of this goal affords the political leadership the time and the opportunity to educate the public to the nature of the threat they face and the careful steps that must be taken to counter it.

One of the perennial difficulties encountered by other democracies in attempting to formulate effective counter-terrorist strategies has been co-ordinating these across different bureaucracies. The difficulty of co-ordination seems to be endemic to complex organizations of any nationality and every function. In India, Northern Ireland, Peru, Sri Lanka and Turkey, both the military and the police forces were engaged in counter-terrorism and all initially experienced considerable problems in co-ordinating their responses. Even those countries in which counter-terrorism policy was firmly in the hands of the police force, like France, Japan, Italy and Spain, there were chronic problems of co-ordination across different agencies. In countries that have been least successful in combating terrorism, such as Russia and Colombia, the problems of poor co-ordination are rampant. In the Colombian case this is because the state has been too weak to enforce co-ordination, and in Russia it is because myriad security units – some regional, some national, some police and some military – all appear to be operating on their own. Having a coherent and clearly articulated objective provides a goal against which all acts can be measured and helps to elaborate a division of labour to ensure mutually reinforcing pursuit of the shared objective.

Successful counter-terrorism almost invariably requires a combination of coercive and conciliatory policies. It is imperative for success to ensure that these policies do not undermine one another by being used against the wrong audiences. Coercive policies should be restricted to the few actual perpetrators of the violence, while conciliatory policies ought to be focused on their potential recruits. To use coercive policies too broadly, as the US has been prone to do, serves to alienate those it should be trying to conciliate, while conciliating the perpetrators of the violence is likely to be successful only if the political objectives are clearly understood and negotiable.

If the US keeps the goal of halting the spread of Islamic militancy firmly in mind it is less likely to be distracted by anger at atrocities

WHAT IS TO BE DONE?

along the way; the immediate urge to retaliate is more likely to be satisfied with an appeal to the longer-term objective. Similarly, a fear of accusations of being soft on terrorism or of rewarding terrorists is likely to be ameliorated if the goal is to end their appeal. A number of policies, such as legislation granting lenience in return for information, have proven to be successful when offered to members of an organization that is on the defensive, as the Red Brigades were when Italy introduced its *pentiti* (repentance) legislation. This policy has been less successful when offered to members of a group who are feeling in the ascendant. The policy can have political costs by appearing not to punish adequately the perpetrators of terrorist violence, but again, if the goal is to halt the spread of militancy and one is confident of acquiring invaluable information to further the achievement of that objective, concerns about rewarding terrorism are less likely to resonate.

Rather than waging a war to eliminate terrorism, the US should be engaged in a campaign to contain threats from terrorists. This is a campaign it can win, but to do so it needs to keep the goal firmly in mind and to measure every policy option against its ability to move towards achievement of that goal.

Rule Number 2: Live by Your Principles

There are a number of principles that should guide a counter-terrorist campaign. The first of these was succinctly expressed by President Bush on September 20, 2001: 'We are in a fight for our principles, and our first responsibility is to live by them.'[12] In this the president was right. There is, nevertheless, a popular and quite fallacious view that democracies are peculiarly vulnerable to terrorism and that the freedoms granted to citizens in democratic societies can be exploited by terrorists and therefore must be curtailed. In the wake of terrorist attacks, governments invariably respond with emergency legislation and the public is generally quite happy to sacrifice some liberty in the name of security. The perspective of Benjamin Franklin on this point is not often quoted. He said: 'They who would give up an essential liberty for temporary security deserve neither liberty nor security.'[13] Support for emergency leg-islation is generally won with the argument that it is a temporary expedient, but, as Laura Donohue has demonstrated in her work on the US and the UK, the one iron law of emergency legislation is that temporary legislation is rarely temporary.[14]

Quite apart from the many reasons of principle why it is unwise to abandon liberal democratic values and practices in the face of a terrorist threat, there are a number of pragmatic reasons as well. To alter one's government in response to a terrorist threat is to concede a victory to the adversary. It is to reward their action by demon-strating their power. It is to provide them with a reaction. It is to miss the opportunity to demonstrate the strength of one's com-mitment to the rule of law and to model the behaviour one advo-cates for others.

If the US is prepared to abandon its principles as soon as they are threatened it demonstrates to those whose support it should be focused on winning that it has double standards, one for itself and one for others. It will detain Arab Americans but not others. Or it holds others to standards like the Geneva Convention that it is not prepared to uphold itself. This undermines the legitimacy of America's position and makes more credible the claims of its enemies that its democratic ideals are a mere smokescreen for baser motives.

During the Revolutionary War General George Washington understood both the principled and the pragmatic position on these points. More Americans died in British prison ships in New York harbour than in all the battles of the Revolutionary War. According to the Department of Defense, there were 4,435 battle deaths during the Revolutionary War, while estimates of the number of deaths on prison ships range from 7,000 to 11,644. The British justified the appalling treatment of American prisoners with the argument that they were merely rebels. In an indignant letter that might have been written on behalf of an enemy combatant in Guantanamo, Abu Ghraib or Bagram today, General George Washington wrote to General Lord Howe on January 13, 1777, in protest: 'You may call us rebels, and say that we deserve no better treatment. But remember, my Lord, that supposing us rebels, we still have feelings as keen and sensible as loyalists, and will, if forced to it, most assuredly retaliate upon those upon whom we look as the unjust invaders of our rights, liberties and properties.'[15]

As it happened, Washington opted not to retaliate. Instead, after taking 221 British prisoners at Princeton, he wrote to the American officer in charge: 'Treat them with humanity, and let them have no reason to complain of our copying the brutal example of the British army in their treatment of our unfortunate brethren.'[16] Instead Washington used the issue as an object lesson for his men on the importance of the principles they were fighting for. According to historian David Fischer, Washington regularly reminded his men that they were fighting for liberty and freedom, which were rights of all humanity and therefore ought to be extended even to their enemies.[17]

The US government in the post-9/11 days might have decided that the rebels America confronted were entitled to the protection of the Geneva Conventions. They might have decided, as General Washington did, that as a defender of democracy and individual freedom America was bound to treat its prisoners humanely, and they might have used the opportunity to demonstrate to US soldiers and the world the difference between America and its adversaries. Had the US government so decided, the abuse of prisoners that took place in American prisons would never have happened. The photographic evidence of this abuse, which has been shown throughout the world, has seriously undermined America's legitimacy in the eyes of its allies and the non-committed and confirmed its perfidy in the eyes of everyone else.

We will never know just how many young men were moved to join terrorist groups in anger and outrage at these photographs, nor how many others resolved that they would never lift a finger to help the US in its campaign against terrorism. I believe we can safely assume that the numbers are very large. These photographs, and the failure to repudiate them conclusively by holding the most senior people responsible, has made the crucial task of driving a wedge between the terrorists and the communities that produce them immeasurably more difficult.

In the campaign against terrorism America's ethics and its interests are completely aligned. Far from its democratic principles constraining its ability to respond to terrorism, those principles are among the strongest weapons in its arsenal. All it has to do is remember them.

Rule Number 3: Know Your Enemy

There is no more important requirement for the success of any encounter than knowing your enemy. There is simply no substitute for good intelligence. The centrality of good intelligence to the successful conduct of warfare has long been recognized. Sun Tzu, the Chinese military strategist thought to have lived in the fourth century BC, wrote: 'Nothing should be as favourably regarded as intelligence; nothing should be as generously rewarded as intelligence; nothing should be as confidential as the work of intelligence.'[18]

We must know how and where terrorists operate, how they organize themselves, how they communicate with one another, how they finance and plan their operations. America's post-9/11 counter-terrorist campaign has actually been fairly successful in this respect. It has captured significant numbers of the leaders of al-Qaeda, including many of the masterminds of the 9/11 attacks. The US has comprehensively impaired their ability to communicate with one another and it has disrupted their organization by forcing the leadership to expend most of their time, energy and resources on avoiding detection. It has successfully seized a great many of their assets and made it altogether more difficult for them to transfer significant amounts of money to finance large-scale operations.

In response they have simply adapted. The threat from al-Qaeda has changed. The west is no longer facing a well-funded, well-led, well-trained and well-run organization. Instead the ideology that inspired al-Qaeda now inspires radicalized Muslims in a broad range of countries from the Middle East to the heart of Europe. Some of these groups have connections through individuals to al-Qaeda, many do not. Al-Qaeda may offer advice and occasional expertise, but it does not direct or finance their operations. One of the biggest advantages of the tactic of terrorism is that it is so inexpensive. The 9/11 operation was the most expensive terrorist attack in history and it cost its organizers, as mentioned earlier, an estimated $500,000 (it cost the insurance industry alone between $25 billion and $50 billion).[19] Subsequent operations in London, Madrid, Bali and Casablanca have been self-financed and have cost only a few thousand dollars each. Turning off the flow of money to al-Qaeda has hurt the organization and weakened it, but it has not and will not stop terrorist attacks, though it does reduce the likelihood of a recurrence of sophisticated attacks like 9/11.

While US intelligence operations have enjoyed some successes against al-Qaeda and especially against what might be called 'al-Qaeda central', America has been singularly unsuccessful in gleaning good intelligence on a range of equally important issues. It needs to understand the basis of al-Qaeda's strength. It needs to understand the nature of al-Qaeda's appeal. It needs to understand the importance they attach to the various goals they articulate. Do they really wish to establish a caliphate or would they be satisfied if the US withdrew from the Middle East? Would they continue to fight until Israel was annihilated or would they stop fighting if they were to succeed in bringing down the Saudi regime and introducing sharia law in Saudi Arabia? We have no idea.

If the US does not even know what its enemies are fighting for, it cannot hope to counter them effectively. It has come to believe its own rhetoric that they are driven by uncontrolled evil and limitless ambition to harm it. Americans have tended to imagine all the terrible things terrorists could do to them and then to attempt the impossible task of defending against all of them. Instead, the US needs to figure out, on the basis of sound intelligence, the things they have (or might soon have) both the motive and the capability to do to it, and defend itself accordingly. It also needs to figure out how it can most effectively weaken them.

All governments that have faced a threat from terrorism have found that good intelligence has been the most crucial weapon in their armoury. This has been true across all types of terrorist movements and across all types of government, from Betancourt's campaign against the FALN in Venezuela in the 1960s to France's campaign against the GIA (Groupe Islamique Armé) in the 1990s. I have already mentioned the key role played by DIRCOTE, the small, specialized intelligence agency with the Peruvian police force that was so crucial to the capture of Abimael Guzman. Israel too has relied heavily on intelligence for information leading to the prevention of particular attacks or to the location of terrorist leaders in the West Bank and the Gaza Strip. In Northern Ireland over time the British security services developed a highly efficient intelligence operation largely based on informants that enabled them to prevent planned attacks. The security services there claimed that by the early 1990s around 70 per cent of all planned IRA operations were abandoned on security grounds. Of the remaining 30 per cent, 80 per cent were prevented or interdicted by the security forces.[20] Good intelligence also afforded the opportunity to ambush terrorist operatives, as the SAS did in Loughgall in 1987, killing eight IRA members, and as undercover army commandos did in Coagh in 1991. In all these cases intelligence was acquired by the sophisticated employment of advanced technologies as well as by the extensive use of personal informants. The US has been highly successful in developing the former and has completely failed to develop the latter, relying instead on often dubious information extracted from those it has captured.

Good intelligence not only helps to weaken the capabilities of the adversary by providing information on planned operations or location of hideouts, it also offers crucial insights into the internal dynamics of the group. Terrorist groups operate under conditions of considerable uncertainty and often suffer from quite understandable bouts of paranoia. When operations and individuals are betrayed, the group often turn against their own. As members of terrorist groups tend to have impeccable intelligence on one another, they can be very effective in eliminating suspected collaborators with cold ruthlessness. For example, in the period 1979–81, more members of the IRA were murdered as informants by their colleagues than were killed by the security forces.[21]

In the Punjab the success of the Indian government in infiltrating Sikh terrorist groups served to weaken the movements by sowing distrust among the membership. One of the abiding characteristics of terrorist groups is their fissiparous tendencies – that is, their tendency to split into smaller groups. Most well-known terrorist groups, whether they be nationalist groups like the IRA or social revolutionary groups like the Red Army Faction, are surrounded by smaller offshoots which have split over some ideological or personal issue (and most often it is a personal issue wrapped up as an ideological one). These splits weaken the movement by distracting attention from the central campaign they are waging, by causing the loss of scarce resources like trained members, as when an expert bomb-maker joins a splinter group. It leaves people outside the control of the leadership with vital information about the core group. One of the most effective means of weakening a terrorist group is to encourage these splits. In order to do so we must have our intelligence operatives deep inside these groups participating in the internal debates and learning about the leanings as well as the plans of the membership.

There is no doubt that penetrating terrorist groups is no easy task. Developing a good intelligence network takes time, connections, language skills, cultural knowledge and deep engagement in the region where the groups come from. It is even more difficult when, as at present, so many new ad-hoc groups are forming which appear to be linked only by personal connection and radical ideology. Nevertheless, if John Walker Lindh can be accepted by the Taliban, and Jose Padilla by al-Qaeda, then other Americans, with a very different agenda, must also be able to join radical jihadi groups. If Richard Reid, the so-called 'shoe bomber', can be recruited in prison and prisons are becoming what Jessica Stern has called 'gateway organizations', we should have our operatives flooding these avenues to militant Islam.

As Israel's very different experience in intelligence gathering in Lebanon and the West Bank can attest, it is a great deal more difficult to acquire good intelligence in a territory one does not control. Nevertheless, there is no real alternative. America must either gather this intelligence itself or persuade enough people on the ground to do so on its behalf. Within the United States the best possible source of information on the emergence of small groups of Islamic militants along the lines of their European counterparts in Britain, Spain, the Netherlands, France, Germany and Belgium is the loyal Muslim American population. If the US treats them as suspect by rounding up and detaining large numbers of them, if it pays lip-service to tolerance while practising racial profiling, then it is likely to deprive itself of invaluable information, quite aside from any real civil-liberties concerns it may have.

The US is not confronting in its war on terror a transnational cabal of psychopaths; rather it is confronting a range of different groups which are prepared to use terrorist violence. Given that the US is not in a position simply to obliterate every suspected terrorist, as some Latin American military regimes sought to do, it must understand the nature of its opponent and fashion its response accordingly. A tactic that works against one terrorist organization will not work against others. Israel has practised a policy of decapitation against radical Palestinian groups for years, and for every Hamas leader Israel assassinates another emerges. The policy has not worked. On the other hand, the policy of decapitation did work against the PKK and the Shining Path. The success of the policy will depend on the nature of the group against which it is deployed. So the first step must be to understand the nature of the group you are facing.

If anything, America appears to know less about the nature of its adversary in the war on terrorism than it did when it began. It has been engaged in a veritable dialogue of the deaf with al-Qaeda over its preferred means of mass communication. It says it fights them because they attacked it first. They say they attacked the US because it attacked them first. The US says they fight it because they hate freedom, they say they fight the US because they want freedom. America says they hate life, they say they love life. The US says that the only language they understand is force. They say that the only language the US understands is force. America hurls accusations against them across the airwaves, not unlike the First World War allegations that German soldiers ate Belgian babies and raped Belgian nuns when they invaded Belgium.

The US takes it as a given that al-Qaeda's demands are so extreme as to be non-negotiable, but it would be worth finding out if that is, in fact, the case. Yet suggestions that their demands might be negotiable are treated with deep suspicion, and suggestions that America should actually talk to the terrorists are considered tantamount to treason. It seems to me that this issue is of such importance that it must be demonstrated (rather than simply asserted) that their demands are indeed non-negotiable. Even if the US could get over the public's inhibitions about talking to the terrorists it would not be altogether easy to do so. The hammer of American military power that descended on al-Qaeda in the autumn of 2001 had the effect of shattering the organization and sending splinters throughout the world, so it is not entirely clear to whom one could talk. That said, Ayman al-Zawahiri has clearly emerged as the chief spokesman and strategist of the al-Qaeda leadership, and while it is far from clear that he has the authority to carry his followers with him, the opportunity to engage him is one that should not be missed, no matter how much opprobrium Americans hold for him.

I have no illusions about how unpopular a suggestion this is likely to be. Governments always resist talking to terrorists for fear that it confers legitimacy on them, or rewards their terrorism. It is also the case that many governments have successfully defeated terrorist groups without ever engaging them, like Italy and the Red Brigades and Germany and the RAF. Nevertheless, it is also the case that Britain ended the IRA's terrorism only through negotiating with the terrorists and that the ceasefire currently enjoyed in Sri Lanka is a result of government talks with the hated Tamil Tigers. The difference between the Red Brigades and the RAF on the one hand and the LTTE and IRA on the other is that the first pair both had non-negotiable goals and were isolated from their communities. The second pair had political and hence negotiable goals and a significant degree of support in their communities. As I mentioned in Chapter One (see Figure 1), the two key characteristics of all terrorist groups are the nature of the goals they seek and the nature of their relationship to their community. Al-Qaeda appears to have non-negotiable goals and a significant degree of community support. The focus of our intelligence, and indeed of all other counter-terrorist policies at the moment, ought to be to establish if that indeed is the nature of their goals and second, to isolate them from their community of support.

Wars are easier to begin than to end; they tend to last much longer than an objective assessment of the interests of the participants suggests that they should. The same is true of terrorism and of counter-terrorist campaigns.[22] In some cases one side has overwhelming power and simply wins the conflict, but this is rare. The First World War, for example, ended in 1918 on terms that had essentially been available two years earlier. The Boer War could have been concluded on the same terms eighteen months earlier. The IRA finally called an end to its campaign seven years after the Good Friday Agreement, and the broad terms of that agreement could have been available many years earlier. There are a variety of reasons for this. The costs of wars are such that participants feel they have to continue fighting to justify the costs already borne. Wars and terrorist campaigns tend to be prolonged by an unlikely alliance of hawks on both sides and generally require an alliance of doves on both sides in order to make peace.

In the case of terrorist groups, delay can be caused by unwillingness to negotiate. Talks with terrorists are not simply an opportunity for negotiating concessions; they are also an invaluable opportunity for gaining information about the opponent. As I have noted, governments tend to be reluctant to get involved in talks with terrorists as they do not want to confer legitimacy on the illegal group or to reward their violent activity. Nevertheless many states have, in fact, talked to terrorists, although most have been inconsistent in their willingness to do so. The Khasavyurt Accord brought the first Chechen war to an end with the promise of resolving the status of Chechnya, but the outbreak of the second Chechen war and Putin's assumption of power and firm refusal to negotiate has meant a bloody prolongation of the conflict.

Throughout the conflict in Northern Ireland the British government held talks with the IRA. These talks often took place during a period when the government had an official line of refusing to talk to terrorists. From the first secret talks in 1972, which served mainly to demonstrate to each side the extent of the differences between them, these meetings helped the British government to size up their opponent. In 1975 a series of meetings were held between the British government and the IRA while the movement maintained a ceasefire. The IRA subsequently concluded that they had been tricked into these meetings. Initially they had been led to believe that Britain was looking for a way to extricate itself from the province, but they concluded that the talks were a ruse by the government to gather intelligence and encourage splits within the movement by trying to draw some members into constitutional politics. The years of direct and indirect public and private talks finally paid off in the signing of the 1998 Good Friday Agreement.

By overcoming the reluctance to talk we could discover a great deal about our adversaries, about the importance they assign to particular goals, about how they make decisions and about their assessment of their own position. These talks do not have to be public nor do they have to be direct. They could be conducted through intermediaries, but it is very difficult to know your enemies if you don't try to engage them.

There are any number of examples of how America's ignorance of its enemies has served only to strengthen them. In his speech to the United Nations in February 2003 when Colin Powell painted the portrait of Abu Mus'ab al-Zarqawi as bin Laden's man in Iraq, he suddenly transformed al-Zarqawi, a hitherto largely unknown two-bit Jordanian thug, into a leader of a global movement. At the time al-Zarqawi was not remotely in the same league as the highly trained, highly educated, experienced leadership of al-Qaeda. By offering a $25 million reward for him the US elevated him into the senior ranks. In fact it took al-Zarqawi a year and a half to declare allegiance to bin Laden in a statement posted on Islamist websites.[23] Two months later, in December 2004, bin Laden in an audio-tape accepted al-Zarqawi's fealty, pronounced him the 'emir' of al-Qaeda in Iraq, and instructed Muslims to listen to him.[24]

By knowing your enemies you can find out what it is they want. Once you know what they want you can then decide whether to deny it to them and thereby demonstrate the futility of their tactic, or to give it to them, or to negotiate and give them a part of it in order to cause them to end their campaign. By knowing your enemies you can make an assessment not just of their motives but also of their capabilities and of the calibre of their leaders and their organizations. Any information one could glean from this encounter would be useful. If one concludes definitively that their demands are non-negotiable, the focus of one's policy must be to isolate them from their communities and to go after them with targeted coercive policies. On the other hand, one might learn that their demands are, in fact, negotiable, and this once again can help to direct counter-terrorist policy. The most likely outcomes would be to discover that they are not a unitary actor and that some have negotiable demands and others do not. Then the direction of policy should be to exploit these differences and sow dissent among them.

In short there is nothing to lose and a great deal to gain by knowing your enemies. The best way to do so is to invest decisively and heavily in a comprehensive intelligence strategy.

Rule Number 4: Separate the Terrorists from Their Communities

The first point, as I have said, is to be clear about the goal one seeks. The US wishes to contain the threat from terrorists. Today this means that it needs to stop the spread of Islamic militancy. In order to stop the spread of Islamic militancy it must understand the nature of its appeal and endeavour to counter it. This means that the focus of America's counter-terrorism strategy should not be, as it has been until now, on the actual perpetrators of the violence; it should rather be on the potential recruits of the terrorist groups, the communities from which they derive their support. Terrorist groups thrive in complicit societies. Without recruits they cannot grow. If they are isolated from their communities they become infinitely weaker as they become dependent upon crime to derive a means of support, and this in turn exposes them to capture. If they are isolated from their communities they cannot travel safely, internal rivalries become more intense, paranoia grows and the group become more susceptible to defection and are at greater risk of betrayal. It becomes more difficult for them to operate and in particular it becomes harder to operate sophisticated weapons arsenals or training grounds.

America's policies in the years since 9/11 have been focused on the perpetrators of the violence. Its focus has been on stopping them, not on figuring out what motivates them or how they manage to win recruits. Its use of force against them has appeared to many on the ground to be indiscriminate, and as a result it has intensified their relationships with their communities and alienated their communities from America. In so doing the US has won them recruits and safe houses and ensured that they will not be turned over to it. Had it more wisely seen this as a two-step process whereby it first isolates them from their community and then goes after the perpetrators with highly discriminate coercive policies, there would today be far less support for Islamic militancy and far more support for the US.

America's purpose in alienating the terrorists from their communities is not to win a popularity contest. The reality is that the extent of its wealth and strength will always breed resentment. It does not need to be loved – great powers rarely are. The only threshold it needs to reach is that ordinary members of society should not be prepared to support those who wish to oppose the US by killing its civilians. That is not such a high threshold to achieve. Nevertheless if by its actions America seems to confirm the view of it held by the terrorists themselves, if its behaviour seems more in keeping with their account of its motives than with its own, then it will immeasurably strengthen its adversaries.

As mentioned earlier, terrorism requires a combination of an alienated individual, a complicit society and a legitimizing ideology. Of the three it is the society that is most susceptible to influence by the US. Individuals become alienated and radicalized in a host of ways and it cannot intercede to prevent this. It can challenge ideologies, whether they be Salafism or communism, but it is not in the best position to influence these debates. The level at which it can intervene and at which it potentially has all the resources needed to intervene effectively is at the level of the societies that produce the extremists. This is where its attention has to be focused.

If America's goal is to contain the threat from terrorists, and the focus of its attention is the communities from which the terrorists derive their support, it has some criteria to consider when deciding policies.

There are surely few who would dispute the appropriateness of the goal of containing the spread of Islamic militancy; the dispute is over how best to do so. America's approach has been to play to what it considers to be its strength, its military prowess, and to stop the spread of Islamic militancy by capturing or killing all the Islamic militants. The problem with this approach is that in its efforts to capture and kill them its use of overwhelming force is in fact generating more of them. This is emphatically the case with the war in Iraq, which has radicalized a whole generation of young jihadists who have been led to believe that the US is establishing a base in the Middle East with which to exploit the resources and dominate the politics of the region.

Secretary of Defense Rumsfeld showed that he understood the difficulty in a memo of October 16, 2003 to four of his subordinates. He asked: 'Today, we lack metrics to know if we are winning or losing the global war on terror. Are we capturing, killing or deterring and dissuading more terrorists every day than the madrassas and the radical clerics are recruiting, training and deploying against us?'[25] He was, in effect, describing a competitive battle for the hearts and minds of potential recruits. Capturing the culprits is one approach and it has the advantage of being action oriented and decisive and of using America's great military strength.

The other approach is to engage in the war of ideas and in effect to try to inoculate the broader community against the appeal of the militants. This approach has less appeal to policymakers as it is more intangible, is likely to take a long time to produce results, appears to reward those close to the terrorists and insufficiently repudiates the evil of the atrocity. Moreover, it requires a deep engagement with the region across a range of policy areas and requires a linguistic and cultural familiarity that is surprisingly rare in the halls of US foreign and intelligence services.

The leaders of al-Qaeda are acutely conscious of the fact that they are engaged in a war of ideas with America. Through their extensive use of the new media, from the internet to audio- and videotapes, they have sought to compensate for their military weakness and to engage in this battle. The term 'hearts and minds' was coined in the British counter-insurgency experience in Malaya in the 1950s, and was much discredited by the US campaign in Vietnam; nevertheless it remains a crucial component in the current campaign against terrorism. It is a term that has even been used by the terrorists: 'I say to you that we are in a battle, and that more than half of this battle is taking place in the battlefield of the media. And that we are in a media battle in a race for the hearts and minds of our umma [community].'[26]

In a missive captured in autumn 2005 from al-Qaeda's second in command, Ayman al-Zawahiri, to Abu Mus'ab al-Zarqawi, one of the leaders of the Iraqi insurgency, the elder terrorist sought to teach the younger firebrand the importance of this aspect of their war. This extraordinary document, dated July 2005 and captured by US intelligence sources in Iraq and posted on the website of the Office of the Director of National Intelligence, spells out the strategy being pursued by al-Qaeda in Iraq and proffers advice on how they should achieve their objectives.

> If we look at the two short-term goals, which are removing the Americans and establishing an Islamic emirate in Iraq, or a caliphate if possible, then we will see that the strongest weapon which the mujahideen enjoy – after the help and granting of success by God – is popular support from the Muslim masses in Iraq, and the surrounding Muslim countries. So, we must maintain this support as best we can, and we should strive to increase it . . . In the absence of this popular support, the Islamic mujahid movement would be crushed in the shadows . . . Therefore, the mujahid movement must avoid any action that the masses do not understand or approve.[27]

He then goes on to counsel against attacks on Shias and gruesome beheadings of hostages on the ground that the Muslim public are troubled by these tactics.

If al-Qaeda believe that their greatest strength is the popular support they enjoy among the Muslim populations, America's energies should be focused on undermining that support. On the contrary, almost everything it has done has served to strengthen that support.

Conducting a war of ideas is a more nebulous notion and a less energizing concept than waging a 'real' war of bombs and bullets. The two kinds of warfare also require somewhat different mindsets. The heavy sacrifices expected of those who participate in conventional warfare require certainty about the rectitude of one's own position in order to justify those sacrifices. In order to win a war of ideas, however, one has to engage with the adversaries and even concede at times that they may have a point.

The fact that someone who has committed heinous crimes makes allegations against the US does not mean that those allegations are without foundation and should be dismissed out of hand. If America's audience is the broader community to which he is appealing, then it needs to listen and to respond to the allegations. Nowhere is the gulf between al-Qaeda's argument and America's more in evidence than in the question of the impact of economic sanctions on Iraq. In his statements over the years bin Laden regularly invoked the hundreds of thousands of Iraqi children killed by US sanctions. 'A million innocent children are dying as we speak, killed in Iraq without any guilt.'[28] Americans simply dismissed these claims as the rantings of a diabolical fanatic. Economic sanctions after all are benign; they are a means of putting pressure on a pariah government without using force. Americans saw their sanctions as evidence of their restraint, and if they caused hardship for Iraqi civilians it was because Saddam Hussein impeded their implementation in the humanitarian way the US intended.

The fact is that the UN sanctions did cause the deaths of hundreds of thousands of Iraqi children. A UNICEF report issued in 1999 indicated that 500,000 children under the age of five died between 1991 and 1998 in Iraq due largely to the impact of the sanctions.[29] The British medical journal *Lancet* reported: 'Infant mortality rose from 47 per 1,000 live births during 1984–89 to 108 per 1,000 in 1994–99, and under five mortality rose from 56 to 131 per 1,000 live births.'[30] Two successive UN officials in charge of the programme resigned to protest against the humanitarian catastrophe over which they were presiding. Hans von Sponeck explained: 'I can no longer be associated with a programme that prolongs suffering of the people and which has no chance to meet even the basic needs of the civilian population.' Later he said: 'Lawlessness of one kind does not justify lawlessness of another kind . . . how long must the civilian population be exposed to such punishment for something that they've never done?'[31] Earlier Fred Halliday, a thirty-year veteran of the UN, had also resigned, insisting that '4,000 to 5,000 children [are] dying unnecessarily every month due to the impact of sanctions because of the breakdown of water and sanitation, inadequate diet and the bad internal health situation.' Halliday went on to describe the complete breakdown in civil society in Iraq as a result of the privations imposed by sanctions and in 1998, remarking on the growth of fundamentalist Islamic thinking, he declared that 'We are pushing people to take extreme positions.'[32]

It is imperative that the US listens to the allegations being made against it and that it examines the impact of its policies on the ground. Public opinion polls have repeatedly indicated that the American people have not blamed the Iraqi people for the actions of their leader and yet the economic sanctions the US imposed on Iraq punished Iraqi civilians. Indeed, more Iraqis died as a result of economic sanctions than have been killed by every kind of weapon of mass destruction throughout history, including the bombing of Hiroshima and Nagasaki.[33] The US cannot hope to win a war of ideas if its actions appear to be so completely at variance with its stated principles.

As well as listening to the allegations being made against it and examining the impact of its policies on the ground to ensure that they are in keeping with its principles, America must also engage with the grievances that give rise to the pools of resentment from which terrorist groups draw. Many of these grievances are political and are difficult to redress. Extremists, however, have been very successful at exploiting such conflicts as the Arab–Israeli problem and the dispute between India and Pakistan over Kashmir. No reasonable person expects the US to resolve these disputes and its support for Israel will always be unpopular. Nevertheless, if it is seen to hold its allies to the same standards of behaviour as it holds its adversaries to and if it makes a concerted effort to facilitate resolution of these political disputes, it will gain the respect of moderate Arab opinion.

The other political arena in which America should act if it wishes to drive a wedge between the extremists and the societies that enable their behaviour is the domestic politics of its allies in the Middle East. There can be little doubt that many of its allies in the region do not share its commitment to democracy and the rule of law. If it wants their populations to believe that it is committed to the principles it espouses, it must be seen to be an advocate for political reforms. It should demonstrate that it is aware that elections alone do not constitute democracy and that democracy cannot successfully be imposed from without. Instead it should support the development of a resilient civil society and moderate opposition political parties. It should see the election of those who disagree with it as evidence of its success, not of failure. Again, this is a very long-term objective, but its commitment to the process will undermine the argument of those who proselytize by pointing to the significant disparity between America's principles and its practices.

As the richest country in the world the US has an enormous comparative advantage in the campaign against terrorists. It should use it. It should adopt a comprehensive development agenda to address the underlying or permissive causes of terrorism. It has often been said that Americans prefer big ideas to small ones, as evidenced by the support for the Marshall Plan after the Second World War or the mobilization behind Kennedy's plan to put a man on the moon, or indeed the support for President Bush's plan to eliminate terrorism. What better way to demonstrate the difference between America and those who attacked it on 9/11 than to respond by redressing economic and social inequities among populations they claim to represent?

The US should have no illusions that these actions would impress, much less mollify, the perpetrators of the violence, but they would not be the target of its policies. In the worst-case scenario a comprehensive development plan would fail to deprive terrorists of support. It would nevertheless significantly improve the quality of life of a great many people, and in all probability develop markets for US products too. On the other hand, if a war on terrorism fails, as I have argued it is bound to do, the lives of many people and the quality of life of a great many more will have been destroyed.

As I have pointed out earlier, there is no direct link between poverty and terrorism, and many of the perpetrators of jihadi violence today have above-average levels of education. The societies that support them, however, are societies which have experienced social and economic dislocation and in which perceptions of relative deprivation and political exclusion are acute. In many instances, ranging from Peru to Egypt, well-meaning policies like providing opportunities for education have backfired because they were taken in isolation. Providing opportunities for education while failing to offer opportunities for employment for those who had been educated and whose expectations had consequently been raised has proven to be a particularly dangerous mistake. In formulating a comprehensive development agenda it is imperative that the various policies be co-ordinated and that they be consistent with the overall objective.[34]

It turns out that perhaps one of America's most successful counter-terrorist policies was one that it implemented quite unwittingly and not under the guise of countering terrorism. Indonesia, the country with the largest Muslim population in the world (almost 200 million), has proven to be a hotbed of support for al-Qaeda. The local militant Islamic group Jemaah Islamiyah has been implicated in numerous terrorist attacks, including a number of attacks on western targets. A bomb outside the Sari Club and another at nearby Paddy's Bar in Bali on October 12, 2003 killed 202 people. When interrogators asked Amrozoi, one of the accused bombers, why he wanted to bomb the Club, he repeatedly told them it was because he 'hated Americans'. Another of the accused, Imam Samudra, elaborated: 'I hate America because it is the real centre of international terrorism, which has already repeatedly tyrannized Islam. I carry out jihad because it is the duty of a Muslim to avenge, so the American terrorists and their allies understand that the blood of the Muslim community is not shed for nothing.'[35]

In the years since the attack Jemaah Islamiyah has been seriously weakened by a combination of government action and internal divisions. In October 2005 three suicide bombers blew up three western restaurants in Bali, killing themselves and nineteen others. This attack had none of the sophistication that marked that of 2003 and appears to have been carried out by a previously unknown group of jihadis.[36] The difference in the two attacks illustrates the declining fortunes of the jihadi movement in Indonesia.

In December 2004 Indonesia was devastated by the Indian Ocean earthquake and subsequent tsunami. The natural disaster is estimated to have cost 280,000 lives, with tens of thousand of injuries and a million people made homeless. Casualties in Indonesia are estimated at 130,000 dead, 100,000 injured and 400,000–700,000 displaced. The US initially offered $35 million in assistance. That was quickly increased to $350 million, and in February 2005 President Bush pledged $950 million in assistance. A public opinion poll conducted by the Pew Global Attitudes Survey found that 79 per cent of Indonesians said they had a more favourable view of the US as a result of American relief efforts. The number of Indonesians who had a favourable opinion of the US increased from 15 per cent in 2003 to 38 per cent in 2005.[37] Consistent with this change is the subsequent finding that 35 per cent of the Indonesian public had confidence in Osama bin Laden as a world leader in 2005, down from 58 per cent in 2003.[38] By its humanitarian efforts to alleviate the suffering caused by the tsunami in Indonesia, the US government have undermined popular support for terrorism against America.

The prospects for the success of any policy initiatives that America undertakes are likely to be significantly enhanced if it engages in a concerted effort to explain its policies and the reasoning behind them. This requires a sustained and significant commitment to public diplomacy. There have been a number of recent reports spelling out details of how the conduct of US public diplomacy might be overhauled.[39] There can be no doubt that if America is to separate the terrorists from their communities it must make its case to these communities. This again is an area in which its wealth and its media and technology skills can be a considerable advantage. These advantages will gain the US nothing, however, if it does not take the time to study the languages and the cultures of the societies with which it is dealing. Currently the public diplomacy budget stands at three-tenths of 1 per cent of the Defense Department budget.[40] America's complete failure to seize the opportunity to

make its case to the Islamic world since 9/11 is difficult to understand. The position of under secretary of state for public diplomacy
has rotated among a series of well-meaning and talented individuals, none of whom has extensive experience in the cultures they are
supposed to engage.

For a campaign of public diplomacy to have any chance of
success it must be a great deal more than window dressing. It must
again have a comprehensive, co-ordinated and well-funded plan
that is developed and implemented by disinterested people inti-
mately familiar with the nuances of the societies America seeks to
influence. Its success will not be measurable on a timeline consistent with electoral politics in the US and therefore America's political leaders need to develop a bipartisan consensus so that the
implementation of these policies is not exploited for short-term
political advantage.

The most sophisticated, well-articulated and well-funded public
diplomacy campaign, however, will probably come to nothing if
the arguments that are being made are inconsistent with what
people are experiencing on the ground. If the US continues to
pursue policies that are widely unpopular and that appear to be
inconsistent with what it is saying, its actions will speak louder than
its words. As long as American troops remain on the ground in
Iraq, and as long as the US is unable to deliver security, stability and
a decent standard of living to Iraqis, those who argue that it is there
either to dominate the region or to acquire Iraqi oil are going to
find a receptive audience.

If America succeeds in separating the terrorists from the communities that produce them there will be real limits to the damage
they can do to it. It will never be able to stop them attacking a soft
western target in some part of the world, but it can prevent them
pulling off a spectacular attack that requires sophisticated and
co-ordinated planning. If it is able to isolate them, it can then focus
its coercive policies on tracking them down and disabling them. It
will not be able to isolate them unless it can persuade others that
what they say about it is wrong.

Rule Number 5: Engage Others in Countering Terrorists with You

Historically most terrorist action occurred within countries or across neighbouring countries. Terrorism was adopted as a tactic to address a local grievance, but very often the issue had international implications. In the case of nationalist movements, terrorism may have affected two neighbouring states, as when a group wanted to secede from one country and join another, for example in the dispute between India and Pakistan over Kashmir, or the desire of some Northern Irish Catholics to secede from the UK and join the Republic of Ireland. On other occasions neighbouring countries are involved because of the wish of a terrorist group to create a homeland consistent with the location of the ethnic group, like the Basques in Spain and France, or the Kurds in Turkey, Iraq and Syria.

While the groups emerged locally, there has often been an international component, as when nationalist groups have relied for support on those who have emigrated abroad. Sikhs in North America have generously supported Sikh nationalists in India's Punjab. The Tamil diaspora has also been a consistent source of support for the LTTE, while Irish Americans have supported the IRA. In a few cases the ideology of terrorist groups has been internationalist, for example the social revolutionary groups in Europe in the 1970s. The German group called themselves the Red Army Faction because they perceived themselves to be just one faction of an internationalist communist army. Terrorism also became international when states sponsored terrorists overseas as a covert instrument with which to conduct their foreign policy. In some instances, such as Iranian and Syrian support for Hezbollah, the support has not even been so covert.

Nevertheless, the transnationalism of recent terrorists appears to have gone a considerable step further. In the case of the London bombing, for example, you have young men born in England radicalized by what they have heard of American action in Iraq. Never having been either to America or to Iraq, they murder commuters in London. This is indeed the globalization of terrorism, when a global conflict ignites a local terrorist group. The US simply cannot hope to counter these types of groups on its own, and yet it is quite vulnerable to them. The 9/11 attacks were planned by a cell in Hamburg. Richard Reid was recruited in a British jail. Zacharias Moussaoui, a would-be member of the 9/11 team, found his calling in a London mosque. Ahmad Rassam, who planned to blow up Los Angeles International Airport, was linked to a network of radicals in France. The US will need extensive co-operation and intelligence sharing with other countries in order to monitor the activities of known and emergent cells of radical militants.

This co-operation is more likely to be successful if other countries believe in the legitimacy of America's position and believe that they are consulted by Washington in defining the problem and devising a response. Inevitably domestic norms and domestic legislation are going to impede action in particular cases, but the terrorists themselves are very adept at operating freely across borders, so the US must become equally adept at traversing borders in response.

America should make it a priority to establish effective multilateral institutions that will facilitate the tracking of terrorists. This must go beyond insisting on specific actions on the part of other countries. Instead the US must develop broadly acceptable norms and procedures so that sharing of information is automatic. The experience of other countries dramatically demonstrates the effectiveness of such collaborative arrangements. As long as Kashmiri separatists could find safe haven in Pakistan, Basques in France and republicans in southern Ireland, these movements thrived. Once the French and Irish governments were persuaded of the legitimacy of the Spanish and British counter-terrorist policies and agreed to prevent the terrorists from operating freely from their side of the border, the terrorist groups were greatly weakened. In the case of Northern Ireland, Britain got this support only after it finally recognized that the Republic of Ireland also had an interest in the question and gave formal recognition to the Irish dimension to the Northern Irish conflict.

There are any number of ways in which engaging the international community in the campaign to contain the terrorist threat can strengthen America's hand. At a practical operational level it can help the US to track and capture militants, curtail their funding and impede their operations. At a political level, it can enhance the legitimacy of America's position by casting the conflict as one between those who believe in the rule of law and those who don't, rather than simply one of the strong against the weak, or the US against the rest.

Members of the international community can also play an important role as a broker in negotiations, as the Norwegians did in brokering the Oslo accords or as the US did in facilitating the Northern Ireland peace process. The international community can also help to address social problems, as in the funding by the World Bank and the Inter-America Bank of the Peruvian micro-development projects designed to address some of the socio-economic grievances that galvanized support for the Shining Path.

Given that the international community shares the US interest in combating terrorism, if not America's assessment of the best way to do so, there are clearly areas of mutual agreement. One of these areas is the subject of 'loose nukes'. There is considerable international consensus on the dangers inherent in the numerous unsecured sites in countries of the former Soviet Union where work on the development of nuclear, chemical and biological weapons was carried out. Securing these sites is probably the best available means of enhancing America's security at the lowest cost. Yet the US government programme set up for that purpose has been poorly run and seriously under-funded. This is an issue that must be addressed, yet the US government have lacked either the will or the interest to do so. It is an ideal subject on which to engage the international community.

The Co-operative Threat Reduction Programme (CTR) was established in 1991 to secure nuclear, chemical and biological weapons sites in the former Soviet Union. The USSR had the most intensive biological weapons programme in history, with the result that stores of dangerous pathogens such as anthrax, smallpox and Ebola virus remain in unsecured sites in parts of the world in which terrorist groups with a declared interest in acquiring them are known to be operating. In 2003 the General Accounting Office reported that security projects were under way at only four of the forty-nine known biological sites and that only two sites had been secured against external threats. The CTR, which is responsible for securing nuclear and chemical as well as biological facilities, has been funded at approximately $1 billion a year since the 1990s, in spite of the recommendation of a bipartisan panel in January 2001 to triple the funding. Given the real need for action on this front and given US unwillingness to act, this seems to be an area that America should be prepared to engage others in addressing.

A second area in which a division of labour would make eminent sense is managing the aftermath of military operations. The Europeans have more extensive experience than the US has of post-war reconstruction (even if the Americans are daily acquiring more experience). Other countries are actively engaged in post-war reconstruction in Afghanistan. NATO currently has more than 12,000 troops stationed there. In order to secure support for post-war reconstruction, however, the US is going to have to be prepared to consult more broadly during pre-war planning. Today we have the curious circumstance that behind-the-scenes co-operation is actually better than anyone cares to admit publicly. The unpopularity of the US-led war on terrorism is such that allied governments have no desire to publicize the degree to which they are helping America, preferring instead for the co-operation to take place quietly. To give one example, small groups of French and German special forces are apparently to be found in Afghanistan and Pakistan searching for the remnants of the al-Qaeda leadership, but without the French and German governments announcing this fact to their publics for fear of unpopularity. It cannot be in America's interest for it to be in the interest of its allies to conceal the extent to which they are helping Washington.

The international community, of course, is not the only level that should be engaged. As I have mentioned, local communities need to be engaged and can be the most powerful force in the repudiation of terrorism. In Egypt, for example, when significant segments of the public concluded that terrorist attacks against tourists, as occurred at Luxor in 1997, were at variance with the Islamic tradition of protection for visitors, and deeply damaging to the tourist industry as well, they helped to put pressure on al-Gama'a al-Islamiyya to stop these attacks.

A recent example occurred in Israel. A nineteen-year-old Israeli soldier, Eden Natan-Zada, who was affiliated with the right-wing Kahanist Kach group, opened fire on a bus carrying Palestinians to protest against the Israeli pull-out from Gaza. At the time he was AWOL from the army. The Israeli public emphatically repudiated the attack. The Israeli media immediately referred to it as a terrorist act (language not usually heard when Israelis kill Palestinians) and the attacker was labelled a terrorist. The Israeli prime minister called Natan-Zada a 'bloodthirsty murderer and terrorist'. The Ministry of Defence in Tel Aviv refused to allow him to be buried among soldiers as he had sullied the honour of the Israeli Defence Forces, and the mayor of his home town refused to allow him to be buried there. Those among the right-wing settler community who might have been inclined to be more sympathetic felt compelled to condemn the action. This kind of comprehensive repudiation by a community of someone claiming to be acting in their name is striking.

We cannot know for sure if this kind of response will deter another young Israeli extremist from acting in the same way, but it is hard to believe that it could not. This young man may have succeeded in exacting revenge but he certainly got no renown nor did he succeed in provoking the desired reaction. If the local communities from which terrorists come were to respond in this way, there can be little doubt that terrorism would hold less attraction for young men seeking glory.

The US does not just need to engage the broader members of a community, it also needs to mobilize moderates. By engaging members of the local community in this way it has to be careful that they are not delegitimized by virtue of being associated with it. America must not insist as a price of its support that the moderates it attempts to mobilize are uncritical. There is no surer way of undermining them. The US needs to engage them and engage with their criticisms of its policies and its practices. It must demonstrate in its reaction to them that it respects the rights of others to oppose it. It simply does not accept their right to express their opposition through terrorism.

Again the experience of other countries provides many examples of how governments have successfully mobilized moderates against extremists. The Italian government's ability to defeat the Red Brigades was immeasurably enhanced by the role played by the Italian Communist Party. In Northern Ireland the British government endeavoured to strengthen the hand of the moderate nationalist party the SDLP (Social Democratic and Labour Party) as a counterweight to the IRA. Later, after the leader of the SDLP, John Hume, had engaged the leader of Sinn Fein, Gerry Adams, in talks, the government then concentrated on strengthening the hand of the pragmatists within the republican movement itself, such as Adams.

In another example, the Indian government assisted in the development of moderate political parties to represent the Sikhs as a counterweight to those who were prepared to deploy violence to achieve their political objectives. Similarly in Spain, the government sought to strengthen the moderate Basque Nationalist Party in an effort to demonstrate the advantages of a political approach to conflict resolution. For a time the government also permitted the emergence of the political party Herri Batasuna as a means of encouraging the ETA to pursue political means, but it revoked that recognition once it decided that Batasuna was no more than a front for the ETA. More recently the Spanish government has responded to the terrorist attacks in Madrid by working with the moderate leaders of Spain's one million Muslims. On the first anniversary of the bombing at Atocha station, which occurred on March 11, 2004 and killed 192 people, Mansur Escudero Bedate, secretary general of the Islamic Commission of Spain, issued a fatwa against bin Laden, al-Qaeda and all who use the Koran to try to justify terrorism.

It is worth pointing out that the experience of others indicates one very clear lesson, that the mobilization of moderates should never extend to the point of supporting one group that is prepared to use violence against another. This tactic invariably backfires. Indeed, one has only to look to American support of the mujahideen in Afghanistan as a counterweight to the Soviet Union for evidence of the folly of this approach. Prime Minister Sadat of

Egypt assisted in the development of the movement that eventually murdered him in his effort to develop a counterweight to communist parties. In Lebanon too, Israel unwittingly assisted in the creation of Hezbollah as radicals within the Amal movement resisted peace negotiations. Similarly, in the West Bank and Gaza, Israel turned a blind eye to the activities of the Muslim Brotherhood in the belief that these groups were more moderate than Fatah, but the result was the emergence of Hamas, which was much less moderate.

The lesson from other countries suggests the wisdom of engaging with moderate opinion and mobilizing and encouraging a moderate alternative to violence. It is not crucial that this moderate voice be supportive of the US position, but it is crucial that it oppose violent forms of political change.

Terrorist groups are often keenly aware of the threat posed to them by moderate leaders of their own community. The Tamil Tigers in particular have been ruthless in targeting moderate Tamil leaders for assassination. The Red Brigades also turned against the reformist Italian Communist Party, of which they were as critical as they were of the conservative Christian Democrats. The Red Brigades' murder in 1979 of Guido Rossi, a popular Communist Party activist, proved to be a major miscalculation. Spontaneous demonstrations and strikes in protest at Rossi's murder erupted in all the major factories of Genoa, previously a stronghold of support for the Brigadistas.

Terrorist groups often do make mistakes and go too far, even for their own supporters. Most commonly this happens when they start killing moderate leaders or particularly vulnerable populations, like children. These mistakes offer a hugely important opportunity for governments to mobilize opinion against the terrorists. In the past, governments have very rarely seized such opportunities. Most often governments react with severe security measures or by introducing draconian counter-terrorist legislation and promptly lose the moderate support they had the chance of gaining. If governments keep their eye on the objective of isolating the terrorists and preventing the spread of their ideology, they will capitalize on these terrorist atrocities and use them to further that objective rather than acceding to the provocation of the terrorists.

On the morning of July 7, 2005, the British prime minister Tony Blair was attending the G8 Summit in Gleneagles, Scotland, when four suicide bombers attacked the London transport system, killing fifty-six people, including themselves. Blair's early and apparently unscripted comments were the very model of how a democratic leader should respond to a terrorist attack. Far from elevating the rhetoric and engaging in the language of warfare or revenge, he spoke calmly of crime scenes and police work and of Britons' quiet determination to defend their values and way of life. The communication between terrorists and their audience is a constant narrative of blame, an unremitting contest to assume the role of victim to the other's aggressor. Blair simply refused to engage in this dialogue and in so doing modelled a different way for democratic leaders to respond to terrorism. In subsequent, and clearly scripted, speeches Blair slipped back into the more familiar and less constructive response mode generally adopted by democratic leaders.

The British government again displayed the good judgement that accompanies experience with countering terrorism when the IRA finally called off their military campaign and decommissioned their arsenal. Rather than treat IRA disarmament as the concession it was and employ the language of victory for political advantage, Blair instead used language that would help the IRA supporters of disarmament deal with their hardline critics.

The task of countering terrorism will be rendered much easier if the US is prepared to engage others, and to pay the price necessary to engage others, in the effort to contain it.

Rule Number 6: Have Patience and Keep Your Perspective

Some terrorist groups have lasted for generations, some have lasted only a few years. A list of the groups active in, say, 1970 reveals some very familiar names and many more that have long since been forgotten. Those that have lasted the longest have tended to be those that have close ties to their communities. These groups tend to be ethnic or nationalist groups seeking political change. Some of these groups too are no longer active. The IRA have finally declared an end to their military campaign and the PKK have been defeated by the action of the Turkish government, though the latent threat of resurgent terrorism among disfranchised Kurds remains real. The social revolutionary movements that posed a potent threat to several western democracies in the 1970s have all disintegrated through a combination of effective police work, popular repudiation and strategic mistakes by the terrorists.

Given the nature of the threat posed to the US by al-Qaeda and the global jihadi networks it has spawned, it is highly unlikely that these groups will disappear quickly. The duration of the threat they pose will in large part be determined by the nature of their relationships with the communities from which they come, and that in turn will depend upon US success in separating them from those communities. As many of the grievances that sustain these groups involve profound socio-economic realities and deeply intractable political problems, like the Arab–Israeli issue, they are unlikely to be redressed quickly. Concerted effort on America's part to address the resentment that drives the animosity against it will not bring immediate results but will serve to stem the growth of that resentment and to roll back the perceived legitimacy of a resort to terrorist tactics.

The language of warfare connotes action and immediate results. The US should replace this language with the language of development and construction and cultivate the patience that goes with it.

Terrorism in one form or another, therefore, is probably here to stay. The impact of globalization means that terrorist acts will be easier to plan and to conduct, weapons will be easier to acquire and to transport, and the enemy will be easier to reach than in the past. Nevertheless, the likelihood that terrorist groups could inflict real harm on the US remains very low. The possibility that a terrorist group could set off a bomb in an American subway, stadium or shopping mall will always be there. The probability that terrorists will kill as many Americans as drunk drivers will in any given year is tiny.

In thinking about the terrorist threat America faces we should always remember the words of Ayman al-Zahawiri himself: 'However far our capabilities reach, they will never be equal to one-thousandth of the capabilities of the kingdom of Satan that is waging war on us.' We can reject his characterization of the US without rejecting his basic point, that they will never have one-thousandth of America's strength. The US should bear this in mind as it contemplates the threat and plans its response. It is infinitely stronger than they are. This does not give it licence for complacency but it does give it the luxury of adopting a deliberative response and a long-time horizon. It also requires that America does not embolden them by confirming their belief in its cowardice by exaggerating the threat they pose.

The only way that terrorists could inflict real and lasting damage on the US is if they were to acquire a weapon of mass destruction, and not just any weapon of mass destruction. A dirty bomb or a chemical weapon could inflict serious damage but pose no real threat. The one way they could truly harm America is if they were to acquire and deploy a biological or nuclear weapon. The likelihood of this was always very low. It is even lower today because the US has deprived al-Qaeda, at least, of their base in Afghanistan and deterred other states from offering them sanctuary. Moreover, while the war on terror may have generated lots of new recruits for the terrorist cause, these new recruits are joining small ad-hoc groups and not those with sophisticated organizations and training sites. The threat nevertheless remains and, as I have mentioned, one of the easiest and least expensive ways of reducing it is to secure immediately all known facilities where these weapons are stored. In contemplating this threat it is also worth remembering that compared to twenty years ago, when the Soviet nuclear arsenal had the power to obliterate the United States, Americans are far less vulnerable to nuclear attack than they have been for a very long time.

The adoption of terrorism as a tactic is to engage in psychological warfare against a stronger enemy. Terrorism is an attractive tactic because it is easy and because it makes the weak seem stronger, but if the US can recognize terrorists' essential weakness, enhance societal resilience and calibrate its reaction to the actual risk it faces, it will make the task of the terrorists more difficult.

On September 16, 2001, President Bush declared America's goal to be 'to rout terrorism out of the world'. He said: 'We will rid the world of the evildoers.'[41] The truth is, we won't. But if the US has a more modest agenda, if its goal is to contain the threat from terrorism and if in doing so it plays to its strengths and abides by its principles, it can definitely succeed.

What Is to Come?

We are likely to encounter terrorism in the future just as we have in the past. We are going to have to learn to live with it and to accept it as a price of living in a complex world. Through improved security procedures and enhanced intelligence we must protect ourselves against the most dangerous weapons and most sophisticated attacks. We must always remember, however, that terrorists cannot derail our democracy by planting a bomb in our midst. Our democracy can be derailed only if we conclude that it is inadequate to protect us. I have argued here, however, that far from being inadequate our democratic principles are our strongest weapons. In the case of counter-terrorism our ethics and our interests are clearly aligned.

The most recent attacks in London, Madrid and the Netherlands all suggest that the Muslim diaspora in Europe will produce the next wave of terrorist attacks. The same ideology that motivated Michael Barrett in the 1860s motivated Seamus Finucane in the 1970s. Nationalism has never ceased in its attraction to those prepared to fight for the 'freedom' of their group. This sense of nationalism is as keenly felt in Sri Lanka, Chechnya, India, Spain and Iraq. Today, however, the 'national' group that young men of the European diaspora identify with is religious and transnational. Their exploitation of new technologies enables them to generate and sustain a sense of belonging to this wider community. In a metaphor that is often used by Muslim extremists, a Jemaah Islamiyah website declared: 'One Muslim to another is like a single body. If one part is in pain, the other part will also feel it.'[42] The fusion of nationalism and religion, as we have seen in Chechnya and Kashmir, is a troubling development as religious groups have always been the most absolutist and nationalist groups have always been most successful in maintaining ties to broader communities. Moreover, it is of course harder to predict where the theatre of operations will be when the cause is transnational. We can predict, based on past patterns of behaviour, that they will hit where we are not looking.

In Europe a generation ago, young, educated, alienated idealists like Mara Cagol who sought to change the world were mobilized by communism. Today young, educated, alienated idealists like Omar Sheikh, Ziad Jarrah and Sidique Khan are mobilized by jihadism. We do not know what ideology will mobilize the next generation of young idealists who want to change the world, who are prepared to sacrifice themselves and others in pursuit of their extremist ambition. We can be confident, however, that there will be another generation mobilized by yet another extremist ideology designed to protest against the inequities evident around them. We should be equally confident that we can withstand the threat they pose.

Notes

Introduction

1. Quoted by Rex A. Hudson in 'The Sociology and Psychology of Terrorism. Who Becomes a Terrorist and Why?' Federal Research Division, Library of Congress, 20540–4840, Washington DC, September 1999
2. For a recent example see the text of an interview I did on Minnesota Public Radio on December 27, 2004. This was a call-in radio show looking back on a year of the war on terror. http://news.minnesota. publicradio.org/programs/Midday
3. This oft-quoted expression dates back to John Bradford, a sixteenth-century Englishman, who commented on seeing a group of criminals being led to their execution. He was burned at the stake a few years later
4. Benjamin Franklin told his co-signatories: 'We must all sign together or most assuredly we will all hang separately.' The Irish signatories were executed by firing squad
5. The nomenclature of the IRA can be confusing to the uninitiated. The generic term, IRA, for Irish Republican Army, is the most commonly used in Ireland. In December 1969, however, a split in the IRA created two groups, the 'Provisional' IRA or 'Provos' for short, and the 'Official' IRA. The IRA before the split became known as the 'Old' IRA. In the course of the Troubles (the term given to the Northern Irish conflict), as the Provisionals became the most dominant group the qualifier 'Provisionals' was gradually dropped and the term IRA returned. In the early 1990s two further splinter groups emerged, the 'Real' IRA and 'Continuity' IRA, each claiming to be the true heirs of the historical IRA
6. Table 4 in Robert J. Art and Louise Richardson (eds), *Democracy and Counterterrorism: Lessons from the Past*, Washington DC: United States Institute of Peace, 2006

7. Comision de la Verdad y Reconciliacion Peru, *Informe Final: Tomo 1: Primera parte: El proceso, los hechos, las victimas*, Lima: Navarrete, 2003
8. This account of the campaign against the Shining Path is necessarily abbreviated. For a fuller account of the Peruvian counter-terrorist campaign against the Shining Path see David Scott Palmer, 'Peru and the Shining Path', in Art and Richardson (eds), *Democracy and Counterterrorism: Lessons from the Past*, Washington DC: United States Institute of Peace, 2006
9. Abu Ubeid Al-Qurashi, in *Al-Ansar*, issue no. 4, March 12, 2002

Part I: The Terrorists

1. Yasser Arafat, speech at the United Nations General Assembly, New York, November 13, 1974. Available at http://www.mideastweb.org/Arafat_at_un.htm

Chapter One: What Is Terrorism?

1. Maximilien Marie Isidore de Robespierre, 1758–94, member, National Assembly and Committee of Public Safety, speech, Paris, February 1794
2. Al-Qaeda statement, October 10, 2001. Reprinted in Barry Rubin and Judith Colp Rubin (eds), *Anti-American Terrorism and the Middle East*, Oxford: Oxford University Press, 2002, pp. 251–3
3. CNN, February 5, 2005. Transcript of interview of Osama bin Laden with Al-Jazeera correspondent Tayseer Alouni in October 2001
4. Interview with Chairman Gonzalo in *El Diario*, July 1988, p. 19. Available on Shining Path website. http://www.blythe.org/peru-pcp/docs_en/interv.htm. Accessed July 26, 1997
5. Interview aired on ABC News, *Nightline*, July 28, 2005
6. Osama bin Laden, interview with John Miller, ABC News, May 1998
7. Transcript of remarks by Jordanian officials. http://newdelhi.usembassy.gov/wwwhpro514b.html. Accessed June 15, 2005
8. Abu Ubeid al-Qurashi in *Al-Ansar*, issue no. 4, March 12, 2002
9. Rubin and Rubin (eds), *Anti-American Terrorism and the Middle East*, p. 261
10. Shamil Basayev, interview on ABC News, *Nightline*, July 27, 2005
11. Osama bin Laden interview, Al-Jazeera, 1998

12. Osama bin Laden, 'Message to America', October 30, 2004

13. Yasser Arafat, speech to United Nations General Assembly, New York, November 13, 1974. Le Monde Diplomatique. http://MondeDiplo. com/focus/mideast/a2288. Accessed June 20, 2005

14. Julie Wolf, 'People & Events: The Iran Contra Affair', available at http:// www.pbs.org/wgbh/amex/reagan/peopleevents/panddeo8.html. New content 1999–2000 PBS Online/WGBH. Accessed June 15, 2005

15. Osama bin Laden, interview with John Miller, ABC News, May 1998

16. Nelson Mandela, *Long Walk to Freedom*, Boston: Little Brown, 1994, p. 240

17. Osama bin Laden, 'Message to America', October 10, 2004

18. Basayev on ABC News, *Nightline*, July 27, 2005

19. Osama bin Laden, 'Letter to the American People', text in English in the *Observer* (London), November 24, 2002

20. Please consult Glossary for descriptions of these groups

21. See Andrew Silke (ed.), *Terrorists, Victims, Society: Psychological Perspectives on Terrorism and Its Consequences*, London: Wiley, 2003. Max Taylor, *The Terrorist*, London: Brassey's, 1988. Walter Reich (ed.), *Origins of Terrorism: Psychologies, Ideologies, Theologies, States of Mind*, Washington DC: Woodrow Wilson Center Press, 1998. Max Taylor and Edith Quale, *Terrorist Lives*, London: Brassey's, 1994

22. Peter Taylor, *Loyalists: War and Peace in Northern Ireland*, New York: TV Books, 1999, p. 8

23. On the PKK see Rex A. Hudson, *The Sociology and Psychology of Terrorism: Who Becomes a Terrorist and Why?*, Washington DC: Federal Research Division, Library of Congress 20540–4840, 1999, p. 47
On Islamist groups, even those who recruit for martyrdom operations see: Anne Marie Oliver and Paul Steinberg, *The Road to Martyrs' Square: A Journey into the World of the Suicide Bomber*, Oxford: Oxford University Press, 2005, p. 119, and Diego Gambetta, *Making Sense of Suicide Missions*, Oxford: Oxford University Press, 2005, p. 107

24. Quoted in *The Economist*, June 8, 2004. http://www.economist.com/ displaystory.cfm?story. Accessed June 20, 2005

25. Bruce Hoffman, 'The Logic of Suicide Terrorism', *Atlantic Monthly*, 291, 5, June 2003, 40–7. R. Pape, 'The Strategic Logic of Suicide Terrorism', *American Political Science Review*, 97, 2003, 343–61. Luca Ricolfi, 'Palestinians 1981–2003', in Gambetta (ed.), *Making Sense of Suicide Missions*, pp. 76–130

26. Quoted by Gregg Zoroya, in 'Woman Describes the Mentality of a Suicide Bomber', *USA Today*, April 22, 2002

27. See Chapter Five for more detailed coverage of suicide bombings. Louise Richardson, 'Blasts from the Past', *Financial Times*, July 5, 2005

28. Bernard Lewis, *The Assassins*, New York: Basic Books, 2002

29. President George W. Bush, Address to a Joint Session of Congress and the American People, September 20, 2001

30. Albert Camus, *Caligula and Three Other Plays*, New York: Vintage Books, 1958

31. Osama bin Laden, 'Declaration of War Against the Americans Occupying the Land of the Two Holy Places', August 1996

32. Vellupillai Prabakharan, interview, March 23, 1986 *The Week* (India), available on LTTE website

33. Nasra Hassan, 'An Arsenal of Believers Talking to the Human Bombs', *New Yorker*, November 19, 2001

34. Quoted in Garrett O'Boyle 'Theories of Justification and Political Violence: Examples from Four Groups', *Terrorism and Political Violence*, 14, 2, Summer 2002, p. 32

35. Mohamed Elmasry, President of the Canadian Islamic Congress, *Toronto Star*, October 23, 2004

36. Osama bin Laden, 'Letter to the American People', text in English in the *Observer*, November 24, 2002

37. Hassan, 'An Arsenal of Believers Talking to the Human Bombs'

38. Taylor, *Loyalists*, p. 92

39. Osama bin Laden, interview with John Miller, ABC News, May 1998

40. Alan Cullison, 'Inside Al Qaeda's Hard Drive', *Atlantic Monthly*, 294, 2, September 2004

41. Osama bin Laden, audiotape broadcast on *Al-Arabiya*, April 15, 2004

42. On the IRA hunger-strikers see David Beresford, *Ten Men Dead: The Story of the 1981 Hunger Strike*, London: HarperCollins, 1987, and Padraig O'Malley, *Biting at the Grave: the Irish Hunger Strikes and the Politics of Despair*, Boston: Beacon Press, 1990

43. See Gambetta (ed.), *Making Sense of Suicide Missions*. Oliver and Steinberg, *The Road to Martyrs' Square*. Pape, 'The Strategic Logic of Suicide Terrorism'. Hassan, 'An Arsenal of Believers Talking to the Human Bombs'

44. Oliver and Steinberg, *The Road to Martyrs' Square*, p. 155

Chapter Two: Where Have Terrorists Come From?

1. Yasser Arafat, speech at the UN General Assembly, New York, December 13, 1988, http://www.mideastweb.org/arafat1988.htm

2. This account relies heavily on Patrick Quinlivan and Paul Rose, *The Fenians in England, 1865–1872*, London: John Calder, 1982

3. Quoted in ibid., p. 95

4. Quoted in ibid., p. 96

5. The seminal piece on the three ancient groups is David C. Rapoport, 'Fear and Trembling: Terrorism in Three Religious Traditions', *American Political Science Review*, 78, 3, 1984, pp. 658–677. On the Fenians see T. W. Moody (ed.), *The Fenian Movement*, Cork: Learning Links, 1978, and F. S. L. Lyons, *Ireland Since the Famine*, Glasgow: Collins, 1973. On the anarchists see James Joll, *The Anarchists*, Cambridge, MA: Harvard University Press, 1980

6. There were, in fact, a number of different groups, some variously called Sicarii and Zealots. I have followed Rapoport in treating them as one

7. Josephus cited in Rapoport, 'Fear and Trembling', p. 670

8. Margaret Thatcher, speech to the American Bar Association, July 15, 1985: 'And we must find ways to starve the terrorist and the hijacker of the oxygen of publicity on which they depend.' Full text available at http://www.margaretthatcher.org/Speeches/displaydocument.asp?docis =106096&doctyp=1. Accessed June 23, 2005

9. Rapoport, 'Fear and Trembling', p. 662

10. 'Report of Saint-Just, February 26, 1794.' Cited in Hippolyte Taine, *The French Revolution*, trans. John Durand, Indianapolis: Liberty Fund, 2002, p. 910, n. 22

11. *Marx/Engels Collected Works (MECW)*, vol. 42, *Marx–Engels Correspondence 1867*, Marx to Engels in Manchester, December 14, 1867, London: Lawrence & Wishart, 1975–2005, p. 501

12. Ibid., Engels to Marx, December 19, 1867, p. 505

13. See Richard E. Rubenstein, *Alchemists of Revolution: Terrorism in the Modern World*, New York: Basic Books, 1987

14. See for example Osama bin Laden, audiotape, broadcast on Al-Arabiya, April 15, 2004

15. See Joll, *The Anarchists*. Paul Avrich, *Anarchist Portraits*, Princeton: Princeton University Press, 1990

Chapter Three: What Causes Terrorism?

1. Osama bin Laden, 'Message to America,' October 10, 2004
2. Ibid
3. George Paynter, interview, BBC, July 16 2002
4. David Shead, head referee of the European Arm Wrestling Federation, quoted in Yosri Fouda and Nick Fielding, *Masterminds of Terror*, New York: Arcade, 2003, p. 55
5. Ibid., p. 56
6. 'Omar Sheikh's Diaries Part II', *Indian Express*, October 11, 2001
7. Osama bin Laden, 'Dinner Party Tape', December 13, 2001, depicting a visit by bin Laden and his lieutenants to a sheikh, presumably in Afghanistan
8. Karl Rove, Remarks to the New York Conservative Party, June 22, 2005. Text available on Washingtonpost.com
9. The most influential psychological studies of aggression and violence have been associated with Freud, Fromm, Lorenz, Pavlov and Skinner
10. Osama bin Laden, statement broadcast on Al-Jazeera, November 3, 2001
11. Michael Baumann, *How It All Began*, Vancouver: Pulp Press, 1997. Donatella Della Porta, *Social Movement, Political Violence and the State: A Comparative Analysis of Italy and Germany*, Cambridge: Cambridge University Press, 1995. Kevin Toolis, *Rebel Hearts: Journeys Within the IRA's Soul*, New York: St Martin's, 1995. Peter Taylor, *The Loyalists: War and Peace in Northern Ireland*, New York: TV Books, 1999
12. 'Tamil National Leader Hon. V. Pirapaharan's Interview', *The Week*, (India) March 23, 1986. LTTE website
13. Chairman Gonzalo, interview in *El Diario*, July 1988, p. 58. Available on Shining Path website. Accessed July 26, 1997
14. Osama bin Laden, Statement, October 7, 2001
15. Osama bin Laden, 'Message to America', October 30, 2004. Translation in Bruce Lawrence (ed.), *Messages to the World: The Statements of Osama bin Laden*, New York: Verso, 2005, p. 239
16. President George W. Bush, Address to a Joint Session of Congress and the American People, September 20, 2001
17. Osama bin Laden, interview broadcast on Al-Jazeera, 1998. Full English text, July 10, 2001, News.telegraph.co.uk
18. Mark Juergensmeyer, *Terror in the Mind of God*, Berkeley, CA: University of California Press, 2000, p. 74

19. Osama bin Laden, interview with John Miller, ABC News, May 1998

20. Seamus Finucane to Kevin Toolis in *Rebel Hearts*, p. 104

21. Osama bin Laden, interview with Al-Jazeera, 1998. Full English text, July 10, 2001, News.telegraph.co.uk

22. Osama bin Laden, interview with Peter Arnett, CNN, March 1997

23. Marc Sageman, *Understanding Terror Networks*, University of Pennsylvania Press, 2004

24. Gilles Keppel, *Muslim Extremism in Egypt: The Prophet and the Pharaoh*, Berkeley, CA: University of California Press, 1995

25. Peter Bergen and Swati Pandey, 'The Madrassa Myth', *New York Times*, June 14, 2005

26. Jerrold M. Post, 'Notes on a Psychodynamic Theory of Terrorist Behavior', *Terrorism: An International Journal*, 7, 3, 1984, pp. 242–56

27. Jillian Becker, *Hitler's Children: The Story of the Baader–Meinhof Gang*, Philadelphia: J. P. Lippincott, 1977

28. Jerrold M. Post, Ehud Sprinzak and Laurita M. Denny, 'The Terrorists in Their Own Words: Interviews with 35 Incarcerated Middle Eastern Terrorists', *Terrorism and Political Violence*, 15, 1, Spring 2003, p. 176

29. Della Porta, *Social Movement, Political Violence and the State*, esp. Chapter 6

30. 'Life History' 12:35, in Della Porta, *Social Movement, Political Violence and the State*, p. 146

31. Anne Marie Oliver and Paul Steinberg, *The Road to Martyrs' Square: A Journey into the World of the Suicide Bomber*, Oxford: Oxford University Press, 2005. Kevin Toolis, *Rebel Hearts*

32. Eamon Collins, *Killing Rage*, London: Granta, 1997, p. 78

33. 'Tamil National Leader Hon. V. Pirapaharan's Interview', *The Week*, (India), March 23, 1986. LTTE website

34. United States Department of State, *Patterns of Terrorist Violence*, Washington DC, April 2003, p. 77

35. President George W. Bush, Address to a Joint Session of Congress and the American People, September 20, 2001

36. Louise Richardson, 'State Sponsorship: A Root Cause of Terrorism?', in Tore Bjorgo (ed.), *Root Causes of Terrorism: Myths, Reality and Ways Forward*, London: Routledge, 2005, pp. 189–97

37. Alan Krueger and Jitka Maleckova, NBER Working Paper no. w9074, Cambridge, MA: National Bureau of Economic Research, 2002. See also Krueger and Maleckova, 'Does Poverty Cause Terrorism?', *New Republic*, June 24, 2004

38. Human Development Report 2005, Chapter 2: Inequality and Human

Development (New York: United Nations Development Programme), http://hdr.undp.org/reports/global/2005. Accessed January 5, 2006

39. Ted Robert Gurr, *Why Men Rebel*, Princeton: Princeton University Press, 1970

40. As a mother of three children I generally come home from work without treats for my children. They do not expect any and are reasonably well behaved. If I were to bring home three candy bars and give one to each of my children one day, they would all be delighted, very appreciative and very well behaved (for a short time, at least). If I were to bring home four candy bars and give one each to my daughters and two to my son I would have two furious children, outraged by the injustice done to them. Now their objective condition would be better than if I brought home no candy bars, and no different than if I had given each child one, but in this instance they would be outraged. This, in essence, is relative deprivation

41. *The World Factbook* (Washington DC: CIA), Appendices: Field Listing – Unemployment Rate, http://www.cia.gov/cia/publications/factbook/fields/2129.html. Accessed January 5, 2006

42. *2005 World Population Data Sheet*, Washington DC: Population Reference Bureau, 2005

43. Scott Atran, 'Genesis of Suicide Terrorism', *Science*, 299, 7 March 2003, www.sciencemag.org

44. Osama bin Laden, interview with John Miller, ABC News, May 1998

45. Barry Rubin and Judith Colp Rubin, *Anti-American Terrorism and the Middle East*, Oxford: Oxford University Press, 2002, pp. 169–72

46. Judy Aita, 'Bombing Trial Witness Describes Nairobi Surveillance Mission', US Department of State, February 22, 2001. http://usinfo.state.gov/is/Archive_Index/Bombing_Trial_Witness_Describes_Nairobi_Surveillance_Mission.html. Accessed January 23, 2006

47. In recent years the Republic of Ireland has often ranked highest on the globalization index. The IRA's terrorism has emerged in the quite distinct economy of Northern Ireland

48. *Foreign Policy Magazine*, Index of Globalization, 2001–5

49. Quoted in Jessica Stern, *Terror in the Name of God: Why Religious Militants Kill*, New York: HarperCollins, 2003, pp. 40–1

50. Bruce Hoffman, *Inside Terrorism*, New York: Columbia University Press, 1998, p. 91

51. *Patterns of Global Terrorism 2003*, Washington DC: Department of State, April 2004

52. John Kifner, 'Israelis Investigate Far Right; May Crack Down on Speech', *New York Times*, November 8, 1995

53. On Aum Shinrikyo, see D. W. Brackett, *Holy Terror: Armageddon in Tokyo*, New York: Weatherhill, 1966, and Ian Reader, *Religious Violence in Contemporary Japan: The Case of Aum Shinrikyo*, Honolulu: University of Hawaii Press, 2000

54. Osama bin Laden, interview with Peter Arnett, CNN, March 1997

55. Ibid.

56. Osama bin Laden, 'Declaration of War against the Americans Occupying the Land of the Two Holy Places', August 1996

Chapter Four: The Three Rs: Revenge, Renown, Reaction

1. The account on pp. 95–8 is based on interviews with various members of the Finucane family in Kevin Toolis's fine book *Rebel Hearts: Journeys within the IRA's Soul*, New York: St Martin's, 1997, pp. 84–191

2. Among those who make this point is Robert Pape in an article in the *American Conservative*, July 19, 2005. In talking to groups this point is regularly made to me too by members of the audience

3. The publication of a book by Alan Dershowitz, *Why Terrorism Works*, New Haven: Yale University Press, New Haven, 2002, sparked a debate on this issue

4. Hannah Arendt, 'Reflections on Violence', *New York Review of Books*, 12, 4, February 27, 1969

5. Osama bin Laden, 'Dinner Party Tape', December 13, 2001

6. See the account in David A. Korn, *Assassination in Khartoum*, Bloomington: Indiana University Press, 1993

7. Peter Taylor, *Behind the Mask: The IRA and Sinn Fein*, New York: TV Books, 1997, p. 127

8. Gututz Jáuregui, 'Del nacionalismo sabiniano a la guerre revolucionaria (1963–1965)', in Antonio Elorza et al., *La Historia de ETA*, Madrid: Temas de hoy, 2000

9. Taylor, *Behind the Mask*, p. 127

10. Ibid., p. 305

11. Barry Rubin and Judith Colp Rubin (eds), *Anti-American Terrorism and the Middle East*, Oxford: Oxford University Press, 2002, p. 21

12. Quoted in Donatella Della Porta, *Social Movements, Political Violence and the State: A Comparative Analysis of Italy and Germany*, Cambridge: Cambridge University Press, 1995, p. 150

13. Interview posted on FARC's website. Available at http://www.farcep. org/pagina_ingles/interview/rrp111082001.html. Accessed July 27, 2005

14. *Al-Safir*, February 16, 1985, quoted in Rubin and Rubin (eds), *Anti-American Terrorism and the Middle East*, pp. 50–4

15. Ibid.

16. Robert C. Tucker, *Marx-Engels Reader*, New York: W. W. Norton, 1972, p. 160

17. Osama bin Laden, interview with Peter Arnett, CNN, March 1997

18. Interview with *El Diario*, July 1988, Peru, p. 54. http://www.blythe. org/peru-pcp/docs-en/interv.htm. Accessed July 26, 1997

19. Paul Reyes, interview with Luis Enrique González of *Prensa Latina*, July 20, 2001. Available at http://www.farcep.org/pagina_ingles/ interview/rrp111082001.html. Accessed July 27, 2005

20. *Sunday Magazine* (India), March 11–17, 1984, interview with Anita Pratap. Also available on LTTE website

21. ABC News, *Nightline*, July 28, 2005

22. Anne Marie Oliver and Paul Steinberg, *The Road to Martyrs' Square: A Journey into the World of the Suicide Bomber*, Oxford: Oxford University Press, 2005, p. 148

23. Ibid., p. 146

24. Ibid., p. 79

25. 'Communiqué on the Attempted Assassination of Hans Neusel, State Secretary in the German Ministry of the Interior, in Cologne on 27 July 1990', in Yonah Alexander and Dennis A. Pluchinsky, *Europe's Red Terrorists: The Fighting Communist Organizations*, London: Frank Cass, 1992, pp. 70–4

26. 'Communiqué on the assassination of Dr José Ramón Muñoz in Zaragoza on 27 March 1990', in ibid., pp. 127–9

27. Taylor, *Behind the Mask*, pp. 151–2

28. Peter Taylor, *Loyalists: War and Peace in Northern Ireland*, New York: TV Books, 1999, pp. 91–2

29. Quoted in Della Porta, *Social Movements, Political Violence and the State*, p. 155

30. Quoted in ibid.

31. Osama bin Laden, 'Message to America', October 30, 2004

32. Osama bin Laden, audiotape, April 15, 2004, broadcast on Al-Arabiya

33. Osama bin Laden, 'Declaration of War against the Americans Occupying the Land of the Two Holy Places', August 1996

34. Osama bin Laden, 'Dinner Party Tape', December 13, 2001

35. Osama bin Laden, Statement shown on Al-Jazeera, November 3, 2001
36. Osama bin Laden, interview on Al-Jazeera, December 27, 2001
37. *New York Times*, July 29, 2005, p. 1
38. Jerrold M. Post, Ehud Sprinzak and Laurita M. Denny, 'The Terrorists in Their Own Words: Interviews with 35 Incarcerated Middle Eastern Terrorists', *Terrorism and Political Violence*, 15, 1, Spring 2003, p. 178
39. Della Porta, *Social Movements, Political Violence and the State*, p. 159
40. Ibid., p. 158
41. Osama bin Laden, Statement shown on Al-Jazeera, November 3, 2001
42. Rubin and Rubin (eds), *Anti-American Terrorism and the Middle East*, p. 274
43. Interview with *El Diario*, July 1988, Peru, p. 54. http://www.blythe. org/peru-pcp/docs-en/interv.htm. Accessed July 26, 1997
44. Jean Marcel Bougereau, 'Memoirs of an International Terrorist: Conversations with Hans Joachim Klein', in *The German Guerrilla*, Orkney: Cienfuegos Press, p. 36
45. Jerrold M. Post, 'The Socio-cultural Underpinnings of Terrorist Psychology: When Hatred Is Bred in the Bone', in Tore Bjorgo (ed.), *Root Causes of Terrorism: Myths, Reality and Ways Forward*, New York: Routledge, 2005, p. 61
46. Ibid., p. 63
47. Kevin Cullen, 'From Terrorist to Priest', *Boston Globe*, Sunday Magazine, August 7, 2005, p. 20
48. Post, Sprinzak and Denny, 'The Terrorists in Their Own Words', p. 177
49. Cullen, 'From Terrorist to Priest'
50. Osama bin Laden, interview with Peter Arnett, CNN, March 1997
51. Interview with Anita Pratap, *Sunday Magazine* (India), March 11–17, 1984. Also on LTTE website
52. Interview aired on ABC News, *Nightline*, July 28, 2005
53. Interview with *El Diario*, July 1988, Peru, p. 54. http://www. blythe.org/peru-pcp/docs-en/interv.htm. Accessed July 26, 1997
54. Osama bin Laden, Statement, November 3, 2001
55. Osama bin Laden, interview with Peter Arnett, CNN, March 1997
56. Eamon Collins, *Killing Rage*, London: Granta, 1997, pp. 59–60
57. See especially Bernard Lewis, *What Went Wrong: Western Impact and Middle Eastern Response*, Oxford: Oxford University Press, 2002
58. Osama bin Laden, interview on Al-Jazeera, December 27, 2001
59. Osama bin Laden, 'Declaration of War Against the Americans Occupying the Land of the Two Holy Places', August 1996, p. 19

60. Abu Ubeid al-Qurashi, Middle East Media Research Institute, report no. 353, March 12, 2002
61. In Rubin and Rubin (eds), *Anti-American Terrorism and the Middle East*, p. 32
62. Osama bin Laden, audiotape, April 15, 2004
63. Osama bin Laden, interview on Al-Jazeera, 1998
64. Osama bin Laden, 'Open Letter to King Fahd', August 1995, part 4
65. Osama bin Laden, 'Fatwa Urging Jihad Against Americans', February 23, 1998
66. Osama bin Laden, interview with Peter Arnett, CNN, March 1997
67. Abu Ubeid al-Qurashi in *Al-Ansar*, issue no. 4. Translation by Middle East Media Research Institute, report no. 353, March 12, 2002
68. Osama bin Laden, interview with Peter Arnett, CNN, March 1997
69. Ed Moloney, *A Secret History of the IRA*, New York: W.W. Norton, 2002, pp. 121–2
70. Tim Pat Coogan, *The IRA: A History*, Boulder, CO: Roberts Rinehart, 1994, pp. 299–302. William Whitelaw, *Whitelaw Memoirs*, London: Aurum Press, 1989, pp. 99–100. Sean Mac Stiofain, *Memoirs of a Revolutionary*, Edinburgh: Gordon Cremonesi, 1975, p. 281
71. Della Porta, *Social Movements, Political Violence and the State*, p. 146
72. Interview with Mullah Umar Muhammad, September 21, 2001 in Rubin and Rubin (eds), *Anti-American Terrorism in the Middle East*, pp 247–249
73. Ayman al-Zawahiri, *Knights Under the Prophet's Banner*, Summer 2001, translation by FBIS (Foreign Broadcast Information Service)
74. *Al-Ansar* is al-Qaeda's online magazine. Abu Ubeid al-Qurashi is thought to be a leader of al-Qaeda. *Al-Ansar*, issue no. 4. Translation by Middle East Media Research Institute, report no. 353, March 12, 2002

Chapter Five: Why Do Terrorists Kill Themselves?

1. 'It is a sweet and glorious thing to die for one's country': Quintus Horatus Flaccus (Horace), *Odes*, 111, 11, 13
2. George La Hir, writing of Verdun in the *New York Times*, 1916, cited in Jeremy Black (ed.), *The Seventy Great Battles in History*, London: Thames & Hudson, 2005, p. 236
3. Quoted in the *Guardian*, July 14, 2005

4. Quoted in the *Guardian*, July 13, 2005

5. Ariel Merari makes this argument in his lectures to students that we have jointly taught at Harvard Law School

6. See Stephen Frederic Dale, 'Religious Suicide in Islamic Asia: Anti-colonial Terrorism in India, Indonesia and the Philippines', *Journal of Conflict Resolution*, 32, 1, March 1988, pp 37–59, on which this account is based

7. Robert A. Pape, *Dying to Win: The Strategic Logic of Suicide Terrorism*, New York: Random House, 2005, p. 139

8. Stephen Hopgood, 'Tamil Tigers, 1987–2002', and Luca Ricolfi, 'Palestinians, 1981–2003', in Diego Gambetta (ed.), *Making Sense of Suicide Missions*, Oxford: Oxford University Press, 2005, pp. 44 and 82

9. Rohan Gunaratna, 'The LTTE and Suicide Terrorism', *Frontline* (India), 17, 3, February 5–8, 2000

10. About 90 per cent of Tamils are Hindu, but the Tamil Tigers are avowedly secular

11. Sumantra Bose, *States, Nations, Sovereignty: Sri Lanka, India and the Tamil Eelam Movement*, New Delhi: Sage, 1994, p. 118

12. Hopgood, 'Tamil Tigers, 1987–2002', p. 74

13. Charu Lata Joshi, 'Ultimate Sacrifice: Faced with Harassment and Economic Deprivation, Young Tamils Are Ready to Give Up Their Lives', *Far Eastern Economic Review*, 1 June 2002

14. Quoted in P. Schalk, 'Resistance and Martyrdom on the Process of State Formation in Tamililam', in J. Pettigrew (ed.), *Martyrdom and Political Resistance*, Amsterdam: VU University Press, 1997, p. 79

15. One has to imagine that the logistics of this are difficult

16. Quoted in Gambetta (ed.), *Making Sense of Suicide Missions*, p. 64

17. Amy Waldman, 'Masters of Suicide Bombing: Tamil Guerrillas of Sri Lanka', *New York Times*, January 14, 2003

18. Quoted in Charu Lata Joshi, 'Ultimate Sacrifice: Faced with Harassment and Economic Deprivation, Young Tamils Are Ready to Give Up Their Lives'

19. Ibid.

20. Ibid.

21. Christoph Reuter, *My Life as a Weapon: A Modern History of Suicide Bombing*, trans. Helena Ragg Kirkby, Princeton: Princeton University Press, 2004

22. Ibid., p. 57

23. Ariel Merari, 'Social, Organizational and Psychological Factors in Suicide Terrorism', in Tore Bjorgo (ed.), *Root Causes of Terrorism: Myths, Reality and Ways Forward*, New York: Routledge, 2005, p. 72

24. Gambetta (ed.), *Making Sense of Suicide Missions*, p. 288

25. See Peter Hill, 'Kamikaze 1943–45', in ibid., pp. 1–42

26. Ibid., pp. 24–5

27. Ibid., p. 23

28. For excellent accounts see David Beresford, *Ten Men Dead: The Insider Story of the 1981 Hunger Strike*, London: HarperCollins, 1987, and Padraig O'Malley, *Biting at the Grave: The Irish Hunger Strikes and the Politics of Despair*, Boston: Beacon Press, 1990

29. Anne Marie Oliver and Paul Steinberg, *The Road to Martyrs' Square; A Journey into the World of the Suicide Bomber*, Oxford: Oxford University Press, 2005, p. 119

30. Daniel Pipes, 'Arafat's Suicide Factory', *New York Post*, December 9, 2001

31. Quoted in Gregg Zoroya, 'Woman Describes the Mentality of a Suicide Bomber', *USA Today*, April 22, 2002

32. Nasra Hassan, 'An Arsenal of Believers', *New Yorker*, November 19, 2001

33. Robert Pape argues that there were 315 suicide attacks worldwide between 1980 and 2003 (*Dying to Win*, p. 15). There were about 400 between the US invasion of Iraq in 2003 and June 2005 (*Washington Post*, July 17, 2005). The most extensive quantitative analysis of suicide attacks has been conducted by Pape in *Dying to Win*. His numbers, however, are lower than those of most other analysts familiar with the cases. Nevertheless the general point about the scale of the tactic in Iraq compared to elsewhere remains

34. The most detailed analysis of the foreign insurgents in Iraq is a September 2005 study by Andrew Cordesman and Nawaf Obaid of the Centre for Strategic and International Studies (CSIS). They argue that of the 3,000 foreign insurgents 600 are Algerians, 550 Syrians, 500 Sudanese, 400 Egyptians, 350 Saudis. Most other reports have assumed the Saudis to be the largest contingent

35. Aparisim Ghosh, 'Inside the Mind of an Iraqi Suicide Bomber', *Time*, July 4, 2005

36. Ibid.

37. Ibid.

38. Barbara Victor, *Army of Roses: Inside the World of Palestinian Women Suicide Bombers*, New York: Rodale (St Martin's), 2003, p. 19

39. Quoted in ibid., p. 30

40. Libby Copeland, 'Female Suicide Bombers: The New Factor in Mideast's Deadly Equation', *Washington Post*, April 27, 2002. Avishai Margalit, 'The Suicide Bombers', *New York Review of Books*, January 16, 2003

41. Victor, *Army of Roses*, p. 33
42. Quotes in ibid., p. 266
43. 'Homicide Bomber-Mom Kills Four at Gaza Border', FoxNews.com, January 14, 2004
44. Quoted in Victor, *Army of Roses*, p. 242
45. Manuela Dviri, 'My Dream Was to Be a Suicide Bomber. I Wanted to Kill 20, 50 Jews, Yes, Even Babies', Daily *Telegraph* (London), June 26, 2005
46. Victor, *Army of Roses*, p. 112
47. This is the argument of Barbara Victor in *Army of Roses*
48. Dviri, 'My Dream Was to Be a Suicide Bomber'
49. Quoted in Victor, *Army of Roses*, p. 253
50. Ibid., p. 35
51. *Daily Star* (Beirut), February 8, 2002. Quoted in Haim Malka, 'Must Innocents Die? The Islamic Debate over Suicide Attacks', *Middle East Quarterly*, Spring 2003, http://www.meforum.org/article530
52. Quoted in Rohan Gunaratna, 'The LTTE and Suicide Terrorism', *Frontline* (India), 17, February 5–8, 2000
53. Stathis Kalyvas and Ignacio Sanchez-Cuenca, 'Killing Without Dying: The Absence of Suicide Missions', in Gambetta (ed.), *Making Sense of Suicide Missions*, p. 211
54. See his *Knights Under the Prophet's Banner*, Summer 2001, translation by FBIS
55. Pape, *Dying to Win*, p. 190
56. Hassan, 'An Arsenal of Believers'
57. Ibid.
58. Quoted in Victor, *Army of Roses*, p. 112
59. Hassan, 'An Arsenal of Believers'
60. Ibid.
61. Merari, 'Social, Organizational and Psychological Factors in Suicide Terrorism'. Nasra Hassan also described these training sessions in 'An Arsenal of Believers'
62. Oliver and Steinberg, *The Road to Martyrs' Square*, p. 31
63. Ricolfi, 'Palestinians 1981–2003', p. 113
64. Oliver and Steinberg, *The Road to Martyrs' Square*, pp. 153–4
65. Merari, 'Social, Organizational and Psychological Factors in Suicide Terrorism'
66. Public Opinion Poll no. 15, Palestinian Centre for Policy and Survey Research, March 2005

67. Public Opinion Poll no. 54, Jerusalem Media and Communications Centre, May 2005

68. Public Opinion Poll no. 9, Palestinian Centre for Policy and Survey Research, October 2003

69. Hassan, 'An Arsenal of Believers'

70. Quoted in Reuter, *My Life as a Weapon*, p. 155

71. Victor, *Army of Roses*, p. 37

72. Ibid., p. 206

73. Hassan, 'An Arsenal of Believers'

74. Thomas L. Friedman, 'Marines Release Diagram on Blast', *New York Times*, October 28, 1983

75. Ghosh, 'Inside the Mind of an Iraqi Suicide Bomber'

76. Oliver and Steinberg, *The Road to Martyrs' Square*, p. 122

77. Ronald Reagan, *An American Life*, New York: Simon & Schuster, 1990, p. 465

78. Texts of the statements can be found on BBC News.com

79. BBC.com, July 7, 2005

80. One of the four, Germaine Lindsay, was born in Jamaica

81. Quoted in *Guardian*, July 13, 2005

Part II: The Counter-Terrorists

1. President George W. Bush, Address to a Joint Session of Congress and the American People, September 20, 2001

2. Osama bin Laden, Sermon for the Feast of the Sacrifice, February 2003. The Middle East Media Research Institute, Special Dispatch Series, no. 476, March 5, 2003

Chapter Six: What Changed and What Did Not on 9/11

1. President George W. Bush, Address to a Joint Session of Congress and the American People, September 20, 2001

2. Lord Campbell, House of Commons, March 19, 1868, Hansard

3. Terry McDermot, *Perfect Soldiers: The Hijackers: Who They Were, Why They Did It*, New York: HarperCollins, 2005, p. 234

4. Text in ibid., p. 231

5. This account relies on ibid.

6. Yosri Fouda and Nick Fielding, *Masterminds of Terror*, New York: Arcade, 2003, pp. 98–100

7. *Patterns of Global Terrorism 2000*, Department of State, Washington DC: April 2001

8. *Patterns of Global Terrorism 1999*, Department of State, Washington DC: April 2000

9. Franz Fanon, *The Wretched of the Earth*, New York: Grove Press, 1963

10. President George W. Bush, Address to a Joint Session of Congress and the American People, September 20, 2005

11. McVeigh was actually pulled over by the Oklahoma Highway Patrol officer for driving without a licence. He was linked to the bombing as he was about to be released two days later

12. NBC News, *Meet the Press*, September 14, 2003

13. CBS News/*New York Times* Poll, October 25–28, 2001, PollingReport.com, Terrorism (7), http://www.pollingreport.com/terror7.htm. Accessed February 14, 2006

14. Osama bin Laden, Sermon on the Feast of the Sacrifice, February 11, 2003, Middle East Media Research Institute Special Dispatch Series, no. 476, March 5, 2003

15. President George W. Bush, Address to the Nation, September 11, 2001

16. President George W. Bush, Nampa, Idaho, August 24, 2005

17. Harris Poll, September 19–24, 2001, PollingReport.com, Terrorism (8), http://www.pollingreport.com/terror8.htm. Accessed February 14, 2006

18. Ipsos-Reid Poll, September 11, 2001, PollingReport.com, Terrorism (10), http://www.pollingreport.com/terror10.htm. Accessed February 14, 2006

19. Figures from the Center for Disease Control (CDC), Total Deaths Data Set, United States 2001, and CDC, Alcohol-Attributable Deaths Report, United States 2001, and National Highway Traffic Safety Administration FARS data

20. Alan Prendergast, 'A Simple Case. How a Drunk Driving Fatality Got Lost in the System', Westword.com, September 25, 2003

21. President George W. Bush, Remarks by the President on Arrival, The South Lawn, September 16, 2001

22. President George W. Bush, Address to a Joint Session of Congress and the American People, September 20, 2001

23. Pew Research Center survey conducted by Princeton Survey Research Associates. August 14–25, 2002, PollingReport.com, Terrorism (5),

http://www.pollingreport.com/terror5.htm. Accessed February 14, 2006

24. President George W. Bush, Address to a Joint Session of Congress and the American People, September 20, 2001

25. President George W. Bush, National Endowment for Democracy, October 6, 2005

26. See Mark Juergensmeyer, 'Religion as a Cause of Terrorism', in Peter R. Neumann and Louise Richardson (eds), *Democracy and Terrorism volume I: The Roots of Terrorism*, New York: Routledge, 2006

27. President George W. Bush, West Point, June 1, 2002

28. ABC News Poll, October 8–9, 2001, PollingReport.com, Terrorism (8), http://www.pollingreport.com/terror8.htm. Accessed February 14, 2006

29. FOX News/Opinion Dynamics Poll, September 8–9, 2002, PollingReport.com, Terrorism (5), http://www.pollingreport.com/terror5.htm. Accessed February 14, 2006

30. Murray Sayle, 'Nerve Gas and Four Noble Truths', *New Yorker*, 1 April 1996, p. 71

31. BBC News.com, 'Factory Bombing: A Matter of Evidence', 5 May 1999

32. John McWenthy, 'Bin Laden Set to Strike Again?', ABC News, 16 June 1999. 'Afghan Alliance – UBL Trying to Make Chemical Weapons', *Parwan Payam-e Mojahed*, 23 December 1999

33. Muhammad Salah, 'Bin Laden Front Reportedly Bought CBW from E. Europe', *Al-Hayah*, April 20, 1999. Muhammad Salah, 'US Said [to be] Interrogating Jihadist Over CBW', *Al-Hayah*, April 21, 1999

34. Guido Olimpio, 'Islamic Group Said [to be] Preparing Chemical Warfare on the West', *Corriere della Sera*, July 8, 1998. Yosef Bodansky, *Bin Laden: The Man Who Declared War on America*, Roseville, CA: Prima, 2001, p. 326

35. Pamela Hess, 'Al Qaeda May Have Chemical Weapons', *United Press International*, August 19, 2002. *Insight*, CNN, August 19, 2002

36. Eric Croddy, 'Chemical Terrorist Plot in Rome?', *CNS Research Story*, March 11, 2002

37. Alan Cullison and Andrew Higgins, 'Computer in Kabul Holds Chilling Memos', *Wall Street Journal*, December 31, 2001. 'Report: Al Qaeda Computer Had Plans for Bio-Weapons', Reuters, December 21, 2001

38. Barton Gellman, 'Al Qaeda Near Biological, Chemical Arms Production', *Washington Post*, March 23, 2003

39. Gwynne Roberts, 'Militia Defector Claims Baghdad Trained Al Qaeda Fighters in Chemical Warfare', *Sunday Times* (London), 14 July 2002

40. Joby Warrick, 'An Al Qaeda "Chemist" and the Quest for Ricin', *Washington Post*, May 5, 2004

41. Chris Summers, 'Questions Over Ricin Conspiracy', BBC News, April 13, 2005

42. Richard Norton Taylor, 'Ricin Plot: London and Washington Used Plot to Strengthen Iraq War Push', *The Guardian*, April 14, 2005. May Ridden, 'With Poison in Their Souls', *Observer* (London), April 17, 2005

43. The eleventh volume of this 5,000-page tome is devoted to instructions on how to construct chemical and biological weapons

44. A. J. Venter, 'Elements Loyal to Bin Laden Acquire Biological Agents "Through the Mail"', *Intelligence Review*, August 1999

45. 'Prague Discounts an Iraqi Meeting', *New York Times*, October 21, 2001

46. 'Al Qaeda: Anthrax Found in al-Qaeda Home', *Global Security Newswire*, December 10, 2001. 'Walker Lindh: Qaeda Planned More Attacks', CNN, October 3, 2002

47. Judith Miller, 'Labs Suggest Qaeda Planned to Build Arms, Officials Say', *New York Times*, September 2002. Michael Gordon, 'US Says It Found Qaeda Lab Being Built to Produce Anthrax', *New York Times*, March 23, 2002. Dominic Evans, 'US Troops Found Afghan Biological Lab', Reuters, March 22, 2002

48. 'Al Qaeda Made Biological Weapons in Georgia – French Minister', *Moscow News*, January 3, 2005

49. James Gordon, 'Feds Find Poison Plot vs. Gulf Troops', *Daily News*, February 10, 2003. Mike Toner, 'Humble Bean Produces a Deadly Toxin', *Fox News Service*, March 20, 2003. Maria Ressa, 'Reports Al Qaeda Operative Sought Anthrax', CNN, October 10, 2003. Judith Miller, 'US Has New Concerns About Anthrax Readiness', *New York Times*, December 28, 2003

50. David C. Rapoport, 'Terrorism and Weapons of the Apocalypse', *National Security Studies Quarterly*, 5 (3), 1999, p. 57

51. Ibid., p. 52

52. FOX News/Opinion Dynamics Poll, September 19–20, 2001, PollingReport.com, Terrorism (9), http://www.pollingreport.com/terror9.htm. Accessed February 14, 2006

53. FOX News/Opinion Dynamics Poll, June 4–5, 2002, PollingReport.com, Terrorism (6), http://www.pollingreport.com/terror6.htm. Accessed February 14, 2006

54. Osama bin Laden, interview with Al-Jazeera, 1998. English text available at News.Telegraph, filed July 10, 2001

55. Riyad Alam al-Din, 'Report links Bin Laden, Nuclear Weapons', *Al-Watran al-Arabi*, November 12, 1998. Emil Torabi, 'Bin Laden's Nuclear Weapons', *Muslim Magazine*, Winter 1998

56. Benjamin Weiser, 'US Says Bin Laden Aide Tried to Get Nuclear Weapons', *New York Times*, September 26, 1998

57. 'Arab Security Sources Speak of a New Scenario for Afghanistan: Secret Roaming Networks that Exchange Nuclear Weapons for Drugs', *Al-Sharq al-Awsat*, December 24, 2000

58. Ibid.

59. 'N-weapons May Be in US Already', *Daily Telegraph* (Sydney, Australia), November 14, 2001

60. 'Al-Qaeda Does Not Have Our Nuclear Bombs, Insists Ukraine', *Scotsman*, February 11, 2004. 'Al-Qaeda Said to Possess Nuclear Arms', Associated Press, February 9, 2004

61. 'Osama Bin Laden's Bid to Acquire Weapons of Mass Destruction Represents the Greatest Threat That Western Civilization Has Faced', *Mail on Sunday* (London), June 23, 2002

62. FOX News/Opinion Dynamics Poll, November 14–15, 2001, PollingReport.com, Terrorism (7), http://www.pollingreport.com/terror7.htm. Accessed February 14, 2006

63. Adam Nathan and David Leppard, 'Al Qaeda's Men Held Secret Meetings to Build a Dirty Bomb', *Sunday Times* (London), October 14, 2001

64. Uthman Tizghart, 'Does Bin Laden Really Possess Weapons of Mass Destruction? Tale of Russian Mafia Boss Simon Mogilevich Who Supplied Bin Laden with the Nuclear "Dirty Bomb" ', *Al-Majallah* (London), November 25, 2001

65. Ed Johnson, 'Report: Al Qaeda Made Bomb in Afghanistan', Associated Press, January 30, 2003

66. Nick Fielding, 'Bin Laden's Dirty Bomb Quest Exposed', *London Times Online*, December 19, 2004

67. 'The case against Jose Padilla', *Online Newshour*, June 1, 2004

68. Osama bin Laden made this assertion in an interview with Rahilullah Yusufzai, who reports for both *Time* magazine and ABC News. See *Time*, January 11, 1999

69. Hamid Mir, 'Osama Claims He Has Nukes: If US Used Narms It Will Get Same Response', *Dawn* (Pakistan), November 10, 2001. There have been doubts expressed about the authenticity of this interview

70. Jamie McIntyre, 'Zubaydah: Al Qaeda Had Dirty Bomb Know How', CNN, April 22, 2002. 'Al-Qaeda Claims Dirty Bomb Know How', BBC, April 23, 2002
71. Max Delany, 'Under Attack Al Qaeda Makes Nuclear Claim', *Moscow News*, March 3, 2004
72. John Mueller and Karl Mueller, 'Sanctions of Mass Destruction', *Foreign Affairs*, 78, 3, 1999, p. 51
73. David C. Rapoport, 'Terrorism and Weapons of the Apocalypse', *National Security Studies Quarterly*, 5, 3, 1999, p. 52
74. Pew Research Center for the People and the Press available at http://people-press.org/reports/print.php3. Page ID 441. Released April 11, 1996
75. Report of the work of Michael J. Flanagan and Michael Sivak in *Science News Online*, January 11, 2003
76. Garrick Blalock, Vrinda Kadiyali and Daniel H. Simon, 'The Impact of 9/11 on Driving Fatalities: The Other Lives Lost to Terrorism', February 25, 2005

Chapter Seven: Why the War on Terror Can Never Be Won

1. General George Grivas, leader of the Greek Cypriot terrorist group EOKA (1955–8), referring to the actions of the British Army, in Charles Foley (ed.), *The Memoirs of General Grivas*, New York: Praeger, 1965, p. 53
2. Bommi Baumann, a leading member of the German terrorist group the June 2nd Movement, explains how he was radicalized by the shooting of a New Left student, Benno Ohnesorg, during demonstrations against a visit by the shah of Iran in June 1967. Bommi Baumann, *Wie Alles Anfing, How it all Began*, translated by Helene Ellenbogen and Wayne Parker, Vancouver: Pulp Press (2nd edition), 1981, p. 40
3. President George W. Bush, Address to the Nation, September 11, 2001
4. President George W. Bush, Address to a Joint Session of Congress and the American People, September 20, 2001
5. http://4.law.cornell.edu/uscode50/usc
6. http://www.ict.org.il/articles/fatwah.htm
7. President George W. Bush, Remarks by the President upon Arrival, The South Lawn, September 16, 2001
8. See for example CBS News/*New York Times* poll, September 20–23, 2001, PollingReport.com, Terrorism (9), http://www.pollingreport.com/terror9.htm. Accessed January 10, 2006

9. The full texts of this and other Weathermen communiqués are available at http://www.sunrisedancer.com/radicalreader/library/weatherman/weatherman45.asp

10. President Ronald Reagan, Address to the 41st Session of the UN General Assembly in New York, September 22, 1986

11. See for example 'The War on Terrorism', *New York Times*, April 2, 1881

12. Jean-Marie Colombani, *Le Monde* (Paris, France), September 12, 2001

13. Stephen F. Szabo, *Parting Ways: The Crisis in German–American Relations*, Washington DC: Brookings, 2004, p. 15, and related to the author by some of those who were present

14. Douglas Feith, as quoted by Fred Kaplan in 'Bush's Many Miscalculations', *Slate*, September 9, 2003

15. United States Department of Defense, News Transcript, 'Secretary Rumsfeld Media Availability En Route to Poland', September 22, 2002

16. See for example Szabo, *Parting Ways*, p. 16

17. The Pew Research Center, *Global Attitudes Survey*, May 2003

18. *Los Angeles Times* poll, September 13–14 2001, PollingReport.com, Terrorism (10), http://www.pollingreport.com/terror10.htm. Accessed January 10, 2006

19. CBS News/*New York Times* poll, September 20–23, 2001, PollingReport.com, Terrorism (9), http://www.pollingreport.com/terror9.htm; and Pew Research Center, November 13–19, 2001, PollingReport.com, Terrorism (7), http://www.pollingreport.com/terror7.htm. Accessed January 10, 2006

20. ABC News/*Washington Post* poll, September 13, 2001, PollingReport.com, Terrorism (10), http://www.pollingreport.com/terror10.htm; and CBS News/*New York Times* poll, September 20–23, 2001, PollingReport.com, Terrorism (8), http://www.pollingreport.com/terror8.htm. Accessed January 10, 2006

21. President George W. Bush, Oval Office, September 28, 2001.

22. President George W. Bush, Warsaw Conference, November 6, 2001.

23. President George W. Bush, Ontario, California, January 5, 2002.

24. President George W. Bush, Remarks by the President on Arrival, The South Lawn, September 16, 2001

25. President George W. Bush, Address to a Joint Session of Congress and the American People, September 20, 2001

26. *Investor's Business Daily/Christian Science Monitor* poll, conducted by TIPP, the polling arm of TechnoMetrica Market Intelligence, November 7–11, 2001, PollingReport.com, Terrorism (7), http://www.pollingreport.com/terror7.htm. Accessed January 10, 2006

27. BBC News.com, 'London Bomber: Text in Full', September 1, 2005
28. Alberto R. Gonzales, Memorandum, 'Decision Re Application of the Geneva Convention on Prisoners of War to the Conflict with Al Qaeda and the Taliban', January 25, 2002. Available at http://msnbc.msn.com/id/4999148/site/newsweek
29. The Pew Global Attitudes Project, June 23, 2005
30. BBC poll available at http://news.bbc.co.uk/1/shared/spl/hi/programmes/wtwta/poll/html/military/global_security
31. ABC News/*Washington Post* poll, October 7, 2001, PollingReport.com, Terrorism (8), http://www.pollingreport.com/terror8.htm. Accessed January 10, 2006
32. For estimates on casualty figures see Robert J. Art and Louise Richardson (eds), *Democracy and Counterterrorism: Lessons from the Past*, Washington DC: United States Institute of Peace, 2006, table 4
33. Congressional Research Service, no. 1B89118, updated June 10, 2005
34. Organization of American States, Inter-American Commission on Human Rights, *Report on the Situation of Human Rights in Argentina*, Washington DC, 1980, p. 135n
35. Guillermo Rojas, *30,000 Desaparececidos Realidad, Mito y Dogma*, Buenos Aires: Editorial Santiago Apostol, 2003. *Nunca Mas: A Report by Argentina's National Commission on Disappeared People*, London: Faber & Faber, 1986
36. Report available at http://www.amnesty.it/Allibtop/1996/AMR/2220001.htm
37. Foley (ed.), *The Memoirs of General Grivas*, p. 71
38. Text of report in Sean Cronin, *Irish Nationalism:A History of Its Roots and Ideology*, Dublin: Academy Press, 1980, appendix XVIII, para 16c
39. Ibid., para 64–5
40. US Secretary of State Colin Powell, Address to the UN Security Council, February 5, 2003
41. *9/11 Commission Report: Final Report of the National Commission on Terrorist Attacks Upon the United States* (official edition), Claitor's Law Books and Publishers' Division, July 22, 2004 pp. 335–6
42. *Washington Post* poll, 'Saddam Hussein and the Sept 11 Attacks', September 6, 2003
43. Harris Poll no. 14, February 18, 2005, Harris Interactive
44. *9/11 Commission Report*, p. 62
45. NBS News, *Meet the Press*, December 9, 2001. NBC, March 24, 2002. NBS News, *Meet the Press*, September 14 2003. This was the Prague meeting, mentioned in Chapter Six, at which Atta was alleged to have been given a vial of anthrax

46. *New York Times*, September 27, 2002
47. NBC News, *Meet the Press*, September 14, 2003
48. President George W. Bush, Fox News, Sunday, September 17, 2003
49. President Discusses War on Terror at National Endowment for Democracy, October 6, 2005
50. President George W. Bush, Remarks of the President, May 1, 2003
51. President Addresses Nation, Discusses Iraq, War on Terror, Fort Bragg, NC, June 28, 2005
52. *9/11 Commission Report*, p. 65
53. Pepe Escobar, 'Zarqawi and Al-Qaeda, Unlikely Bedfellows', *Asia Times*, October 22, 2004
54. Letter from al-Zawahiri, to Al-Zarqawi, October 11, 2005, Office of the Director of National Intelligence. Available at http://www.dni.gov/ Privacy_Security_Notice.html
55. The Pew Global Attitudes Project, June 23, 2005
56. 'Pew, Global Opinion: The Spread of Anti-Americanism', *Trends 2005*, Chapter 7
57. President George W. Bush, Remarks by the President on Arrival, The South Lawn, September 16, 2001
58. President Rallies the Troops in Alaska, February 2002
59. Tom Templeton and Tom Lumley, '9/11 in Numbers', *Observer*, August 18, 2002
60. Statement by the President in his Address to the Nation, September 11, 2001
61. Radio Address of the President to the Nation, September 29, 2001
62. Osama bin Laden, April 15, 2004, in an audiotape offering conditional reconciliation with Europe
63. President George W. Bush, Statement by the President in his Address to the Nation, September 11, 2001
64. President Addresses Military Families, Nampa, Idaho, August 24, 2001
65. President Rallies the Troops in Alaska, February 2002
66. President Discusses War on Terror at National Endowment for Democracy, October 6, 2005
67. Osama bin Laden speech in a videotape sent to Al-Jazeera, October 30, 2004
68. President George W. Bush Addresses Military Families, Nampa, Idaho, August 24, 2005
69. President Discusses War on Terror at National Endowment for Democracy, October 6, 2005

70. President George W. Bush Addresses Military Families, Nampa, Idaho, August 24, 2005
71. Bin Laden in audiotape offering conditional reconciliation with Europe, April 15, 2004
72. President George W. Bush, Remarks by the President on Arrival, The South Lawn, September 16, 2001

Chapter Eight: What Is to Be Done?

1. Osama bin Laden, 'Message to America', October 30, 2004
2. W. E. Gladstone in a letter to his wife, quoted in J. L. Hammond, *Gladstone and the Irish Nation*, London, new impr., 1964, p. 51
3. *The Banner of Ulster*, December 17, 1867. Quoted in Patrick Quinlivan and Paul Rose, *The Fenians in England, 1865–1872*, London: John Calder, 1982, p. 97
4. *Impartial Reporter*, 7 May 1868. Quoted in Quinlivan and Rose, *The Fenians in England, 1865–1872*, p. 97
5. Queen Victoria to Lord Cranbrook, May 1, 1868. Quoted in Quinlivan and Rose, *The Fenians in England, 1865–1872*, p. 133
6. Quoted in Quinlivan and Rose, *The Fenians in England, 1865–1872*, p. 117
7. *The Times*, April 21, 1868. Quoted in Quinlivian and Rose, *The Fenians in England, 1865–1872*, p. 117
8. Quoted in Quinlivan and Rose, *The Fenians in England, 1865–1872*, p. 117
9. Ibid., p. 135
10. Hammond, *Gladstone and the Irish Nation*, p. 80
11. Pearse, Padraic H, *Political Writings and Speeches*, Dublin: Talbot Press, 1966, pp. 133–137.
12. President George W. Bush, Address to a Joint Session of Congress and the American People, September 20, 2001
13. Benjamin Franklin, Pennsylvania Assembly: Reply to the Governor, November 11, 1775. *The Papers of Benjamin Franklin*, ed. Leonard W. Larabee, vol. 6, 1963, p. 242
14. Laura K. Donohue, *Counterterrorist Law and Emergency Powers in the United Kingdom, 1922–2000*, Dublin: Irish Academic Press, 2001
15. George Washington, 1732–1799. The writings of George Washington from the original manuscript sources: vol. 7 Electronic Text Center, University of Virginia Library

16. David Hackett Fischer, *Washington's Crossing*, Oxford: Oxford University Press, 2004, p. 379

17. Ibid., p. 276

18. Sun Tzu, 6th century BC. *The Art of War*, as translated by R. L. Wing, in *The Art of Strategy: A New Translation of Sun Tzu's Classic, The Art of War*, New York: Doubleday, 1998, p. 151

19. Tom Templeton and Tom Lumley, '9/11 in Numbers', *Observer*, August 18, 2002

20. Peter R. Neumann, *Britain's Long War: British Strategy in the Northern Ireland Conflict, 1969–1998*, New York: Palgrave Macmillan, 2003, p. 157

21. Louise Richardson, 'Britain and the IRA', in Robert J. Art and Louise Richardson (eds), *Democracy and Counterterrorism: Lessons from the Past*, Washington DC: United States Institute of Peace, 2006

22. Louise Richardson, 'How Terrorist Campaigns End: Lessons from War Termination', paper delivered at the International Studies Association Annual Convention, New Orleans, LA, March 25, 2002

23. CNN.com. David Ensor, 'U.S. Officials: Al-Zarqawi Group's Statement Credible', October 18, 2004

24. 'Voice on Tape Is Bin Laden Say US Investigators', MSNBC, December 28, 2004

25. October 1, 2003. Text available at http://usatoday.printthis.clickability.com/pt/cpt?action

26. Letter from al-Zawahiri to al-Zarqawi, Office of the Director of National Intelligence, October 11, 2005

27. Ibid.

28. Osama bin Laden, October 7, 2001

29. www.unicef.org/newsline/99pr29.htm

30. Globalpolicy.org

31. Ibid.

32. BBC News, September 30, 1998

33. John Mueller and Karl Mueller, 'Sanctions of Mass Destruction', *Foreign Affairs*, 78, 3, 1999, pp. 43–53

34. For details on the kind of policies that might be included in a comprehensive development plan see the Madrid Agenda produced by the Club de Madrid on March 11, 2005. The background papers upon which the agenda is based provide a wealth of detailed policy recommendations

35. Greg Foley, 'Hating Americans: Jemaah Islamiyah and the Bali Bombings', *IIAS Newsletter*, no. 31, July 2003

36. Raymond Bonner, 'Bali Suicide Bombers Said to Have Belonged to Small Gang', *New York Times*, October 7, 2005, p. A3

37. The Pew Global Attitudes Survey, June 23, 2005
38. The Pew Global Attitudes Project, July 14, 2005
39. Report of the Independent Task Force Sponsored by the Council of Foreign Relations, *Finding America's Voice: A Strategy for Reinvigorating U.S. Public Diplomacy*, New York, 2003. The Djerejian Report, *Changing Minds, Winning Peace: A New Strategic Direction for U.S. Public Diplomacy in the Arab and Muslim World*, Report of the Advisory Group on Public Diplomacy for the Arab and Muslim World, Washington DC, 2003
40. Djerejian Report, p. 25
41. President George W. Bush, Remarks by the President upon Arrival, The South Lawn, September 16, 2001
42. Quoted in Foley, 'Hating Americans: Jemaah Islamiyah and the Bali Bombings'

Glossary

Abu Sayyaf Group (ASG): A small Muslim separatist group operating in the southern Philippines, which split from the larger Moro National Liberation Front in the early 1990s.

Action Directe: A French social revolutionary terrorist group active in French cities in the 1980s.

Action for National Liberation (ALN): Ação Libertadora Nacional, a revolutionary movement formed in Brazil in 1967. Led by Carlos Marighella, the group engaged in urban guerrilla activity. Declined after Marighella's death in 1969.

Adams, Gerry (1948–): Leader of the Irish republican movement. President of Sinn Fein and member of parliament for West Belfast since 1983.

African National Congress (ANC): South Africa's governing party since the first free election in South Africa in 1994. Dedicated to majority rights. Formed in 1912, abandoned non-violence in 1960.

Al-Aqsa Martyrs Brigades: Militant Palestinian group associated with Arafat's Fatah movement. Specialize in suicide terrorism. Originally named after the al-Aqsa Mosque, one of Islam's holiest sites and an icon for the Palestinian movement. Emerged shortly after the outbreak of the al-Aqsa intifada in 2000.

al-Qaeda: 'The Base'. Radical Islamic movement founded in Afghanistan in the 1980s. Led by Osama bin Laden. Responsible for 9/11 and many other terrorist attacks.

Amir, Yigal: Right-wing Israeli who assassinated Prime Minister Yitzhak Rabin in November 1995.

Arafat, Yasser (1929–2004): Chairman of the Palestine Liberation Organization (PLO), founder of Al-Fatah, recipient of the 1993 Nobel Peace Prize along with Shimon Peres and Yitzhak Rabin.

Armed Islamic Group (GIA): Formed in 1982. An Islamic extremist group based in Algeria and operative in North Africa and France.

Asahara, Shoko (1955–): Founder and leader of Aum Shinrikyo in Japan.

Convicted, among other crimes, of the 1995 sarin-gas attack on the Tokyo subway. Sentenced to death in 2004, appealing the ruling.

Assassins: A violent radical Muslim sect that operated from the eleventh century to the thirteenth.

Atta, Mohammad (1968–2001): Egyptian leader of the 9/11 attack team. Piloted AA flight 11 into the North Tower of the World Trade Center.

Aum Shinrikyo (Aum Supreme Truth): Japanese religious millenarian cult established in 1987 by Shoko Asahara. Released sarin gas on the Tokyo subway in March 1995.

Baader, Andreas (1943–1977): Leader of the Red Army Faction, also known as the Baader–Meinhof Gang, in West Germany in the early 1970s. Sentenced to life imprisonment, Baader committed suicide in jail in October 1977.

Baader–Meinhof Gang: Popular name of the Red Army Faction.

Ba'ath Party: Founded in 1945 as a left-wing, secular, pan-Arab nationalist political party. Came to power in Syria and Iraq in 1963. Subsequently split into rival groups in 1966. After the overthrow of Saddam Hussein's Ba'athist regime in 2003, occupying authorities banned the Iraqi party.

Barayev, Movzar (c.1975–2002): Chechen separatist, leader of the Special Purpose Islamic Brigade (SPIR), killed during the seizure of the Dubrovka Theatre in Moscow, which he led in October 2002.

Barrett, Michael (1841–1868): Irish nationalist, member of the Fenians, hanged in 1868 for the Clerkenwell bombing.

Basayev, Shamil Salmanovich (1965–): Chechen leader, briefly prime minister (1998), currently leader of Islamic International Peacekeeping Brigade (IIPB) and Riyadus-Salikhin Reconnaissance and Sabotage Battalion of Chechen Martyrs (RSRSBCM). Believed responsible for the Beslan school siege in 2004.

Baumann, Michael 'Bommi' (c.1948–): Member of the German terrorist group the June 2nd Movement. The Movement's name was a reference to June 2, 1967, the date on which German police killed Benno Ohnesorg, a German university student attending his first political demonstration.

Begin, Menachem (1913–92): Prime minister of Israel 1977–83. Leader of the Irgun movement in the 1940s. Awarded Nobel Peace Prize in 1978.

Benchellai, Menad (c.1975): Radical Islamist arrested in France on terrorism charges. Known as 'the chemist' because of his alleged chemical-weapons training.

Betancourt, Rómulo (1908–81): President of Venezuela (1945–8, 1959–64).

bin al-Shibh, Ramzi: Born in Yemen in 1973, captured in Pakistan in 2002, in US custody. A key member of al-Qaeda who helped plan the 9/11 attacks.

bin Laden, Osama (1957–): Founder and leader of al-Qaeda. Born in Saudi Arabia, his citizenship was revoked in 1994. Son of a construction magnate, he studied management and economics at King Abdul Aziz University. He established al-Qaeda in the 1980s to aid the mujahideen in Afghanistan against the Soviet Union. Believed to be in hiding.

Birds of Freedom (Suthanthirap Paravaikal): The female wing of the Tamil Tigers (LTTE) in Sri Lanka.

Black September: A terrorist group set up following Jordan's expulsion of PLO guerrillas in the 'Black September' of 1970. Responsible for the kidnap and murder of the Israeli Olympic team in Munich in 1972. Al-Fatah dissolved Black September in December 1974.

Clan na Gael (Irish Family): Organization formed by Irish republican sympathizers in the United States in the nineteenth century. Maintained close ties to the Fenians and to the IRB.

Communist Combatant Cells (CCC): A small social revolutionary group active in Belgium in the mid-1980s.

Continuity IRA: A splinter group from the IRA formed in 1994 in opposition to the Northern Irish peace process.

Contras: A US-backed force that opposed the left-wing Sandinista government of Nicaragua between 1979 and 1990. Disbanded following the electoral defeat of the Sandinistas in 1990.

Curcio, Renato (1941–): Leader of the Red Brigades in Italy.

Dawa, al-: Shia Islamic party founded in the late 1950s and supported by Iran.

Dev Sol (Devrimci Sol or Revolutionary Left): Small Turkish Marxist–Leninist group formed in 1978, and split into two factions in the early 1990s. Dev Sol's original founder changed the group's name to DHKP-C. The group have continued to conduct violent attacks against Turkish government targets as well as against western interests in Turkey.

Dirección de Inteligencia Nacional (DINA): Chilean intelligence service until late 1977, when it was renamed the Central Nacional de Informaciones. Acted as a secret police force under the direction of Augusto Pinochet, head of the military government that ruled Chile from 1973 to 1990.

Dohrn, Bernadine (1942–): A leader of and spokesperson for the Weather Underground.

ETA (Euzkadi Ta Askatasuna, or Basque Fatherland and Liberty):

Basque nationalist group founded in 1959 and still operating in Spain with the aim of establishing an independent homeland encompassing the Spanish Basque provinces of Vizcaya, Guipúzcoa, Álava, the autonomous region of Navarra and the south-western French departments of Labourd, Basse-Navarra and Soule.

FARC (Fuerzas Armadas Revolucionarias de Colombia, or Revolutionary Armed Forces of Colombia): Established in 1964 by the Colombian Communist Party, the FARC are Latin America's oldest and largest terrorist group, led by Manuel Marulanda.

Fatah, al- (Palestine National Liberation Movement): Military wing of the Palestinian Liberation Organization, founded in 1959 by Yasser Arafat.

Fenians (Fenian Brotherhood): Nineteenth-century Irish republican organization dedicated to the use of force to gain independence for Ireland. The name is taken from the mythical hero Fionn MacCumhall and his warriors, the Fianna. The term Fenians is loosely used to describe the republican movement incorporating several separate organizations.

Gama'a al-Islamiyya, al- (Islamic Group): Egypt's largest militant group, active since the 1970s. The group's spiritual leader, Sheikh Umar Abd al-Rahman, is serving a life sentence in the US for his role in the 1993 World Trade Center attack. In 1998 the group signed Osama bin Laden's fatwa calling for attacks against the United States.

Ghamidi, Ahmad al-Haznawi al- (1980–2001): Born in Saudi Arabia. One of the hijackers of United Airlines flight 93 (which crashed in Pennsylvania) on September 11, 2001.

GRAPO (Grupo de Resistência Anti-Fascista Primero de Octubre): A small extremist Marxist–Leninist group formed in Spain in 1975. Vehemently anti-American, the group also advocates the overthrow of the Spanish government.

Grivas, George Theodore (1898–1974): Leader of the Greek Cypriot terrorist group EOKA, advocated union with Greece and led the guerrilla campaign against British rule in the 1950s. After Cyprus's independence in 1959, he formed the paramilitary organization EOKA-B opposed to President (and Archbishop) Makarios.

Guevara, 'Che' (1928–67): Born Ernesto Guevara de la Serna, the Argentine revolutionary and guerrilla leader served in Fidel Castro's government in Cuba in the early 1960s. He was captured and shot in 1967 while training guerrillas for an uprising against the Bolivian government.

Guzman, Abimael (1934–): Founder and leader of Peru's Maoist terrorist group, the Shining Path. A former philosophy professor, he was captured in 1992. Often referred to by his followers as 'President Gonzalo' and the 'Fourth Sword of Marxism', following Marx, Lenin and Mao.

Habash, George (1925–): Marxist Palestinian and founder in 1968 of the Popular Front for the Liberation of Palestine (PFLP).

Hamas (Islamic Resistance Movement): Radical Islamic Palestinian group formed in late 1987 with the goal of establishing an Islamic Palestinian state in Israel. Hamas's strength is concentrated in the Gaza Strip and the West Bank and it competes for support with the secular PLO and the smaller Palestinian Islamic Jihad. In January 2006 Hamas won a surprise victory in Palestinian parliamentary elections.

Hanif, Assaf Mohammed (c.1979–2000): British suicide bomber who blew up a bar in Tel Aviv in April 2003. Believed to have been recruited by Hamas.

Hezbollah (Party of God): Radical Shiite organization formed in Lebanon in the early 1980s dedicated to opposing Israel and establishing an Islamic state in Lebanon. Currently led by Secretary General Hassan Nasrallah, and supported by Iran and Syria.

HUM (Harakut ul-Mujahideen): An Islamic militant group based in Pakistan that operates primarily in Kashmir. Signed bin Laden's 1998 fatwa against the US. Its longtime emir, Fazlur Rehman Khalil, was replaced by popular commander Farooq Kashmiri in 2000. Coalition airstrikes destroyed HUM terrorist training camps in autumn 2001.

Hussain, Hasib (1986–2005): One of four British suicide bombers who attacked the London transport system on July 7, 2005, killing themselves and fifty-two others.

Idris, Wafa (1975–2002): The Red Crescent volunteer was the first female Palestinian suicide bomber when she exploded her backpack in the middle of a Jerusalem market. Al-Aqsa Martyrs Brigade claimed responsibility for the attack.

Irgun: Zionist organization founded in Palestine in 1931 to fight for the establishment of a Jewish state. Led for a time by Menachem Begin, later prime minister of Israel (1977–83).

Irish Republican Army (IRA): Formed in the early twentieth century to fight for Irish independence from Britain. The 'Old' IRA split in 1969 into the 'Provisionals' and the 'Officials'. The 'Provisionals' soon became synonymous with 'IRA' and waged a thirty-five-year violent campaign for Irish unity. They called an end to their campaign in summer 2005.

Irish Republican Brotherhood (IRB): A militant Irish republican organization which grew out of the Fenian movement in the mid-nineteenth century and was the precursor to the contemporary IRA. The IRB organized the Easter Rising of 1916 but was gradually replaced by the IRA in the course of the War of Independence. Disbanded in 1924.

Islamic International Peacekeeping Brigade (IIPB): Chechen terrorist group created in 1998 by Shamil Basayev who leads it jointly with Arab mujahideen leader Abu al-Walid. Membership includes Chechens, Arabs and other foreign fighters. Involved in the seizure of the Dubrovka Theatre in Moscow in October 2002.

Izz al-Din al-Qassam Brigades (al-Qassam): The military wing of Hamas, named after Sheikh Izz al-Din al-Qassam (1882–1935).

Jama'at al-Tawhid wal-Jihad (JTJ): Islamist terrorist network in Iraq formed by Abu Mus'ab al-Zarqawi in the late 1990s. In 2004 the group changed their name to 'al-Qaeda in Iraq'.

Japanese Red Army (JRA): Small Japanese social revolutionary terrorist group operative for thirty years from the early 1970s. The only known terrorist group to be led by a woman, Fusako Shigenobu, arrested in 2000. Responsible for the Lod Airport massacre in 1972.

Jarrah, Ziad (1975-2001): Lebanese member of the 9/11 attack team. Piloted UA flight 93 (which crashed in Pennsylvania).

JEM (Jaish-e-Mohammed or Army of Mohammed): Radical Islamic group based in Pakistan. Founded in 2000 by Masood Azhar with the goal of uniting Kashmir with Pakistan.

Jemaah Islamiyah (JI): Islamic terrorist group based in south-east Asia. Their goal is to create an Islamic state comprising Brunei, Indonesia, Malaysia, Singapore, the southern Philippines and southern Thailand. Linked to al-Qaeda and responsible for Bali bombings in 2002 and 2005.

'Jihad Mosque': The Jihad Mosque soccer team was started in 1998 by Muhsin Kawasmeh, a sixteen-year-old, in Hebron. Beginning in 2002, it provided eight volunteers for suicide missions out of its eleven-man team.

Kach (also Kahane Chai): Far-right Israeli terrorist group founded in the early 1970s by Rabbi Meir Kahane (1932–90) and dedicated to restoring the biblical state of Israel. Banned by Israel in 1994, the group officially disbanded; unofficially, however, they remain active.

Khaled, Leila (1944–): Famous female terrorist and member of the PFLP. In August 1969, Khaled was part of a team that hijacked TWA flight 840. In September 1970, she and Patrick Arguello, a Nicaraguan, attempted the hijack of El Al flight 219.

Khan, Mohammad Sidique (1974–2005): British-born leader of the four British suicide bombers who attacked the London transport system on July 7, 2005, killing themselves and fifty-two others.

Kherchtou, L'Houssaine (1964–): Moroccan member of al-Qaeda, testified as a government witness in the 'embassy bombing' trial in 2001, which tried and convicted four men accused of bombing US embassies in Africa in 1998.

Kumaratunga, Chandrika (1945–): Fourth president of Sri Lanka (1994–2005).

Lindh, John Walker (1981–): The 'American Taliban'. An American captured in Afghanistan in November 2001, while fighting for the Taliban. He was sentenced to twenty years in prison in 2002 for supplying services to the Taliban and for carrying explosives.

Lindsay, Germaine (Jamal) (1985–2005): Jamaican-born, one of the four British suicide bombers who attacked the London transport system on July 7, 2005, killing themselves and fifty-two others.

McGuinness, Martin (1950–): One of the leaders of the Irish republican movement. Chief negotiator for Sinn Fein. One-time IRA leader. Elected MP for Mid Ulster in 1997. Became education minister in the Northern Ireland Assembly in 1998.

Mac Sweeney, Terence (1879–1920): Nationalist lord mayor of Cork, died on hunger strike in Brixton prison in 1920 during Ireland's war of independence against Britain.

Marighella, Carlos (1911–69): Brazilian revolutionary. Member of the ALN. Author of *The Mini-manual of the Urban Guerrilla* (1969).

Marín, Pedro Antonio (1928–): The leader of Colombia's FARC, better known as Marulanda.

Masood Azhar, Maulana (1968–): Militant Islamic leader, founder of Jaish-e-Mohammed (JEM) dedicated to uniting Kashmir with Pakistan.

Mawdudi, Sayyid Abul A'la (1903–79): One of the most influential Muslim theologians of the twentieth century and founder of Jamaat-e-Islami, which was established in pre-partition India to promote Islamic values and practices. Together, Mawdudi and Qutb are considered the founding fathers of the global Islamic-revival movement.

Meinhof, Ulrike (1934–76): Leader with Andreas Baader of the Red Army Faction (Baader–Meinhof Gang) in West Germany. Committed suicide in prison.

Mohammed, Khalid Sheikh (1965–): Architect of the 9/11 attacks. Senior Kuwaiti member of al-Qaeda. Captured in Pakistan in 2003. Currently held by the US in an unknown location.

Movement of the Revolutionary Left (MIR): Left-wing revolutionary movement, founded in Chile in the 1960s, engaged in sporadic terrorist attacks in the 1970s and 1980s.

Mugabe, Robert Gabriel (1924–): Leader of Zimbabwe since 1980. Prime minister (1980–7) and since 1987 executive president. Founder and leader of the Zimbabwe African People's Union (ZAPU) liberation movement.

Muslim Brotherhood (Majallar al-Ikhwan al-Musalamin): Islamist organization in the Middle East. The original Muslim Brotherhood was founded by Hassan al-Banna in 1928 in Egypt where it remains the largest political opposition group. Branches of the Muslim Brotherhood have since been founded in Syria, Jordan, Palestine, Kurdistan and Iraq.

Narodnaya Volya (People's Will): A Russian revolutionary anarchist group active between 1878 and 1883. Responsible for the assassination among others of Tsar Alexander II in 1881.

Nasrallah, (Sayyed) Hassan (1960–): Lebanese secretary general of Hezbollah.

Nepalese Communist Party (Communist Party of Nepal-Maoists): Maoist terrorist group founded in 1994 and led by Pushpa Kamal Dahal. The group's objective is to take over the Nepalese government and transform Nepal into a communist society.

New People's Army (Communist Party of the Philippines): Maoist military wing of the Philippines Communist Party, formed in 1969, dedicated to overthrowing the government. Their leaders, José Maria Sison and Luis Jalandoni, live in the Netherlands.

November 17 (Revolutionary Organization 17 November): Small radical leftist group operating in Greece. Founded in 1975 and named for the student uprising in Greece in November 1973. Most of the leadership were arrested in 2002 and were sentenced to multiple life terms in December 2003.

Ocalan, Abdullah (1948–): Founder (in 1974) and leader of the Kurdish terrorist group the PKK. Captured in 1999 and sentenced to life in prison.

Okamoto, Kozo (c.1948–): Member of the Japanese Red Army (JRA). Sole survivor of the Lod Airport attack team in 1972. Sentenced to life in prison by Israel but released in 1985 in a prisoner exchange with the PFLP-GC, he fled to Libya. Subsequently arrested in Lebanon, granted asylum in 2000.

Omar, Mullah Mohammad (1959–): Leader of the Taliban and Afghanistan's de facto head of state from 1996 to 2001. He has been in hiding since the US invasion in 2001.

Palestine Liberation Organization (PLO): Political and military umbrella organization dedicated to creating an independent Palestinian nation state. Formed by the Arab League in 1964 and led by Yasser Arafat from 1969 to 2004. Arafat was succeeded by Mahmood Abbas, who was elected president of the Palestinian Authority in 2005.

Palestinian Islamic Jihad (PIJ): Formed in the Gaza Strip in the late 1970s by Fathi Shaqaqi as a branch of the Egyptian Islamic Jihad, the group are active in the West Bank and Gaza and dedicated to the creation of an Islamist Palestinian state and the destruction of Israel.

People's Revolutionary Army (ERP): Armed wing of the Argentinian Workers' Revolutionary Party, founded in 1969, led by Roberto Santucho. Active 1973 to 1977.

PKK (Kurdistan Workers' Party): Large terrorist group founded by Abdullah Ocalan in 1974 with the aim of establishing an independent Kurdish state in Kurdish areas of Turkey, Iraq and Iran.

Popular Front for the Liberation of Palestine (PFLP): Secular left-wing Palestinian group founded in 1967 by George Habash; opposed the Oslo peace process.

Popular Front for the Liberation of Palestine-General Command (PFLP-GC): Palestinian terrorist group opposed to the PLO. Split from the PFLP in 1968, led by Ahmad Jibril, former captain in the Syrian army.

Prabakharan, Vellupillai (1954–): Leader of the LTTE, sole surviving founder of the organization.

Premadasa, Ranasinghe (1924–93): President of Sri Lanka (1989–93), assassinated by the LTTE.

Provisional IRA (PIRA): In December 1969 the IRA split into two groups. The Provisional IRA, or 'Provos', soon became the largest group synonymous with 'IRA'. The group declared an end to their campaign of violence to secure a united Ireland in 2005.

Qadaffi, Muammar Abu Minyar al- (c.1942–): Leader of Libya since 1969.

Qurashi, Abu Ubeid al-: Aide to Osama bin Laden and al-Qaeda spokesman based in London. Wrote for now defunct al-Qaeda website, *Al-Ansar*.

Qutb, Sayyid (1906–66): Egyptian Islamic theologian, theoretician and writer. Influenced the development of Islamic fundamentalism, especially the concept of jihad (holy war) and the view of the illegitimacy of secular rule. Executed in 1966 for plotting to overthrow the state.

Rantisi, Abdul Aziz (1947–2004): Paediatrician and leader of Hamas. Assassinated by an Israeli missile attack.

Rassam, Ahmad (c.1967–): Algerian convicted of plotting to blow up Los Angeles International Airport on the eve of the millennium. Sentenced to twenty-two years in prison.

Real IRA: Militant offshoot of the IRA formed in 1998 in opposition to the Northern Irish peace process.

Red Army Faction (Rote Armee Fraktion, or RAF): German social revolutionary terrorist group, sometimes known as the Baader–Meinhof Gang, operative in Germany in the late 1960s and 1970s. Officially dissolved in 1998.

Red Brigades (Brigate Rosse, or BR): Italian social revolutionary terrorist group active in the 1970s and early 1980s. Responsible for the kidnap and murder of the elder statesman Aldo Moro in 1978.

Renamo (Resistência Nacional Moçambicana): Right-wing force opposed to the FRELIMO government of Mozambique. Founded in 1975 and currently led by Afonso Dhlakama.

Riyadus-Salikhin Reconnaissance and Sabotage Battalion of Chechen Martyrs (RSRSBCM): Chechen group, led by Shamil Basayev, involved in siege of Dubrovka Theatre in Moscow in 2002. The name translates as 'Requirements for Getting into Paradise'.

Reyashi, Reem al- (c.1981–2003): First Palestinian mother to be a suicide bomber, in January 2004. Claimed by Hamas and Al-Aqsa.

Rossa, Jeremiah O'Donovan (1831–1915): Irish Fenian leader who inspired generations of Irish republicans.

Salafiya Jihadia (Jihad for Pure Islam): Moroccan extremist Islamist movement responsible for suicide bombings in Casablanca in 2003.

Salim, Mamduh Mahmud (c.1958–): Sudanese, reputed to be al-Qaeda's chief of finance, arrested in Munich, Germany, in 1998 on charges of trying to obtain nuclear materials.

Santucho, Mario Roberto (1936–76): Leader of the People's Revolutionary Army (ERP) in Argentina. Killed in 1976.

Sendic Antonaccio, Raúl (1926–89): Founder and leader of the Tupamaros, a terrorist group active in Uruguay in the 1960s and 1970s.

Shanab, Ismail Abu (1950–2003): Third-ranking Hamas leader in Gaza. Assassinated in an Israeli helicopter-missile attack in 2003.

Sharif, Omar Khan (c.1976–2003): British jihadist, one of two suicide bombers who attacked a bar in Tel Aviv in April 2003.

Sheikh, Omar (Ahmed Omar Saeed Sheikh) (1973–): British citizen and radical Islamist member of JEM convicted of the murder of *Wall Street Journal* reporter Daniel Pearl in Pakistan in 2002. Sentenced to death in 2002, appeal pending.

Shigenobu, Fusako (1945–): Leader of the Japanese Red Army. Only woman to lead a terrorist group. Forged an alliance between the JRA and the PLFP in 1971. Arrested in 2000. Currently in prison in Japan.

Shining Path (Sendero Luminoso): Maoist terrorist group in Peru founded in the late 1960s and led by Abimael Guzman. Began armed operations in 1980. Seriously weakened by arrest of the leadership in 1992.

Sicarii: Literally 'dagger men'. Jewish zealots violently opposed to Roman rule in the first century after Christ.

Sinn Fein ('Ourselves'; commonly rendered 'Ourselves Alone'): Political party dedicated to Irish independence established in 1905 by Arthur Griffith. Currently the political arm of the IRA, which seeks the unification of Ireland, and the largest Catholic political party in Northern Ireland.

SLA (South Lebanese Army): Pro-Israeli Lebanese militia during the Lebanese Civil War (1975–1990). Founded in 1976.

Special Purpose Islamic Regiment (SPIR): Chechen group dedicated to independence. Led by Movzar Barayev until his death in the seizure of the Dubrovka Theatre in Moscow in 2002. Barayev was succeeded by Khamzat Tazabayev, who was reported killed in 2004.

Stern Gang (Lehi): Splinter group of Irgun, founded in 1940 by Abraham Stern. Sought to expel British forces and Arab people from Palestine, and refused to observe a truce during the war with Germany. A Lehi leader, Yitzhak Shamir, subsequently became prime minister of Israel (1983–4, 1986–92).

Taliban ('students of Islamic knowledge'): Came to power in the course of the Afghan civil war. An Islamist and Pashtun nationalist movement led by Mullah Mohammad Omar, the Taliban effectively ruled most of Afghanistan from 1996 to 2001 and enforced a strict interpretation of sharia. After the US invasion, the Afghan Interim Authority (AIA) replaced the Taliban government in December 2001.

Tamil Tigers (Liberation Tigers of Tamil Eelam, LTTE): Large Sri Lankan guerrilla and terrorist group founded in 1976 and led by Vellupillai Prabhakaran. They began armed conflict in 1983 to achieve an independent Tamil state. Currently observing a tenuous ceasefire.

Tanweer, Shehzad (1982–2005): One of four British suicide bombers who attacked the London transport system on July 7, 2005, killing themselves and fifty-two others.

Thugi: Large violent Hindu cult that operated in the thirteenth through nineteenth centuries in India.

Tsuchiya, Masami (c.1965–): Chief chemist of Aum Shinrikyo. Sentenced to death in 2004 for role in sarin-gas attack, appealing the ruling.

Tupac Amaru Revolutionary Movement (MRTA): Peruvian Marxist–Leninist revolutionary movement formed in 1983. Most famous for their seizure of the Japanese embassy in Lima in 1996.

Umkhonto we Sizwe (MK): Meaning 'Spear of the Nation'. Military wing of the African National Congress (ANC). Founded 1961, suspended operations 1990.

UNITA (União Nacional para a Independência Total de Angola): Angolan national liberation movement founded by Jonas Savimbi in 1966 to fight for independence from Portuguese colonial rule.

Weather Underground Organization (The Weathermen): A violent offshoot of the SDS (Students for a Democratic Society) student protest movement. Active in the US in the early 1970s.

Yassin, Sheikh Ahmed (1936–2004): Founder and spiritual leader of Hamas. Assassinated by Israeli helicopter gunship.

Zarqawi, Abu Mus'ab al- (1966–): Jordanian leader of the Iraqi insurgency group Jama'at al-Tawhid wal-Jihad (Unification and Holy War Group), also known as 'al-Qaeda in Iraq'.

Zawahiri, Ayman al- (1951–): Egyptian doctor, formerly leader of Egyptian Islamic Jihad, second in command of al-Qaeda.

Zealots: Violent Jewish group opposed to Roman rule in the Judaea province in the first century AD.

Index

Index

References in *italics* refer to glossary entries.